THE LEGEND OF

THE LEGEND OF

JEFFREY L. RODENGEN

For Charlie Strang
Who pointed the way...

Also by Jeff Rodengen

The Legend of Chris-Craft

IRON FIST: *The Lives of Carl Kiekhaefer*

Evinrude-Johnson and The Legend of OMC

Serving The Silent Service: The Legend of Electric Boat

The Legend of Honeywell

The Legend of Dr Pepper/Seven Up

The Legend of Ingersoll-Rand

The Legend of The Stanley Works

WRITE STUFF SYNDICATE

Write Stuff Syndicate, Inc.

1515 Southeast 4th Ave
Fort Lauderdale, FL 33316
1-800-900-Book
(1-800-900-2665)
(305) 462-6657

Library of Congress Catalog Card Number
95-060793

ISBN 0-945903-11-1

Completely produced in the United States of America

10 9 8 7 6 5 4 3 2 1

TABLE OF CONTENTS

INTRODUCTION

BRIGGS & STRATTON began in 1908 as an informal partnership between recent college graduate Stephen F. Briggs and grain company executive Harold M. Stratton. Briggs was the inventor and Stratton was the investor, and together they were going to enter the crowded field of automakers, manufacturing and marketing an innovative six-cylinder, two-cycle engine designed by Briggs. When this plan proved too costly, they quickly shifted gears and decided to assemble cars from parts manufactured elsewhere. Once again, the venture proved unprofitable. But the young entrepreneurs refused to give up. Henry Ford had just introduced the Model T, and his innovative method of mass production made automobiles affordable to average Americans. Hoping to profit from this burgeoning market, Briggs & Stratton began selling locks, ignition switches and other specialty parts for automobiles. Finally, the struggling company had found its niche.

Over the ensuing decades, the company dabbled in many markets, selling, among other things, washing machine engines, radios and refrigerators. The company displayed a talent for quickly adapting to changing market conditions. Eventually, Briggs & Stratton established two solid businesses — automotive locks and small engines.

Briggs & Stratton began producing small engines in 1920. Company executives and engineers constantly searched for ways to improve both the product and the manufacturing process. The breakthrough came in the early fifties, when Briggs & Stratton pioneered an aluminum alloy engine. Lightweight and inexpensive, the new engines made lawn and garden equipment accessible to the growing masses of Americans migrating to the nation's new suburbs. Around this same time, distribution of lawn and garden equipment began to shift from independent dealers to mass merchandisers, creating an even larger opportunity for Briggs & Stratton engines.

Technological innovations over the years contributed to engines that were stronger, quieter and easier to operate. The company purchased foundries and manufactured its own components, creating a vertical integration that decreased costs. New methods were continually explored to increase the efficiency and speed of production.

Briggs & Stratton prospered despite increasing competition from foreign manufacturers. In the early eighties, a weak yen encouraged Japanese manufacturers to invade traditional Briggs & Stratton markets. The company responded swiftly, introducing new engine lines and attracting customers with engines tailored to their specific needs. In 1989, Briggs & Stratton experienced a rude awakening when it lost money. The response was swift, beginning with a company-wide reorganization. Innovative new management methods, such as the Economic Value Added Program, were established.

Adding to the company's challenges was the emergence of a deteriorating relationship with its labor unions. When a radical union leadership staged work slowdowns and refused to discuss industry-wide concepts such as focused factories, which shifted employee focus from an individual process to responsibility for the final product, Briggs & Stratton had little choice than to establish several non-union facilities in Southern states. As a result of efficiencies and increased quality, the company emerged from a potentially devastating situation stronger than ever.

Briggs & Stratton's ability to respond to changing requirements of its marketplace provides a virtual textbook of how to succeed in business. Another key to the company's success is its remarkable continuity, with only three CEOs in more than 60 years. Frederick P. Stratton Jr., CEO since 1977, is the son of former Chairman Frederick P. Stratton and grandson of co-founder Harold Stratton. President John Shiely is the son of Vincent Shiely, who was chairman of this unique company.

Briggs & Stratton recently spun Briggs & Stratton Technologies into a new company called Strattec Security Corporation, with Fred Stratton's brother, Harold Stratton II, as president and chief executive officer.

Together these strategies have allowed Briggs & Stratton to focus on what it does best — producing the best high-quality, durable engines in the world. Director Peter Georgescu, Chairman of the renowned Young & Rubicam advertising firm, said Briggs & Stratton has worked hard to remain the industry leader.

"The reason that Briggs & Stratton has succeeded, in my opinion, is because of the power of the brand, and because they took aggressive action to streamline themselves, to take the fat out, to become competitive. So there was not enough room for a Japanese company to come in and attack, on the basis of either cost or reputation. That is something that should not go unnoted in the history of this company. I give Fred Stratton enormous credit for recognizing the challenge and doing whatever was necessary to meet it," he said.

ACKNOWLEDGMENTS

A great many individuals and institutions assisted in the research, preparation and publication of *The Legend of Briggs & Stratton.* Of singular value was the time and dedication of Briggs & Stratton employees and retirees, who eagerly gave hours of their time in interviews and assistance. This book would not be possible without them.

Particular gratitude is extended to Fred Stratton Jr., chief executive officer of Briggs & Stratton; John Shiely, president and chief operating officer of Briggs & Stratton; and Harold Stratton II, president and chief executive officer of Strattec Security Corporation. These men provided candid and valuable insights into the company's present and future, as well as invaluable memories of the past. They are continuing a proud legacy, as their fathers, Frederick P. Stratton and Vincent Shiely, were both chairmen of Briggs & Stratton.

Research of this book was greatly assisted by the critical insights made available by Jim Wier, executive vice president of Operations; Michael Hamilton, executive vice president for Sales and Service; Hugo Keltz, vice president of the International Division; Erik Aspelin, vice president of the Distribution Sales and Service Division; Stephen H. Rugg, vice president of Sales and Marketing; Gregory D. Socks, vice president and general manager of the Large Engine Division; Dick Fotsch, vice president and general manager of the Small Engine Division; Charles O. Brown, vice president of Engineering and Quality Assurance; Curt Larson, vice president and general manager of the Industrial Division; Paul O. Farny, president and general manager of Daihatsu Briggs & Stratton; Edward Bednar, vice president and general manager of the Castings Division; Paul Neylon, vice president and general manager of the Vanguard Division; Allen Nitz, general manager of the Die Cast Division; George R. Thompson, vice president of Communication; Marketing Director William Reitman; and Corporate Compliance Officer Kassandra Preston.

The author would also like to thank retired engineers Leo Lechtenberg, Jack Ebershoff and Ed Mueller, retired supervisor Charles Graf, and especially Colet Coughlin, who shared her warm and loving memories of her father, former Briggs & Stratton President Charles Coughlin. Gratitude is also extended to Director Peter Georgescu, chairman of Young & Rubicam, Inc., for his valuable insights.

In addition to interviews, other resources provided valuable information on the history of Briggs & Stratton. Much of this information was located and organized by research assistant Robert Carter, who approached the project with considerable zeal and attention to detail. Cheerful assistance was provided by the Briggs & Stratton Records and Information staff, including Sharon LaPlant, Jackie Stribling-Cason, Mike Pitz and Manager Barb Kufalk. Cathy Ritter's detailed proofreading contributed greatly to the quality of this book.

Gratitude is also extended to the Codington County Historical Society, of Watertown, South Dakota; Jenny Crickard of South Dakota State University; Director Tim Ericson and Archivist Mark Vargas at the Milwaukee Urban Archives, and the American Geological Society Collection, both at the Golda Meir Library, University of Wisconsin-Milwaukee; the helpful staff of the Milwaukee Public Library; the Walworth County Historical Society in Elkhorn, Wisconsin; the Milwaukee County Historical Society; the State Historical Society of Wisconsin, in Madison, Wisconsin; The East Troy Historical Society; the United States Department of Labor-Bureau of Statistics; the National Archives in Washington D.C.; *The Milwaukee Journal*; *The Milwaukee Sentinel*; and *The Milwaukee Journal Sentinel*.

The author also wishes to thank Andrew Cochrane, technical writer for the Central Sales and Service Division; Ann Abshier, who provided valuable historical information; Mike Ertl of Briggs & Stratton Technologies; Scott Alderton of Graphic Services, who helped locate many photographs; and Sue Kletzke, who helped analyze financial information.

Finally, a very special thanks to the dedicated staff at Write Stuff Syndicate, Inc., especially my Executive Assistant and Office Manager Bonnie Bratton, Creative Director Kyle Newton, Graphic Designer Anne Boeckh, Executive Editor Karen Nitkin, Project Analyst Karine N. Rodengen, and Logistics Specialist Joe Kenny.

Original patent of the Gas Engine Igniter invented by Stephen Briggs. The patent was granted February 22, 1910, and the product enjoyed modest success.

Chapter One

BEGINNINGS

"I wired most of the town for electricity and fixed most of the autos."

— Stephen F. Briggs

STEPHEN FOSTER BRIGGS was born December 4, 1885 in Watertown, a small frontier community in the Dakota Territory, an area that later became the northeastern part of South Dakota. His parents, Stephen Albro and Flora Foster Briggs, had migrated west from Rhode Island, lured by the abundance of cheap land during the Dakota Land Boom of 1879.

Shortly after settling in Watertown, Stephen A. Briggs established S.A. Briggs & Company, working as both an insurance agent and a tailor. He was elected justice of the peace for the city of Watertown, which had grown to more than 1,000 residents. In 1892, he started the Summer Trinity Episcopal Church, and helped organize a local board of insurance underwriters. An advertisement placed in the local newspaper by Briggs read, "Money to loan on farms ... long time low interest ... loan completed in four days if title is perfect."[1]

He had two children, Gertrude and Grace, with his first wife, Mary Sickle, who died in 1879; and three children, Daisy, Stephen and George, with Flora Foster, whom he married in 1880. When Briggs' oldest daughter, Gertrude, was married September 4, 1888, the wedding announcement acknowledged his high standing in the community.

"The bride is the daughter of Mr. S.A. Briggs, one of Watertown's substantial and highly respected businessmen, who was among the founders of the city, and identified with all its best interest."[2]

Stephen F. Briggs

In his early childhood, Stephen F. Briggs showed an unusual aptitude for mechanics. He spent hours experimenting with different items he had discovered in town, taking them apart to see how they were made, and fixing them if broken. He later recalled, "I wired most of the town for electricity and fixed most of the autos."[3]

In 1903, the year Stephen graduated from high school, the city directory listed the Briggs family as follows: S.A. Briggs, manager of the opera house; Daisy B., student; and Stephen F., electrician. That year, Briggs enrolled at South Dakota State College (SDSC) in Brookings, about 50 miles south of Watertown, to pursue a degree in electrical engineering. His leadership abilities were apparent from the start, and he became president of both his college yearbook, *The Jackrabbit,* and

Above: Early print of the Gas Engine Igniter, dated around 1910.

the campus Electrical Engineering Club. In addition to these activities, he worked his way through college as a fix-it man, doing, as Briggs put it, "the type of odd jobs the village mechanic does."[4] His most significant accomplishment during this period was the design and manufacture of a six-cylinder, two-cycle engine, which he hoped to use to break into the new and exciting world of automotive manufacture.

While at SDSC, Briggs became friends with fellow engineering student Charles L. Coughlin, from Carthage, South Dakota. Coughlin, a lettered athlete in several sports, had 14 brothers and sisters, noted his daughter, Colet Coughlin, in a recent interview. "Everyone had to work their way through high school and college. Everyone went to college. Their mother ran the general store in Carthage, and their father bought, sold, traded and broke horses for the Army," she said.[5]

"Steve was a year ahead of Dad," she said. "They were on the basketball team together and they were good friends. Dad had 19 major letters in sports when he graduated from college, plus he worked his way through school."[6]

The SDSC basketball coach was William (Bill) Juneau. Both Coughlin and Juneau would play important roles in the future of Stephen Briggs. Coughlin began working at Briggs & Stratton in 1910, and would be president of the company from 1935 to 1971. Juneau and his family were friends and one-time neighbors with a Wisconsin family named Stratton. It was Bill Juneau who introduced Stephen Briggs to Harold Stratton.

Following his junior year at SDSC, Briggs traveled to Milwaukee and spent the summer working as a machinist for the A.O. Smith Company. When he graduated

Stephen Foster Briggs in the South Dakota State College yearbook, *The Jackrabbit*. This photograph was taken in 1906, the year he designed his first engine.

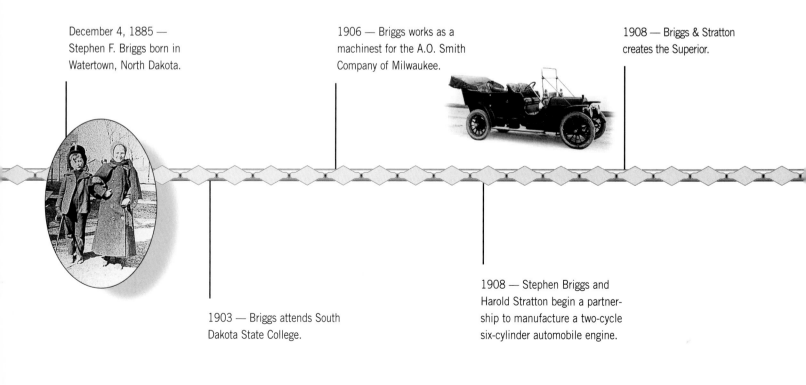

December 4, 1885 — Stephen F. Briggs born in Watertown, North Dakota.

1906 — Briggs works as a machinest for the A.O. Smith Company of Milwaukee.

1908 — Briggs & Stratton creates the Superior.

1903 — Briggs attends South Dakota State College.

1908 — Stephen Briggs and Harold Stratton begin a partnership to manufacture a two-cycle six-cylinder automobile engine.

the following year, Briggs returned to Milwaukee with his recently widowed mother, Flora, his sister Daisy, who had become a school teacher, and his brother, George, who was in college.[7]

Briggs joined with Oertel H. Lemke, president of the Sherman-Lemke Coil and Supply Company, which manufactured and distributed electrical apparatus. The new venture, renamed the Lemke-Briggs Electric Company, manufactured "high-grade ignition apparatus," as described in an advertisement in Wright's Directory of Milwaukee.[8] One of the items manufactured at Lemke-Briggs was an electric starter coil used in automotive and marine engines. A customer of this product was Ole Evinrude, president of the Evinrude Motor Company, and future business partner of Stephen Briggs.

Briggs wanted to start a manufacturing business based on the two-cycle engine he had designed in college. He had abundant skills and intelligence, but he did not have the capital. He needed an investor.

Harold M. Stratton

Harold Mead Stratton was born in Troy Center, Wisconsin, on November 12, 1879, to Prescott B.

and Martha Lull Stratton. Prescott Stratton was station agent for the Chicago, Milwaukee and St.

Stephen Briggs was president of the South Dakota State College Electrical Engineering Club. In this 1906 photograph, he is standing in the back row on the far left.

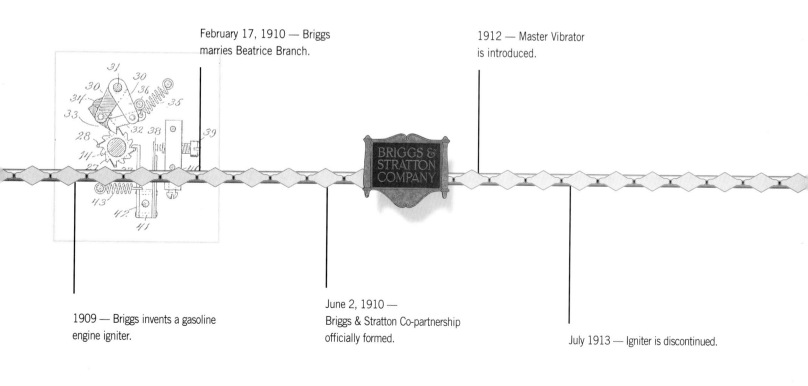

February 17, 1910 — Briggs marries Beatrice Branch.

1912 — Master Vibrator is introduced.

1909 — Briggs invents a gasoline engine igniter.

June 2, 1910 — Briggs & Stratton Co-partnership officially formed.

July 1913 — Igniter is discontinued.

The South Dakota State College basketball team in 1907. Stephen Briggs is standing on the far left, and Charles L. Coughlin, the future president of Briggs & Stratton, is standing next to him. Basketball coach William Juneau, seated, introduced Briggs to Harold Stratton.

ly had a farm in the area.[9] The couple had two sons, John Frantz and Frederick Prescott, and a daughter, Elizabeth Mary. In 1907, Stratton became a partner in his uncle's grain company, remaining at Charles R. Lull & Company in an executive capacity until 1910.

In 1910, Stratton organized a new business venture with Patrick P. Donahue, called the Donahue-Stratton Grain Company, where he served as vice president. The grain business would always be primary to Harold Stratton, though his involvement in Briggs & Stratton would prove substantial.

In addition to the Stratton Grain Company, Harold Stratton participated in at least one other grain business, the Stratton-Ladish Milling Company. His partner was Herman W. Ladish, founder of the Ladish Malting Company and Ladish Company, which makes forgings for milling companies and other customers. When Charles Coughlin briefly left Briggs & Stratton in 1918, he went to work for Ladish Company before returning to Briggs & Stratton in 1923.[10]

Paul Railroads in Troy Center, and it was probably at the request of his employer that he moved his family to nearby North Greenfield, Wisconsin, which later became West Allis. Harold graduated from high school in North Greenfield in 1896, and attended the Milwaukee Business College, where he earned a degree in general business practices. While in school, he worked for his mother's brother, Charles R. Lull, at Charles R. Lull & Company.

On October 21, 1903, Stratton married Bessie Adell Frantz, the daughter of Captain Henry Frantz, a Civil War veteran who farmed a plot of public land, and Nellie Stone, whose fami-

The first executives of the Briggs & Stratton Co-partnership of June 2, 1910. Harold Stratton, left, vice president; Stephen Briggs, center, president; Frank Manegold, right, secretary-treasurer.

Partnership

In 1908, Stephen F. Briggs and Harold M. Stratton began an informal partnership to manufacture and market a six-cylinder, two-cycle automobile engine similar to the one Briggs had designed in college. Stratton invested $50,000 for the business, while Briggs was the hands-on engineer. The office of the tiny Briggs & Stratton Company, rented monthly from the Pfeiffer and Smith Machine Company, was barely large enough to contain a desk.

Unfortunately, this early version of Briggs & Stratton was over almost before it started. Although sound in design, Briggs' engine was simply too expensive to manufacture, much less mass-produce. This early failure did not discourage the partners, for they soon decided to create their own line of automobiles. Their plan was to build the automobiles from parts manufactured elsewhere, a less expensive proposition than manufacturing the parts themselves.

The result was the Superior, a car with a four-cylinder engine manufactured by Continental, a frame from the A.O. Smith Corporation, and a body from a local carriage builder. Two touring cars and a roadster were built before the fledgling company again hit a brick wall. "They were sound cars," explained Briggs, "but we ran out of money, or rather Stratton did, and that was that."[11]

In less than one year, the Briggs & Stratton Company had struck out twice and was out of the automobile manufacturing industry for good. But Briggs was not a man to give up easily. In the early 1900s, the automotive industry showed excellent prospects for future growth, and Briggs was determined to find a niche in which he could excel. He decided to supply a line of specialty products to established automobile manufacturers.

Briggs began in 1909 with a gasoline engine igniter that could replace the magneto, the ignition system utilized by auto manufacturers at the time. Briggs' igniter was more efficient than the magneto at all speeds. The igniter worked by combining the induction coil, timer and distributor into a single mechanism that provided a period of uniform contact in the primary circuit. Also significant was the ease with which the ignition timing could be adjusted. The gas-engine igniter was patented February 22, 1910.[12] But when the prototype was displayed at the New York Auto Show in 1910, it was virtually ignored. Fortunately, the igniter did win some contracts for Briggs & Stratton, including one with the Velie Motor Company of Moline, Illinois, which manufactured roadsters. Encouraged by this limited success, Briggs prepared plans to design, manufacture and distribute an entire line of automobile electrical specialty parts.

The spiffy-looking Superior was assembled by Briggs & Stratton from parts manufactured elsewhere.
Although it ran well, the Superior was expensive to build. Only two touring cars and a roadster were built before the line was discontinued.

A Successful Niche

After only a short period of manufacturing and distributing these automobile specialty supplies, the informal partnership was successful enough to incorporate. The Briggs & Stratton Co-partnership was incorporated in Wisconsin June 2, 1910, with a working capital of $50,000.[13] Stephen F. Briggs was listed as president and Harold M. Stratton as vice president. Frank W. Manegold was secretary-treasurer, and Briggs' friend from college, Charles L. Coughlin, was the factory works manager and secretary.

In 1911, the company reported a gross income of $21,336.17, which, although it was listed as an operating loss of $1,251.86, was indicative of the company's growth.[14] By 1912, it was fast becoming evident that Briggs & Stratton would be successful, as net sales for the first nine months more than doubled those of the entire previous year, to $54,308.90, a net gain of $7,907.52.[15] The following year witnessed an even more substantial increase, with net sales of $116,758.81 for the 12-month period.[16] In 1914, sales again nearly doubled, reaching $222,354.71.[17]

On February 17, 1910, Briggs married Beatrice Branch of Vermillion, South Dakota. This union lasted 66 years, until Briggs' death in 1976, and produced four children, Stephen Albro, John Newton, James Branch and Barbara. None of the Briggs children or grandchildren would ever join the business.

The Briggs & Stratton Company moved into a small section of this Milwaukee Street building in 1909. By 1915, the growing company occupied the third and fourth floors, plus the basement. Unable to expand further, Briggs & Stratton began construction of another facility later that year.

Within a year, Briggs & Stratton had out-grown its home on Clinton Street, and moved to the northeast corner of Milwaukee and Buffalo streets. The company rented three-fourths of the third floor from the Feister-Owens Press Company, for $79.68 per month.[18] In the new location, Briggs & Stratton utilized just under 1,000 square feet of floor space and employed about a dozen men.[19]

The company won several contracts for its gas igniter, including one with the Barr Manufacturing Company of Detroit, for 100 four-cylinder igniters at $13.50, and 20 six-cylinder marine igniters at $15.75.[20] Another contract, with the Morton and Morton Company, called for 500 igniters at $13.50 each.[21] But in 1912, the igniter represented for only $10,500, or about 17 percent of gross sales.[22] By July 1913, the igniter was

The Gas Engine Igniter was the first product developed by Briggs & Stratton at the Milwaukee Street facility. This photo displays an igniter recently refurbished by members of the Tool Room at the Burleigh Plant.

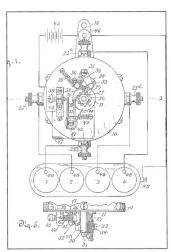

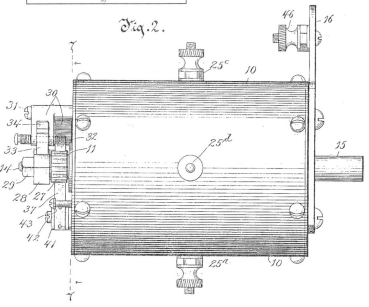

Briggs' original patent drawings for the Gas Engine Igniter, which he filed in February 4, 1909, and which was granted February 22, 1910. Although a marginal success, this was the first item manufactured and sold by the Briggs & Stratton Company that was not a complete failure.

discontinued, accounting for less than 2 percent of gross sales.[23]

One of the more successful specialty parts was the Master Vibrator, a regulator used to control automotive dynamometers, which measured engine horsepower. In 1912, the Master Vibrator led all Briggs & Stratton products in sales, accounting for 47 percent of total gross sales. Although this percentage dropped off in the following few years, the device accounted for $44,260.51 in 1913, $49,230.50 in 1914, and $29,274.51 in 1915. It was not until 1916, when sales fell to $8,956.33, that the Master Vibrator was discontinued.[24]

In 1912, Briggs & Stratton won several valuable distribution contracts from automobile merchandise and parts dealers. On May 15, the company signed a contract with the Arthur Storz Auto Supply Company in Omaha, Nebraska, for a years' supply of Master Vibrators, igniters, switches and other electrical equipment.[25] On August 1, a five-year contract allowed the Fulton-McCutchan Company of Chicago to market and sell the vibrators independently.

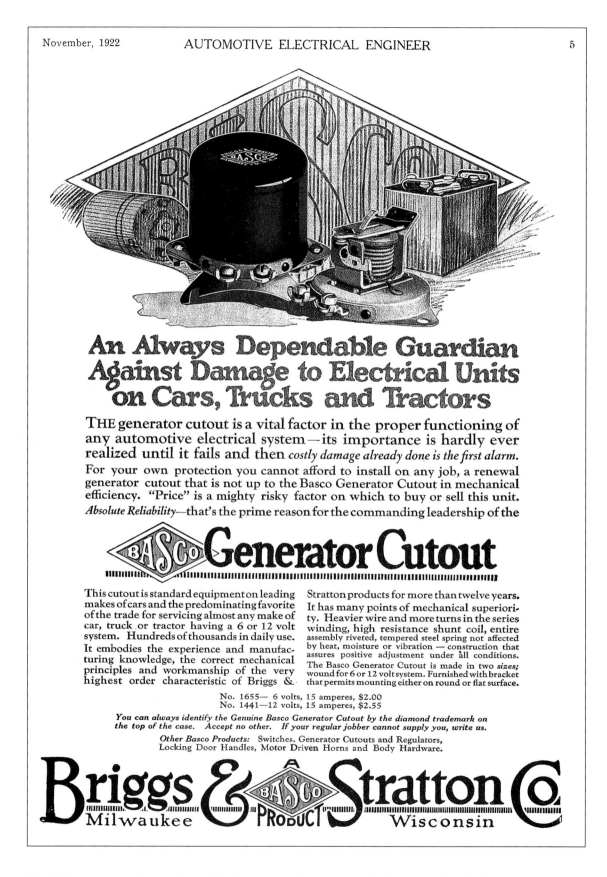

An Always Dependable Guardian Against Damage to Electrical Units on Cars, Trucks and Tractors

THE generator cutout is a vital factor in the proper functioning of any automotive electrical system—its importance is hardly ever realized until it fails and then *costly damage already done is the first alarm.*

For your own protection you cannot afford to install on any job, a renewal generator cutout that is not up to the Basco Generator Cutout in mechanical efficiency. "Price" is a mighty risky factor on which to buy or sell this unit.

Absolute Reliability—that's the prime reason for the commanding leadership of the

BASCO Generator Cutout

This cutout is standard equipment on leading makes of cars and the predominating favorite of the trade for servicing almost any make of car, truck or tractor having a 6 or 12 volt system. Hundreds of thousands in daily use.

It embodies the experience and manufacturing knowledge, the correct mechanical principles and workmanship of the very highest order characteristic of Briggs &

Stratton products for more than twelve years. It has many points of mechanical superiority. Heavier wire and more turns in the series winding, high resistance shunt coil, entire assembly riveted, tempered steel spring not affected by heat, moisture or vibration — construction that assures positive adjustment under all conditions.

The Basco Generator Cutout is made in two *sizes;* wound for 6 or 12 volt system. Furnished with bracket that permits mounting either on round or flat surface.

No. 1655— 6 volts, 15 amperes, $2.00
No. 1441—12 volts, 15 amperes, $2.55

You can always identify the Genuine Basco Generator Cutout by the diamond trademark on the top of the case. Accept no other. If your regular jobber cannot supply you, write us.

Other Basco Products: Switches. Generator Cutouts and Regulators, Locking Door Handles, Motor Driven Horns and Body Hardware.

Briggs & BASCO PRODUCT Stratton Co.
Milwaukee   Wisconsin

This 1922 advertisement for the Briggs & Stratton Generator Cutout appeared in *Automotive Electrical Engineer* magazine.

Chapter Two

AUTOMOTIVE SPECIALTIES AND BASCO

"Merit of product, economy of cost and adequate serving have played a part in gaining almost universal acceptance for Basco Products among the leading car, truck and tractor manufacturers."

— 1923 Basco Brochure

THE GAS IGNITER had opened the door to the world of automotive specialty parts for Briggs & Stratton. Though the igniter itself did not remain long on the market, it led to other products that established the company as a leading manufacturer of automotive components.

Basco

As early as 1913, Briggs & Stratton had developed a niche within the highly competitive automotive industry. To present the company and products to the world in a way that could easily be remembered, the trademark of Basco was developed, standing for the **B**riggs **A**nd **S**tratton **Co**rporation. The Basco trademark and trade name were incorporated within the company structure in December 1913. The trademark patent was filed on January 14, 1914 and granted on January 26, 1915. The easy-to-remember name soon became synonymous with quality.

Until 1919, Basco products included only electrical specialty parts, but the logo evolved and was applied to new products as the marketing department deemed necessary.

The Simple Switch

Although the Master Vibrator was the mainstay of Briggs & Stratton products before 1915, it was the simple, all-purpose electrical switch that took the world of automobile supply by storm. Sales of these remarkably versatile components began at $19,948.81 in 1912, grew to $34,358.08 the following year and then jumped to $89,230.50 in 1914. By 1915, sales had skyrocketed to $177,443.51.[1] Between 1912 and 1916, switches accounted for roughly one-third of gross sales, an impressive statistic considering that each one rarely sold for more than a couple of dollars.[2]

These switches were produced in various forms tailored to different functions. The switch itself was manufactured from drawn steel, with

---

Above: A Briggs & Stratton lock was used in 1935 to protect the spare tire on automobiles from theft.

brass plating and fiber insulation. The face plate was a steel stamping baked in black enamel, with the letters spelling off-dim-on engraved for ease of identification. The switch was lever-operated, and could be modified to control other lights on the outside of the car, as well as the dash lights. It could also be equipped with a locking ignition operated by key.

Early switches, used primarily to control ignition and lighting, were often provided as a combination switch to perform both functions. The combination switch became the most popular

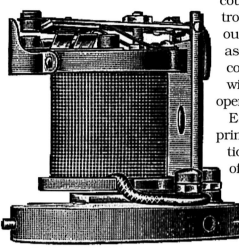

Above: This Reverse Current Cutout automatically connects and disconects the generator and the battery to charge the battery, preventing a drain of current from the battery.

switch product manufactured by Briggs & Stratton. Between 1912 and 1917, some 250,000 combination lighting-ignition switches were sold to such automobile manufacturers as the Willys-Overland Company and the Milburn Wagon Company, both of Toledo, Ohio; the Princess Motor Car Company of Detroit; the Sun Motor Car Company of Elkhart, Indiana; and the Peerless Motor Car Company of Cleveland. These companies would order anywhere from 1,000 to 80,000 at a time, and were charged from $1.15 to $1.60 each.[3]

Electrical Cutouts

Briggs & Stratton sold other automobile specialty items in addition to combination and single-use switches. Plug Transformers and Timers (ignition coils), sold steadily until 1914, when they were replaced by an electrical apparatus called the cutout, which became a company mainstay for several years. Briggs & Stratton also produced several electrical support items that helped modify, simplify, and streamline automotive electrical systems. These items, which began production in

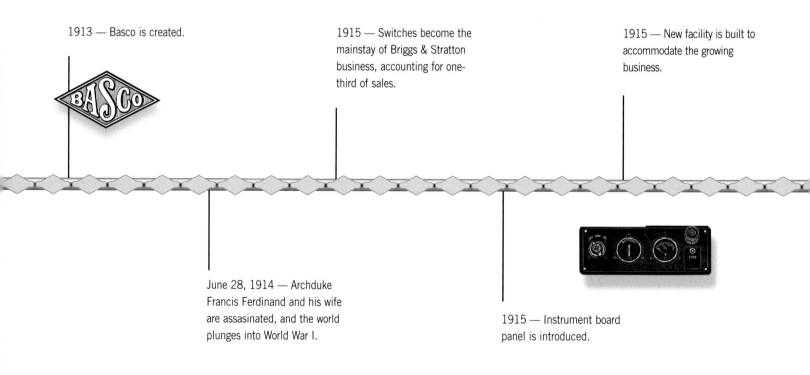

1913 — Basco is created.

1915 — Switches become the mainstay of Briggs & Stratton business, accounting for one-third of sales.

1915 — New facility is built to accommodate the growing business.

June 28, 1914 — Archduke Francis Ferdinand and his wife are assasinated, and the world plunges into World War I.

1915 — Instrument board panel is introduced.

1915, included synchronizers, resistance coils, fuse boxes and circuit breakers. Together, they accounted for almost $50,000 in gross sales between 1915 and 1916.[4]

Electrical cutouts, also known as controllers, became important products for the company beginning in 1913, accounting for $35,762 in sales that year alone. In October 1914, the voltage regulator was introduced, bringing in $17,802.46 in three months. Between 1913 and 1916, regulators and cutouts represented more than $250,000, or about 18 percent of gross sales.[5]

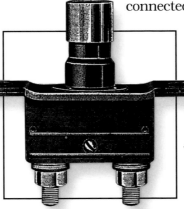

The cutout, reverse current cutout, and eventually the generator cutout, had two functions relating to the flow of electricity from the battery to the balance of the automobile's electrical system. First, it connected the generator to the battery when the generator output was sufficient to charge the battery; and second, it disconnected the generator from the battery when output levels were too low to charge the battery, thus preventing battery drain. The importance of this component was explained in a 1922 advertisement.

"The generator cutout is a vital factor in the proper functioning of any automotive electrical system — its importance is hardly ever realized until it fails and then costly damage is already done in the first alarm."[6]

The regulator was designed to regulate the flow of electricity from the battery to the generator, preventing system overload. It was often sold in conjunction with the cutout, and later, both components were combined into a product called the Universal Regulator Cutout.

Before 1918, the most successful product for Briggs & Stratton was the instrument board

Above: The pedal-operated starting switch was developed in 1917. Between 1912 and 1916, automotive specialties such as these switches comprised roughly one-third of sales.

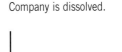

May 16, 1918 — Briggs Loading Company receives contract to assemble, load and pack 1 million rifle grenades.

1924 — Briggs Loading Company is dissolved.

May 7, 1918 — Briggs Loading Company is incorporated.

November 12, 1918 — Armistice Day ends World War I.

panel, also known as the dash panel or switch panel. This was simply a panel designed and manufactured for the needs of the individual automotive manufacturer. A 1916 product catalog described the product and its applications.

"The design of the panel and the group of instruments is optional and in accordance with the wishes of the automobile engineer. ... The instruments included vary with the equipment used. ... Lighting and ignition switch combined or separate, oil gauge, ammeter, dash light and fuse box. The speedometer, carburetor control and clock may be included, or any other combination"[7]

The versatility and quality of this product became readily evident in 1915, its initial year of production. Introduced in May, sales reached $171,752.87 by December 31, and grew to $342,077.13 in 1916.[8] The instrument board panel represented a full 47 percent of sales during this period.

In 1915, Briggs & Stratton really seemed to come into its own, with annual net sales doubling that of the previous year, to $454,049.82, a gain of $121,807.75.[9] Net sales in 1916 again nearly doubled to $740,729.03.[10] In five years, the company had gone from average monthly gross sales of $1,778 in 1911, to $61,727.43 in 1916.[11] In 1917, sales passed the million-dollar mark, totaling $1,014,881.70.[12]

A New Facility

By the fall of 1915, the Briggs & Stratton Company, still at the corner of Milwaukee and Buffalo streets, was renting the entire third floor of the building, plus seven-eighths of the fourth floor and the entire basement. But even the 10,000 feet it occupied wasn't enough.

Stephen Briggs tried to acquire more space in the Feister-Owens building, and even offered to purchase it outright. He also drafted plans to build a

Locking Your Car

Around 1915, the company introduced a combination switch/lock for use on automobile ignitions. This line of Basco products would prove remarkably successful and enduring. The switch/lock was simply a standard Briggs & Stratton switch with a lock built into it, requiring a key for operation. Installed in a wood or metal dash, it operated on either a magnetic or battery-operated electrical system.

Also popular was the use of the transmission switch/ lock, which, when in the locked position, prevented operation of the car. These locks provided a high degree of security from theft and accident. The ignition switch/lock had the advantage of requiring the shut-off of the ignition before the key could be removed, ensuring that the lock would be engaged. This particular unit was also designed to prevent the driver from leaving a running car unattended. As the advertisement claimed:

"Removal is impossible in the unlocked position. ... Using an ignition lock not only leads to more frequent locking of the car, but also protects the driver against forgetfulness in shutting off the ignition."[13]

AUTOMOTIVE ELECTRICAL ENGINEER
February, 1921   5

Universal BASCO

DIM OFF ON

Fits Them All

THE best switch in the world *will* wear out some time. When it finally goes, Mr. Owner wants another — quick! He wants *a* switch — one that fits, looks trim, does its work well and will last.

Old Man Overhead won't let you carry *all* the good switches folks *might* need some day!

Stock the Basco Universal — the switch that's a whole stock in itself!

Interchangeable with switches on practically all makes of cars. The *ideal* renewal switch, *designed* to take care of *any* system — single or double wired; battery or magneto; two-bulb, resistance or series parallel dimming; metal or wood dash; 6 or 12 volts! And it fits them all correctly—efficiently.

The Basco Universal (No. 2051) comes with two keys, a 6-volt dimming coil (12-volt if specified), and extra connectors so that the switch can readily be adapted to battery or magneto-equipped cars.

Makers also of Generator Cut-outs; Current Regulators; Motor Driven Horns; Locking Door Handles for Ford Closed Cars, etc.

Write for Latest Catalog of Basco Automotive and Electrical Components.

Briggs & Stratton Co.
Milwaukee   BASCO PRODUCT   Wisconsin

fifth floor. But these efforts proved fruitless. So that year, Briggs began planning a modern, concrete, fire-proof production facility about five miles from the Milwaukee Street location. This $250,000 facility was to be five stories high, containing 69,030 square feet and equipped with the latest technology in manufacturing and production. Located at the junction of 13th and Center streets, the facility became known as the East Plant.[14]

"Nothing less than a personal visit ... can give the reader a true conception of the unusual size and thorough completeness of the Briggs & Stratton Company's equipment, facilities and organization. ... The Briggs & Stratton plant is

A promissory note signed by Stephen Briggs and Frank Manegold for $7,000.

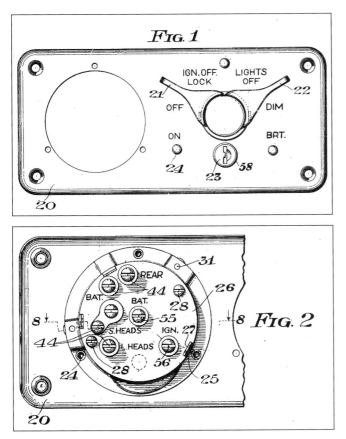

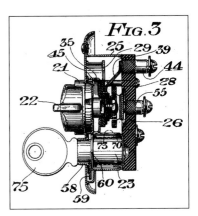

completely and modernly equipped for quantity production of quality units at a minimum cost. Each of the many departments is a complete factory in itself, yet all are so efficiently coordinated that the question of delivery occasions no worry to the manufacturer."[15]

The building was referred to as a "manufacturing institution, not a mere factory."[16] It housed 16 departments, including two in punch press, one in drill press, two in machining, plating and enameling, and others focusing on tooling, finishing, assembly, inspection, testing, heat treatment, as well as shipping and receiving.

In 1918, Briggs & Stratton vacated the building on Milwaukee Street. By this juncture, the Briggs & Stratton Company was supplying specialty parts to the majority of North American automotive manufacturers. A Briggs & Stratton catalog proclaimed:

Above and right: Original patent drawings of various switches and electrical specialty items manufactured at Briggs & Stratton, including lighting and ignition switches, a dash panel, a latch switch and a pedal starting switch.

"Merit of product, economy of cost and adequate serving have played a part in gaining almost universal acceptance for Basco Products among the leading car, truck and tractor manufacturers. No

individual endorsement of Basco products could be so strong as that unstinted approval accorded them by the entire automotive industry. In the roster of companies whom the Briggs & Stratton Company is supplying units are found the names of nearly a hundred manufacturers who are using Basco units. The names in that list speak volumes for Briggs & Stratton."[17]

Electrical specialties by far were responsible for the bulk of Briggs & Stratton sales and revenue. In 1920, electrical specialties amounted to $2.1 million, or 76 percent of total sales.[18] Throughout the twenties, Briggs & Stratton averaged annual net sales of just over $850,000 in electrical specialties alone.[19]

Above: The Press Department on the first floor of the East Plant.

Middle: The third floor housed the Assembly Department, where the electrical switches and specialties were assembled.

Right: The Motor Wheel Machining Department on the fourth floor of the East Plant.

upon to contribute production facilities and labor to the war effort. Though Briggs & Stratton's new facility was large enough to handle both war production and the manufacture of electrical specialties, another facility was necessary to assemble, load and test additional defense production.

The Briggs Loading Company

On May 7, 1918, the Briggs Loading Company was incorporated with a capital stock of $75,000, primarily for ordnance production, as stated in the organizational proceedings.

> *"The business and purposes of this corporation shall be to load grenades, shrapnel, bombs, and shells of every kind and description, and all other explosive containers; to manufacture, buy, sell, trade and deal in guns, ammunition, explosives, air craft, grenades, shrapnel, bombs, shells and all other explosive containers."*[20]

The Briggs Loading Company assembled, tested and packed V.B. Rifle Grenades-Mark I and detonating fuses. It was located

World War I

On June 28, 1914, while on a diplomatic mission in Sarajevo, Austrian Archduke Francis Ferdinand and his wife were assassinated by a Bosnian nationalist, an event which plunged all of Europe, and eventually the world, into war. America managed to stay out of the conflict until 1917, until prompted into action by German resumption of unrestricted submarine warfare, and the coincidental overthrow of the Czarist rule in Russia. On April 6, President Woodrow Wilson declared war on the German Empire.

Like almost every manufacturer in the nation, Briggs & Stratton was called

Above: The Briggs Loading Company was established in 1918, primarily to produce ordnance for World War I. The security post shown on the right was established to meet War Department requirements.

Right: A Briggs Loading Company stock certificate, dated June 27, 1918, shortly after the company was established.

Left: A worker transfers finished grenades and fuses ready for shipment overseas to the loading dock for transport to the East by truck and rail.

Right: Workers at the Briggs Loading Company pose for a group photograph during World War I. Most of the employees were women, since male workers were scarce during the war.

along the Milwaukee River across from the northern end of Estabrook Park. The facility was near abandoned quarries along the river, which were used to test the completed grenades. The remote location preserved the secrecy of the plant and protected the civilian population in case of accident or sabotage.

On May 16, 1918, the company received its first contract from the U.S. Army Ordnance Department, to assemble, load and pack 1 million rifle grenades for $81,250. By the end of the war, Briggs & Stratton and the Briggs Loading Company had received contracts to manufacture and process 13.5 million rifle grenades. However, the contract was never completed because the war ended in November 1918, three months before the agreed delivery date.

The United States government furnished the Briggs Loading Company with components necessary to build the grenades, including "the metal parts of the grenades, fuse containers and all explosives," and the loading company provided "powder for the fuses, the primers, the detonators and the packing boxes."[21] The contract further stated that, "All of the grenade bodies shall be cleaned, varnished and painted with gray stripes."[22]

Women in the Work Force

With most of the work force enlisted for service, the Briggs Loading Company needed to find additional employees to manufacture the grenades. For the first time in history, large numbers of American women found employment outside the home. Though there were many satisfactions to this new status of women, there were logistical problems to overcome. These trailblazers soon discovered that their long Victorian-style dresses were serious hazards, since they could become caught in rotating machinery and belts. Women took to wearing "bloomers," pants-like garments originally intended as undergarments. They also wore pants or overalls when these items were available.

Later in the war, the government required war production facilities to issue pants uniforms to women employees. This requirement helped avoid accidents, and, most likely, quelled the controversy of women wearing bloomers in factories.

The End of the War

When the armistice ending World War I was signed on November 12, 1918, the Briggs Loading Company had yet to build 7.6 million grenades to complete its contract, at a potential profit of $143,023.78. On March 2, 1919, Congress passed a law titled, "An act to provide relief in cases of contracts connected with the prosecution of the war and other purposes," and the Briggs Loading Company filed a claim for compensation. The company estimated the total costs of grenades completed but not delivered, overhead costs and labor, and the loss of potential profits as $252,686.56. Regardless, the company would receive only $64,688.18 of the total amount.[23]

Receiving less than a third of its claim, the Briggs Loading Company faced financial difficulties. The following two years were also difficult for the company, as a post-war depression caught America off-guard. In addition to these chal-

Women production workers marched behind the Briggs & Stratton banner in a 1918 Fourth of July parade.

Employees making grenade casings during World War I. Their jumpsuits were issued by the War Department.

lenges, the Briggs Loading Company had disagreements with the United States Internal Revenue Service. In September 1922, assessments on war profits and excess profits amounted to $74,146.94.25. After about two years of haggling and reassessment, the Briggs Loading Company was actually granted a refund of $3,048.94. The company had actually been taxed on the entire grenade contract, even though it had only completed about half.[24]

When the war ended, Briggs tried to develop a replacement industry for his loading company. He came up with the idea of producing a resin-based composition molding to manufacture radio parts and other items. Unfortunately, the reality of retooling the facility for an entirely new line of manufacture did not make financial sense, and following extensive research, the idea was abandoned.

The combination of under-compensation and tax problems had taken its toll, and the Briggs Loading Company forfeited its corporate rights on January 1, 1923. The IRS refund was all the company had left, and after distribution of funds to the stockholders, all that remained of the Briggs Loading Company was $50.46. In late 1924, the Briggs Loading Company was dissolved.

Another photo reflecting a work force dominated by women during the war. It is interesting to note that the only man in the room (standing, right center) seems to be a supervisor, a situation that was common in this time period.

A close-up view of the Briggs & Stratton Motor Wheel.

Chapter Three

THE MOTOR WHEEL

"There is a fascination about motor wheeling that is simply irresistible. The motor wheel has transformed the labor of bicycling into the pleasure of motoring. With the new Type D Briggs & Stratton Motor Wheel attached to a bicycle, the great open country is within reach of all. The problem of getting to work or business and home again becomes a pleasing anticipation."

— 1920 Company Pamphlet

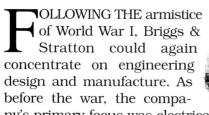

FOLLOWING THE armistice of World War I, Briggs & Stratton could again concentrate on engineering design and manufacture. As before the war, the company's primary focus was electrical specialties for the automotive industry. But in 1919, Briggs & Stratton pursued a new direction, by acquiring the Motor Wheel.

Known as the Wall Auto Wheel, the Motor Wheel was developed in 1910 by Arthur William Wall of Birmingham, England, and manufactured by the International Auto Wheel Company, Ltd., in Kensington, England. It was a 20-inch-spoke bicycle wheel with a 1-horse-power, single-cylinder engine attached laterally to the wheel, driven by a chain attached to the crankshaft. It weighed about 40 pounds and could be fitted to any standard bicycle frame alongside the rear wheel, with an attachment clip. Engaged, it could propel the bicycle to speeds up to 20 miles per hour. It held about a half-gallon of gasoline, enough to travel 50 or 60 miles.[1]

In 1912, the American manufacturing rights for the Wall Auto Wheel were purchased by the A.O. Smith Company, the same company that had employed Stephen Briggs as a machin-

ist in 1906. The name was changed to the Smith Motor Wheel, and several improvements were implemented.

The Model A Smith Motor Wheel, introduced in 1914, was similar to the Wall Auto Wheel except that the chain-driven motor and the spoke wheel were replaced. By utilizing a four-lobe camshaft, the gearing was increased to an 8:1 ratio, thus creating a direct drive locomotion through a 20-inch disc that articulated the wheel directly to the camshaft. Two "horns" attached the engine to the wheel via the crankshaft, holding the fender and gas tank in place. An orifice-type oil system was implemented, and the entire unit was painted bright red.[2]

In 1916, A.O. Smith rolled out the Model B Smith Motor Wheel, which featured a deeper crankcase, a spring-loaded oil pump and an oil gauge. Later that year, the Model BA was introduced, with bronze bearings instead of roller bearings, and an oil drain plug to allow for easier maintenance. The Model C, introduced in 1918,

---

Above: Briggs & Stratton's East Plant in the background, with the Motor Wheel in the foreground.

SEE MY NEW
Type D
Briggs & Stratton

MOTOR-WHEEL
ATTACHMENT for BICYCLES
Don't delay - buy one to-day

featured only a change in the intake cage, which was held on with a clamp instead of screws.[3]

On May 19, 1919, the Briggs & Stratton Company acquired Smith Motor Wheel for $200,000.[4] Later that year, Briggs & Stratton released the Model D Briggs & Stratton Motor Wheel, with several improvements over previous models. A larger cylinder was added, increasing the bore size from $2\frac{3}{8}$ inches to $2\frac{1}{2}$ inches, along with a new, all-steel connecting rod and flywheel

Left: Advertising was an integral part of the early success of the Motor Wheel. Window display posters, such as this one, were used extensively.

Right: A Motor Wheel from the cover of a 1920 promotional booklet.

magneto. These improvements increased the power output to 2 horsepower.[5]

The Motor Wheel Craze

The primary application for the Motor Wheel was to propel the standard bicycle. It was estimated that in 1920, some 3.5 million people owned bicycles, and to Briggs & Stratton, they were all potential customers. The virtues of the Motor Wheel were explained in a 1920 promotional brochure.

"There is a fascination about Motor Wheeling that is simply irresistible. The Motor Wheel has transformed the labor of bicycling into the pleasure of motoring. With the new Type D Briggs & Stratton Motor Wheel attached to a bicycle, the great open country is within reach of all. The

---

1910 — Wall Auto Wheel developed by Arthur William Wall of Birmingham, England.

May 19, 1919 — Briggs & Stratton purchases Smith Motor Wheel for $200,000.

1912 — American manufactuing rights for the Wall Auto Wheel are purchased by the A.O. Smith Company.

1919 — Promotion of Motor Wheel launched at Chicago Cycle Show and Dealer's Convention.

problem of getting to work or business and home again becomes a pleasing anticipation." [6]

In 1920, efforts were directed at exploiting the high sales potential of bicycles and the potential market available for Motor Wheels. "The natural sales of bicycles for 1920 should be 750,000," forecast a Briggs & Stratton pamphlet.

"Last year, bicycle dealers all over the country did a business of more than a million dollars on Motor Wheels. ... The Motor Wheels have created a revival of bicycling that is spreading like wildfire. Old bicycles are going to be resurrected and the Briggs & Stratton Motor Wheel is going to be the power behind this resurrection." [7]

Briggs & Stratton also produced the Model J, a four-wheeled motorized vehicle comparable to a go-kart. Originally known as the Smith Flyer under the ownership of the A.O. Smith Company, it was popularly referred to simply as the Flyer.

The most popular application of the Motor Wheel was as a power source for bicycles.

"The Flyer consists of a buckboard with four wire wheels equipped with pneumatic rubber tires. Two seats are provided, upholstered in

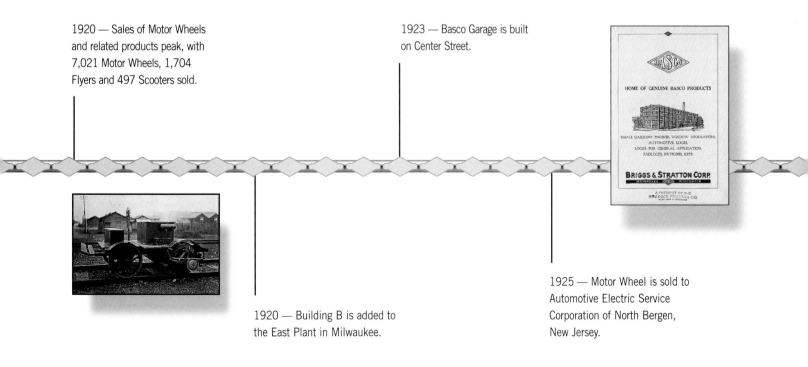

1920 — Sales of Motor Wheels and related products peak, with 7,021 Motor Wheels, 1,704 Flyers and 497 Scooters sold.

1923 — Basco Garage is built on Center Street.

1920 — Building B is added to the East Plant in Milwaukee.

1925 — Motor Wheel is sold to Automotive Electric Service Corporation of North Bergen, New Jersey.

In late 1920, the Model SD Motor Scooter was unveiled to a less-than-enthusiastic market. The Motor Wheel was mounted directly into the rear wheel assembly, and the frame of the scooter was designed with a central footrest. Since it didn't have a cross member to straddle, it was more comfortable than the standard bicycle.

Marketing the Motor Wheel

Promotion of the Motor Wheel was launched in November 1919, at the Chicago Cycle Show and Dealer's Convention, where the Motor Wheel and related products were proudly displayed. This was followed up with full-page and double-page "sales stories" in six national magazines and a cooperative advertising campaign with bicycle dealers nationwide.[9] "A sweeping advertising campaign has been launched and the story of the Motor Wheel will be told to more than five million worthwhile buyers every month

Moroccaline leather. The conveyance is steered by means of a wheel, just like that of an automobile. A foot brake is provided to facilitate stopping the car. Power is derived from a Type D Motor Wheel attached at the rear of the Flyer by means of a pivot pin. A lifting device is provided for the purpose of taking the Motor Wheel off the ground when starting or when coming to a standstill without stopping the engine. When ready to start, the Motor Wheel is lifted from the ground with the lifting lever and motor is started by a few turns of the wheel. Rider takes his place in the seat, throttles the motor down to a slow speed and lowers the lifting device, which brings the Motor Wheel in contact with the ground, and the rider's off."[8]

Briggs & Stratton takes its Motor Wheel show on the road, setting up an impromptu promotion outside of a local jeweler.

Briggs & Stratton founders Harold Stratton (left) and Stephen Briggs take a Type J Flyer for an afternoon ride.

throughout the year," boasted one dealer ad.[10] Another ad was even bolder.

> *"LOOK TO THE FUTURE. ... Opportunity is knocking loudly at the door of every bicycle dealer in America. ... Never was opportunity more insistent ... never before was there such a demand for action, never before was there such a need for the bicycle in speeding up the merchant's business of today. Now is the time for dealers to grasp this new business and take the lead in perpetuating the bicycle for commercial use as well as pleasure."[11]*

With an enlightened marketing strategy, Briggs & Stratton coordinated its advertising to coincide with that of the bicycle dealers. The company stressed the importance of "mat" advertising, a sort of template ad created and distributed to dealers nationally. This format was inexpensive to produce, could be kept on file at the local newspaper, and could easily be customized to include the name of a local dealer. Window ads were also produced and distributed to local bicycle dealers nationwide.

One of the most innovative strategies by Briggs & Stratton was the publication of the *Motor Wheel Age*, a monthly publication written primar-

For a promotional stunt, these men drove a Flyer from St. Louis to Glacier National Park in Montana.

ily for Motor Wheel dealers, with the intention of promoting Motor Wheel products. The magazine featured sales information, tips on caring for the Motor Wheel, information on promotions, and other information relevant to the sales and marketing of Motor Wheels. *Motor Wheel Age* also included human interest features, comic pages, and even songs such as *The Song of the Motor Wheel*, and *Me and My Motor Wheel*.[12]

A Motor Wheel exhibition.

Some of the more interesting articles in this publication focused on the formation of Motor Wheel Clubs, organizations that gathered to swap information, socialize, and, of course, Motor Wheel. Briggs & Stratton marketing officials noted, "There is nothing that will stimulate local interest in Motor Wheeling as the organization of Motor Wheel Clubs."[13]

No one was immune from the media onslaught launched by Briggs & Stratton. "Motor Wheeling is for the youngster as for the grown-ups, for the girl as well as the boy," noted one advertisement. "It is the lady's and the gentleman's mode of conveyance."[14] Young people in general and children in particular were especially targeted.

"The 'Red Bug' so easily handles that it is perfectly safe for any youngster to own. And what a perfect gift it is for a real red-blooded boy or girl. Just imagine hopping into your "Red Bug" and speeding out to the open country ... enjoying the thrill of a big motor car. And you can ride to school in your "Red Bug," do all sorts of errands for your mother. ... Take your folks and friends out. You will be the most popular boy or girl in your crowd."[15]

Commuters were another target for the Briggs & Stratton marketing blitz. One advertisement stated that Motor Wheels will, "soon pay for themselves in car fare and shoe leather, yet economy is not their only virtue. They save time, they eliminate the annoyance of long waits and crowding into congested cars."[16]

A Variety of Uses

Unconventional applications of the Motor Wheel were common. One of the more innovative uses was to power maintenance carts.[17] Another was its attachment to an old horse coach, an application which gave an entirely new meaning to the term "horseless carriage." Stephen Briggs himself designed a towing device for ice skaters, by attaching an old lawn mower handle to a Motor Wheel. A man in Michigan designed a "Snow Machine" from sled runners and a home-built frame with a Motor Wheel attached to the back.[18] One of the more interesting devices was an "Ice-Cycle," a partial bicycle frame with a Motor Wheel in place of the front wheel and spikes on the rear tire for traction on ice.[19]

The Motor Wheel was deemed especially useful in the delivery of goods from market to private residence. Everything from newspapers to groceries were carried throughout major cities via the Motor Wheel.

"Grocers, Butchers, Confectioners, Bakers, Druggists, Milliners, Florists, Dyers, Cleaners, Department Stores, Telephone and Telegraph Companies. ... The mechanical reliability of the Briggs & Stratton Motor Wheel has made it a necessary adjunct to business. Merchandise may be delivered quickly at less expense than by any other present-day method."[20]

One man from New Jersey, whose father had purchased a Flyer in the twenties, beat the gas shortage caused by World War II by using it as reliable transportation over a quarter-century after it left the factory.[21]

A Strong Start

Sales of the Motor Wheel roared to life. In 1919, 798 Motor Wheels and 55 Flyers were sold. In 1920,

This young man bought a Flyer to help him expand his newspaper route. He also used it to travel, in this case driving to Chicago with his cousin.

Different applications for Motor Wheels in winter. Above: A Motor Wheel attached to the rear of a sled turns it into a zippy snowmobile. Below: The Motor Wheel's tremendous versatility was part of its appeal. Here, it propels a sled.

7,021 Motor Wheels and 1,704 Flyers were delivered, as well as 497 Scooters, which had been introduced in September. Net sales for the Motor Wheel and related products topped $661,000.

Though still substantial, 1921 sales decelerated to 2,500 Motor Wheels, 150 flyers, and 442 Scooters, 28 without Motor Wheels.

Export sales grew substantially in 1921, with Motor Wheels sold to Argentina, Canada, Mexico, Central America, the South Pacific and Europe. The most notable customer was Japan, which received 388 Motor Wheels, 20 Flyers, and 70 Scooters. The Japanese found that Motor Wheels were ideal for powering the rickshaw, an ancient mode of transportation that traditionally used foot power, as well as the bicycle. Japan became the most lucrative export market for Briggs & Stratton during the Motor Wheel years. Total sales for Motor Wheel products in 1921 was $211,746.16.

Between 1922 and 1925, sales of the Motor Wheel and related items continued to fall. In 1922, 1,125 Motor Wheels were sold, of which 646 were sent to Japan. In 1923 the number dropped to 493.

Motor Wheel sales dropped slightly again in 1924, and both the Flyer and Scooter were pulled off the market. The last year of Motor Wheel production was 1925, with delivery of only 214 units. That year, Briggs & Stratton sold the Motor Wheel and its related products to the Automotive Electric Service Corporation of North Bergen, New Jersey, which continued distribution of the Flyer and an electric conversion of it until 1928.

In six short years, the Motor Wheel had skyrocketed to success and plunged to extinction. The rapid growth of automobile sales, which in turn created a sudden availability of used automobiles, is often credited for the demise of the Motor Wheel. For the $75 cost of a Motor Wheel, or the $150 needed to buy a Flyer or Scooter, a customer could buy a used Ford Model T. In fact, a brand new Model T in 1923 cost $260.[22]

More Manufacturing Space

The Briggs & Stratton work force more than quadrupled in 1920, swelling from 300 in 1919 to 1,300 in 1920.[23] The company's facilities expanded accordingly. In 1920, Briggs & Stratton built an addition to the company's still-new East Plant at 13th and Center streets in Milwaukee. Completed in June 1920, the addition was actually a second five-story building, known as Building B, which contained 55,520 square feet. In 1923, the Basco Garage was built along Center Street, just east of Teutonia Avenue, to replace the rented property at 1064 Teutonia Avenue, north of the main plant.[24]

Electrical specialties, the products that historically carried Briggs & Stratton to success, were still the principal source of the company's sales and profits. In 1920, the most profitable year of the Motor Wheel, electrical specialties still accounted for $2.1 million in sales, more than three times the revenue of all Motor Wheel products combined.

The Motor Wheel did not survive, but its legacy continued. Early in 1921, Stephen Briggs and his corps of engineers developed an experimental product similar to the Motor Wheel, but with a stationary application. This new version of the Motor Wheel would eventually revolutionize the world of compact power sources. From the death of the Motor Wheel came the birth of the small stationary engine.

Right: Stephen Briggs demonstrates a towing device for use on an ice skating rink. He built the ice tow with a lawn mower handle.

The Nickle Bean Picker, manufactured in 1927 by the Nickle Engineering Works of Saginaw, Michigan, was powered by an F Series engine.

Chapter Four

THE BIRTH
OF THE SMALL ENGINE

"The wide range of its utility and adaptability is shown by the success of its use by manufacturers of garden-cultivators and seeders, air-compressors ... water pumps, water systems, washing machines, ice cream freezers, cream separators, milking machines and electric generators."

— 1920 Promotional Bulletin

THOUGH THE MOTOR Wheel lacked sustained sales, it proved valuable to the company because it led to the development of the stationary engine. As early as 1919, the year the Motor Wheel was acquired by Briggs & Stratton, engineers created a working model of a stationary engine, called the Type S. It is likely that Briggs had the idea for a stationary engine in mind when he purchased the rights to the Motor Wheel.

This working model was a success, and the first Briggs & Stratton small engine, the Type P, or "Portable," engine, was introduced in October 1920. The Type P utilized a $2^1/_2$-inch bore, and could generate 1 horsepower at 2,200 revolutions per minute (rpm). It was similar to the Motor Wheel, except it didn't have the double-wing mounting configuration to connect the engine to the Motor Wheel.

On December 27, 1920, Briggs & Stratton signed a contract with Frank Held of Columbus, Ohio, for a minimum of 1,150 Type P General Utility Engines, at $65 each, supplied over a two-year period.[1] The contract gave Held exclusive rights to use the engine in the garden tractor he manufactured,

with the sole exception of a man named A.G. Bryerly, of Salem, Ohio, who had already begun using the engine in his line of garden cultivators.[2] The Held contract was revised in March 1921, and the price was reduced to $60 per engine.

Pleased with the success of the Type P, Briggs & Stratton began developing other models of the stationary engine. In 1921, the company introduced the Model F "Fullpower" engine, which featured improvements to the ignition, flywheel and cooling fan. This engine was discontinued in early 1923, when several new models were introduced. The New Type P, with a magneto ignition, replaced the old Type P when it was introduced in March. Other models introduced in 1923 were the Model FB, introduced in April; the Type PB "Portable," introduced in October, and the Model FC, introduced in November. The most significant new model developed in 1923 was the Type

Above: The Levitre Tobacco Lath Pulling Machine was used by tobacco growers.

PB, which was used extensively by the Gilson Manufacturing Company of Port Washington, Wisconsin, for the manufacture of lawn and garden equipment. An agreement signed in December 1924 called for the sales and delivery of 1,000 Type PB engines, complete with Zenith carburetor, (less gas tank and muffler), for $42.50 per unit. It is interesting to note that the Gilson representative who signed the agreement was none other than H.W. Bolens, a future magnate in the lawn and garden power equipment industry.[3]

Between 1925 and 1930, 12 engine models were developed and introduced by Briggs & Stratton. These models included the FE, FH, FHI and Q in 1925; FG and FI in 1927; FJ-1 and the R Series in 1929; and the FJ-2, M Series, the T Series, S, SC, and the L Series in 1930.[4] All of these engines ranged from $1/2$ to $2 1/2$ horsepower, and each was developed with a specific application, and special features tailored to that purpose.

Although these engines were intended primarily for use in agricultural machinery, it quickly became evident that the nearly universal application for a small gasoline engine was its strong point. A promotional bulletin released by Briggs & Stratton in 1920 listed some of the uses for the Type P General Utility Engine.

"The wide range of its utility and adaptability is shown by the success of its use by manufacturers of garden-cultivators and seeders, air-compressors ... water pumps, water systems, washing machines, ice cream freezers, cream separators, milking machines, electric generators ... storage battery chargers, portable and isolated electric light plants, power lawn mowers, railway speeders, grindstones ... saws, and other similar applications."[5]

Though the uses for this small engine were virtually limitless, the product was mainly used for lawn and garden applications. Companies such as Moto-Mower and RED-E Engine purchased hundreds of Briggs & Stratton engines for use on lawn mowers, garden cultivators and farm tractors. These companies often featured the Briggs & Stratton engines as the main selling point of their products.

Briggs & Stratton engines were also used as a power source for home washing machines. Although electric motors were the industry standard, much of rural America did not have access to electricity. F.B. Zieg, who manufactured washing machines for the Sears, Roebuck & Company, also held an exclusive contract with Briggs & Stratton for Type F engines.

Serving the Navy

Beginning in 1929, Briggs & Stratton engines were used by the military. Models FJ-1, intro-

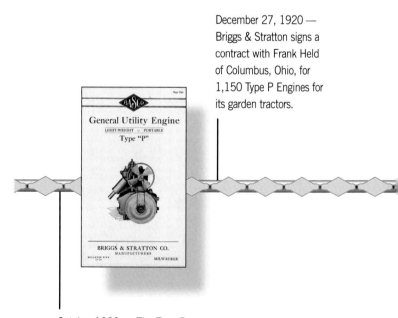

December 27, 1920 — Briggs & Stratton signs a contract with Frank Held of Columbus, Ohio, for 1,150 Type P Engines for its garden tractors.

October 1920 — The Type P "Portable" Engine is introduced.

Above: The 1–horsepower Model FG Engine, introduced in 1929.

duced in 1929, and FJ-2, introduced in 1930, were designed for the United States Navy, which needed a lightweight engine to power portable generators and radio sets. Briggs & Stratton designed an amazingly lightweight engine, utilizing a new type of aluminum alloy for the casting of the engine base, which decreased the total engine weight to less than 40 pounds. This new engine design was perfectly suited to the needs of the Navy, and it set a precedent for later designs and applications, particularly during World War II. The use of aluminum as a major component of engine manufacture was an invaluable innovation.

By the mid-twenties, it was clear that this new engine was no passing fad, as the Motor Wheel had been. In 1921, net sales of gasoline engines reached $58,875.66. In 1922, the number rose to $63,671.66, and in 1923 it jumped dramatically to $248,378.48.[6] By

1930, a cumulative total of 187,759 engines had been manufactured at Briggs & Stratton, representing combined net sales of $6.9 million.[7] A new Briggs & Stratton had emerged.

Financial Difficulties

Despite the success of the stationary engine, Briggs & Stratton faced financial difficulties. The steady sales of previous years were not enough to pull the company out of the

The Model PB powered this fruit-gathering machine, developed in 1927 by P.H. Lint of San Jose, California.

1929 — Briggs & Stratton creates lightweight engines for the United States Navy.

1924 — Briggs & Stratton Company reorganized under state of Delaware law as the Briggs & Stratton Corporation.

1930 — Briggs & Straton acquired window regulator patents from Locliff Company of Toledo, Ohio.

Bolens, Inc., of Port Washington, Wisconsin, was one of Briggs & Stratton's biggest customers. This garden cultivator was one of many products produced by Bolens.

red, and from 1920 to 1922, the company had shown only marginal improvement.

Board Chairman John I. Beggs attempted to explain the difficulties in a letter to stockholders:

"Your Company, which prior to the World War, had grown from small beginnings to very substantial proportions, and had prepared itself for large and continuous operations, in 1920 and 1921 suffered from a sudden cessation of business, and a violent reduction in the value of supplies, materials and parts, and of finished goods. ... Furthermore, contracts which the company had with buyers ... were, without notice, repudiated and other un-looked for and un-expected un-favorable conditions arose in rapid succession which put the Company itself in serious jeopardy."[8]

An early lawn mower powered by a Briggs & Stratton engine.

The other "un-looked for and un-expected un-favorable conditions" arising that Beggs spoke of in his letter were probably the post-war economic slump, slipping sales and financial overextension caused by construction of the new production facility on Center Street, the "B" building.

The company had invested heavily in the Motor Wheel, and an innovative new invention, the Electric Frigerator, which had been purchased from local inventor Alfred Mellowes, who was also retained to continue development of the product. Several thousand dollars had been invested, and neither product lived up to expectations. A disappointing return on war claims, combined with an extended Internal Revenue Service struggle, amplified the worsening situation.

By 1923, these conditions conspired to push the company into a total indebtedness of $726,938. The future of Briggs & Stratton was in jeopardy. However, the board of directors was aware of these problems as early as 1921, and made arrangements with prominent investors in Milwaukee to assist. An agreement was drawn up between the Briggs & Stratton Company and three prominent Milwaukee investors: J.H. Puelicher, Robert W. Baird and Morris F. Fox. Referred to as the Briggs & Stratton Company Stock Trust Agreement, it called for a monitor of financial activities, as well as immediate planning for the recapitalization and reorganization of the company.[9]

On June 30, 1924, the Briggs & Stratton Company, under the guidance of the Briggs & Stratton Trust Agreement Trustees, was liquidated and reorganized under Delaware law as the Briggs & Stratton Corporation.

Hardware

In the late twenties, the company also introduced a new line of automotive support products referred to as hardware. This product line included outside door handles, inside door levers, door knobs, and ornamental plates and hinges for keyholes. Briggs & Stratton promoted these items as "Automobile Body Hardware of Distinctive Character."[10] The Briggs & Stratton catalog summed up the rationale for this line of production.

"Instead of designing a full line of stock types of body hardware similar to the products of other firms ... the Briggs & Stratton policy has been to ... study the field, ascertain the actual need for a certain piece of hardware, then to proceed to develop a unit to meet the requirement. ... During the twelve years that Briggs & Stratton engineers have been closely associated with leading automobile builders, they have

The East Plant, located at 13th and Center streets, was the primary manufacturing site for automotive products until 1973, when lock production was moved to the Good Hope plant in Glendale.

*observed that in the majority
of body hardware there is, and
has been, a marked absence of
those finer details that show real engineering
thought. As a result, they have perfected a number
of body hardware units that have met with enthu-
siastic acceptance by the industry and are now
being used as standard equipment. ... The same
effectiveness and thoroughness that has always
characterized the production of Basco Electrical
Equipment is supplied in Basco Body Hardware."[11]*

Between 1913 and 1920, a new application for
electrical specialty products emerged when Briggs
& Stratton created a Basco switch for use aboard
aircraft. Essentially a lever-type starter switch, it
was used in both single- and twin-engine aircraft.
Airplanes also used light switches similar to those
used in automobiles. The company's customers
included Boeing Aircraft, Curtiss Aeroplane, Pratt-
Whitney Air Craft, Ford and the United States War

Department, for whom Briggs & Stratton also
supplied gun-control switches.[12]

Briggs & Stratton also began supplying
electrical switches for use on boats.
Again, the primary products were starter
switches, some with locking mechanisms, as well as lighting and electrical
switches. One switch was designed
and used as a control for an anchor
hoist. Briggs & Stratton marine customers included Chris Smith & Sons
(later Chris-Craft), U.S. Motor
Corporation, Evinrude and Moto-
Meter Gauge.[13] This line of specialty products for the marine industry
remained a lucrative market until
the end of World War II.

In 1929, Briggs & Stratton
shipped more than 11 million locks to
approximately 130 manufacturers,
including General Motors, Ford, Dodge
Brothers and Chrysler.[14] By 1930, Briggs &
Stratton was the largest manufacturer of automobile locks in the world, producing more than two-
thirds of the automobile locks in the United States.

Briggs & Stratton acquired Metal Spring
Covers from the I-X-L Spring Cover Company
of Milwaukee in March 1930. Used to cover
and protect the rear leaf springs of automobiles, the primary function of the covers was to keep the spring fully lubri-
cated while preventing contamination
from dirt and water.

Above: A Model P engine was used on this 1924 "Star" walk-
behind garden tractor.

Right: The Red E reel type mower received its power from Briggs &
Stratton engines.

THE CYLINDER LOCK

In the early twenties, Briggs & Stratton expanded from simple lock/switches into a cylinder lock, which became a quick success. During the mid-twenties, it overtook electrical specialties to become the company's number one product.

Standard cylinder locks could be used on various access areas located on the automobile. Their primary use was on doors, but they could also secure a car's ignition, transmission, radio and spare tire. A smaller version of the same lock was used for the glove compartment, trunk and rear deck, or rumble seat. It was common for as many as 12 locks to be used on a single car. Since each required a separate key, the simple task of getting into a car and starting it up could be overwhelming.

To solve the problem of key overload, Briggs & Stratton offered a system that could be installed on any new car manufactured with its locks. For a 75-cent fee, the owner could streamline his key chain. One option was to order combinations of keys to work in sets, with one key for access to the ignition, tire and door, and the other for compartments on the car. A second option was to order one master key for every lock on the car.

The locks produced at Briggs & Stratton were manufactured from lock cylinders purchased from the King Lock Company of Chicago. But the cylinders were expensive and not always available. Ever the engineer, Stephen Briggs decided to die-cast his own lock cylinders. Once the process proved successful, Briggs went to Charles Nash of the Nash Motor Car Company, Kenosha, Wisconsin, and sold him on the idea of developing a new type of zinc die-cast transmission lock.

This conversion of lock cylinders from machined brass to die-cast zinc was a major contribution to the industry. "From that point on it pretty much revolutionized the construction of automotive locks," recalled Harold Stratton II, vice president of Briggs & Stratton Technologies before it was spun off into STRATTEC Security Corporation. "Virtually every car in the world is running ... with zinc die-cast locks."[15]

Briggs, in December 1924, began this innovative method of lock cylinder production. Lacking the facilities needed to cast metal, he contracted this work out to the Stroh Die Moulded Casting Company of Milwaukee.

To complement auto lock service and sales, Briggs & Stratton developed a variety of accessories. Several key-cutting tools and jigs were developed for service centers and distributors, as well as key depth decoders, key code books, coding tools and various specialized tools for servicing the locks. In the late thirties, the company introduced the Universal Automotive Key Cutting Machine, a device developed to accurately cut keys for locks made not only by Briggs & Stratton, but Yale, Hurd and Chicago lock companies as well.

Branching out from auto locks, Briggs & Stratton introduced the Basco Padlock in 1929. A die-cast lock made of case-hardened steel, it was guaranteed for "lifetime service," which in actuality was two years from the purchase date. "You will be given a new padlock absolutely free if your Basco is tampered with and thereby damaged, causing failure to operate," the company promised.[16]

The success of the Basco line of locks was almost overwhelming. Between 1926 and 1930, net sales of locks averaged more than $1.5 million per year, with sales reaching almost $2.5 million in 1929.[17] That year, 70 percent of Briggs & Stratton business was in the manufacture and sales of locks. The company supplied about 75 percent of the automotive industry, representing two-thirds of lock production nationwide.[18]

The Nash Motors Company was a typical customer, buying a year's requirements of the springs, which came in a set of eight covers, since it required a set to cover the two leaf springs in each wheel, at $1.20 per set.[19] During the first five months, sales of Metal Spring Covers generated nearly $10,000, but this item was never a major success. Though it averaged between $15,000 and $20,000 a year in net sales, Briggs & Stratton discontinued the line during World War II.

Also manufactured under the Basco name was the Window Regulator, acquired for $275,000 on July 15, 1924 from the Toledo Automotive Product Company. This gear mechanism was used to raise and lower windows in automobiles, and later was used on railway passenger cars. A steady seller, net sales from the Window Regulator averaged just under $400,000 a year between 1925 and 1930.[20] In 1929, Briggs & Stratton introduced a new window lifter that was lighter and less expensive than those already in use.

Because it was so difficult to operate the existing lifters, this design was immediately adapted for use on railroad coaches. On September 23, 1929, it was reported that a prototype was installed for use on the Chicago, Milwaukee, St. Paul and Pacific railroad cars "for thorough experimental tests under actual operating conditions."[21]

In March 1930, Briggs & Stratton acquired from the Locliff Company of Toledo, all of its patents relating to window regulators. Within a year, Briggs & Stratton window regulators were used on board the observation cars of the Pennsylvania, New Haven and Hartford, Union Pacific and Northern Pacific railroads, as well as those of the Pullman Company.[22]

In what was becoming a Briggs & Stratton tradition, the Window Regulator met with more success in an alternative market than that for which it was intended. The regulator remained a quiet success until 1945, when the Locliff Company was liquidated. The design and patents were assigned to Nash-Kelvinator in December 1948.

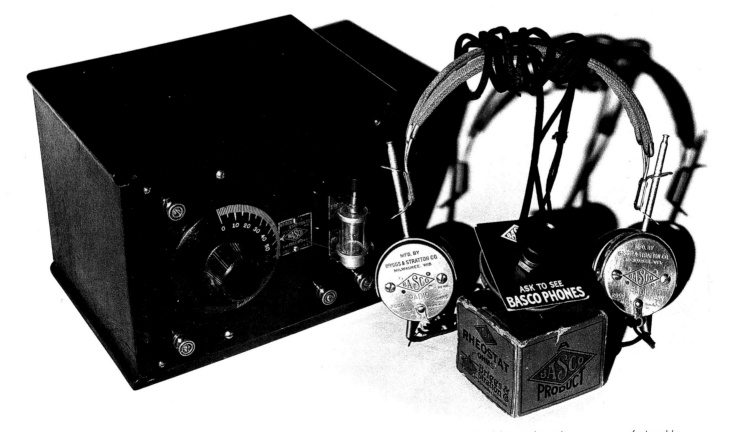

The Briggs & Stratton Basco Crystal Radio Set, introduced in 1922. Even the tuning dial and headphones shown here were manufactured by Briggs & Stratton.

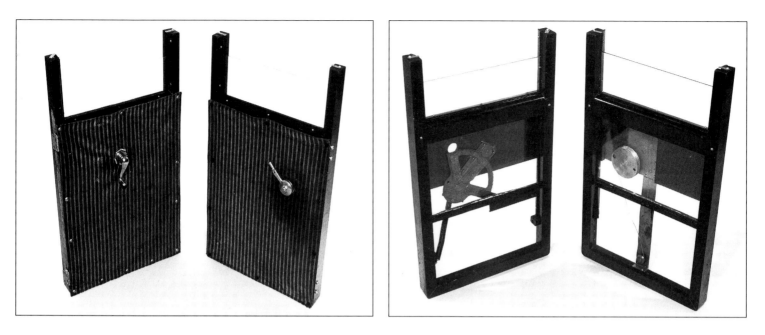

The Window Regulator, developed in 1924, was used to open and close windows in railway cars. The view at left depicts the regulators the way they would appear to passengers. The open view, at right, reveals the mechanism that lifts the windows.

Specialty Products

In addition to its automotive products, Briggs & Stratton produced several specialty lines under the Basco label. These products included a line of radio accessories, including crystal sets, radio cabinets, headphones, and an innovation known as the battery eliminator, designed to convert AC power to DC.

The Basco name was even attached to the gas engine, a line of manufacture that would dominate Briggs & Stratton sales. By the late twenties, gas engines would compete with automotive locks and hardware as the principal source of revenues.

But after 1930, the Basco name was dropped from gas engine manuals and advertising. And electrical specialties, which dominated the company until the mid-twenties, would be virtually eliminated by 1945.

The Basco Distribution Network

In order to support products in the field, Briggs & Stratton created the Basco Distributors and Central Service Network. This corporate philosophy was summed up in the 1923 catalog.

"We do not believe that our obligation to the manufacturer ends when we ship him the components that are supplied by us. We recognize the fact that the ultimate success of any manufacturer's product depends upon the service rendered the owner. To this end we have built a network of distributors and service stations to service Basco equipment. In addition ... there are a great number of sub service stations. A complete stock of service parts is carried by these distributors assuring prompt servicing for any owner when occasion demands.[23]

The first Briggs & Stratton Distributor and Central Service Station representative for Wisconsin was the Lemke Electric Company, where Stephen Briggs had been a partner years earlier. This relationship, however, lasted only a short time. By the late 1920s, Briggs & Stratton had formed a new affiliation with Wisconsin Magneto of Milwaukee, a business relationship that survives to the present day.

The concept of a centralized distribution and service system eventually grew into an international system of product support, among the reasons for the continuing success of the Briggs & Stratton Corporation.

This window card assured customers that the dealer within sold and serviced Basco radios and power units.

Chapter Five

FRIGERATORS AND RADIOS

"The Briggs & Stratton Frigerator is a complete, scientifically built, self–contained, cold storage plant of a size suitable for homes. In addition to the food compartments and cooling coils, it consists of an electrically driven frigerating machine, which automatically controls and continually reuses, an unfailing Frigerant which maintains a perfect cold for the preservation of food."

— Frigerator Brochure

IT COULD NEVER be said that the engineers and designers at Briggs & Stratton either lacked innovation or were afraid to risk a new idea. The company dabbled in many markets, including some which later became substantial. Refrigerators and radios were not invented by Briggs & Stratton, and are not Briggs & Stratton products today. But Briggs & Stratton technology was essential to the development of both. Stephen Briggs was an inventor and an experimenter, and his influence could be seen in the company's willingness to explore new directions.

The Frigerator

The electric "Frigerator" was developed by Milwaukee native Alfred Mellowes. (Refrigerators referred at the time to units that used ice for coolant.) Mellowes first produced the Frigerator in 1915 under the name of Domelre. In 1916, he moved his operation to Detroit, and changed the name of his company to the Guardian Frigerator Company. In 1918, it was purchased by William Durant, then president of General Motors, who sold his interests to General Motors a year later. General Motors subsequently moved the operation to Dayton, Ohio, and renamed the company Frigidaire.

Around the same time Mellowes was looking for investors, Briggs & Stratton was exploring investment opportunities. Briggs & Stratton became intrigued with the improvements Mellowes had incorporated into the Frigerator, making it safer, quieter and cleaner. Mellowes still held several of the original patents on critical components of the Frigerator, including the evaporator, a device that allowed operation of the Frigerator without the production of poisonous ammonia gas as an unwelcome byproduct.

After Mellowes sold his company to Durant, he was hired by Briggs & Stratton to be head of its new Frigerator Division. Following additional research and exhaustive testing, the Briggs & Stratton Frigerator was ready for market.

The Briggs & Stratton Frigerator of 1919 was similar to an icebox, except it was powered by electricity. At the heart of the unit was a small

Above: The compressor and motor of a Briggs & Stratton Mellowes Electric Frigerator.

electric motor situated beneath the frigeration unit, within a closed compartment that kept the operation quiet and hidden from view, with "No spoiling of pretty kitchens ... no danger to children."[1] Within this compartment were the internalized components designed by Mellowes, including the sealed valve, cooling chamber, thermostat, pressure controls, frigerating apparatus and the evaporator.

The evaporator was most significant, for it was the principal component that revolutionized the refrigeration industry. Designed by Mellowes during his short tenure at Briggs & Stratton, the evaporator replaced the system of cooling the frigeration compartment through a brine tank. The evaporator utilized several frigerant tubes, which ran laterally along and above a water-freezing compartment. These tubes, when filled with cold water, absorbed heat at an

Display model of a Briggs & Stratton Mellowes Electric Frigerator. The motor, condenser and evaporator were housed under the compartment and hidden behind a door.

1915 — Frigerator first produced by Alfred Mellowes.

1919 — Durant sells Frigerator to General Motors.

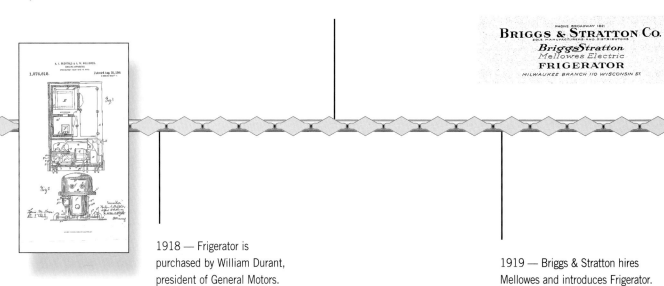

1918 — Frigerator is purchased by William Durant, president of General Motors.

1919 — Briggs & Stratton hires Mellowes and introduces Frigerator.

extremely fast and efficient rate, forcing cooled air to descend into the food compartments.

A company pamphlet described the unit:

"The Briggs & Stratton Frigerator is a complete, scientifically built, self-contained, cold storage plant of a size suitable for homes. In addition to the food compartments and cooling coils, it consists of an electrically driven frigerating machine, which automatically controls and continually reuses, an unfailing Frigerant which maintains a perfect cold for the preservation of food." [2]

The Mellowes Electric Frigerator was indeed a fine piece of engineering. It stood about 5 feet high, 3 feet wide, 2 feet deep, weighed 700 pounds, and was available in cabinets made of oak, ash or white enamel. Within were two food compartments (one small with one shelf, one large with five shelves), and a freezer compartment that contained two smaller compartments

A company brochure in 1920 touts the new Mellowes Electric Frigerator. The compartment at the upper left held ice cube trays.

1921 — Frigerator discontinued.

1922 — Briggs & Stratton radio set is introduced.

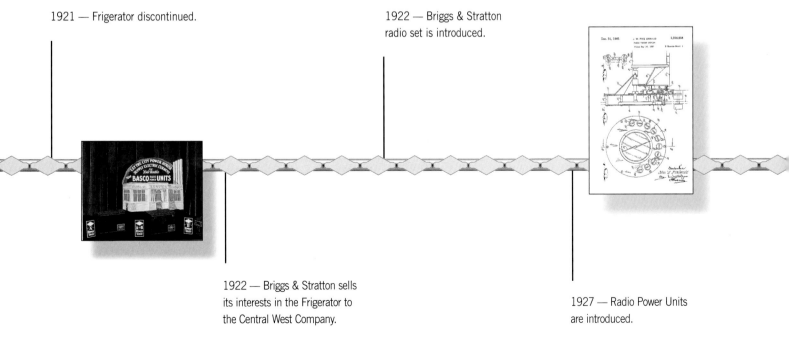

1922 — Briggs & Stratton sells its interests in the Frigerator to the Central West Company.

1927 — Radio Power Units are introduced.

for making ice cubes. The interior of the Frigerator contained 10 cubic feet of storage space, and maintained the environment within 4 degrees of the thermostat setting.

One advantage of the electric Frigerator over the conventional icebox was that it eliminated the problem of using ice as a coolant. As it melted, ice led to mold and mildew, damp and musty odors, and a moist cold that was at best inconsistent, and at worst caused food to spoil. "The Briggs & Stratton Frigerator keeps food in a uniform, pure air," stated a sales brochure.[3] "Instead of moisture from melting ice, you have a perfect dry cold, which guards against deterioration,

taints and musty smells."[4] Also significant was the "icemaker" included with the unit, though it was nothing more than two small freezer compartments that held ice cube trays, a feature which had never been offered in a household refrigeration unit.

One of the most attractive features of the Frigerator was its low cost of operation, which averaged about $3.50 per month, including electricity and water for use in the condensing coils. It was considerably less expensive and more convenient than purchasing ice several times a month. One ad noted that, "Refrigerators melt ice and waste money; Frigerators make ice and save money."[5]

Despite these advantages, the Frigerator never sold well, partly because, at $600, it was

Above: A sales brochure from the Frigidaire Corporation extolls the benefits of the "iceless refrigerator." The Frigidaire used patents developed by Mellowes before he joined Briggs & Stratton.

Right: The Briggs & Stratton Mellowes Electric Frigerator stood more than 5 feet tall, weighed 700 pounds and occupied 16 square feet of floor space.

too expensive for the average family. For the two years it was on the market, 1920 and 1921, it recorded total sales of only $22,614.31.[6] It was never accepted as a standard household appliance like the modern refrigerator of today. Unfortunately, Briggs & Stratton spent $154,114.65 on research and development of this product, nearly seven times the amount of its total net sales.

When the Frigerator was discontinued in 1921, Stephen Briggs commented that Mellowes was simply ahead of his time.

"His ideas at the time were already years ahead of anything else and were thoroughly practical. But unfortunately we ... couldn't afford to go ahead. The Frigerator, our latest development, had to be given up."[7]

On March 22, 1922, Briggs & Stratton sold its interests in the Frigerator to the Central West Company for $28,000, a pittance considering how significant the device would be in future years.

The Radio

First developed in the early 1910s, the Basco Radio fared much better than the Frigerator. Briggs & Stratton had already established a tradition of improving existing products, and the company improved the radio by developing a crystal detector radio set.

The Briggs & Stratton Radio Set consisted of a standard crystal set, housed in a mahogany cabinet 6 inches high, 8 inches wide and 6 inches deep. The crystal detector set utilized two different battery power sources, known as "A" battery and "B" battery power, which heated the filament and energized the plate of the crystal respectively. The filament, also known as a cat whisker, would rectify the crystal, which would in turn detect high-frequency signals located within the electromagnetic spectrum via the antenna. These signals would be transferred to the tuning coil, which would allow the listener to tune into the station of choice.

In 1922, a Crystal Radio Set sold for $12. It was sold through several dealers, though it was primarily offered through large department and catalog stores such as Montgomery Ward and

Above: The inside of a Basco Radio. One battery heated the coil and another energized the crystal, which detected signals through the antenna.

Left: Stephen Briggs consults with a radio production engineer in 1922.

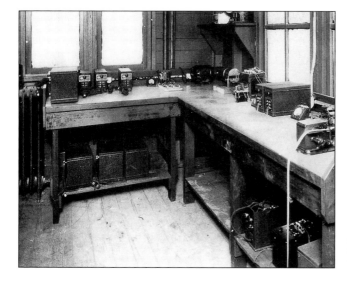

Above, left to right: An assembly station and a testing station in the Radio Department.

Tresco. The set was also sold independently through advertisements in trade magazines such as *Radio News* and *Radio Retailing*.

Several radio accessories were developed by Briggs & Stratton, including the innovative tuning dial, which selected the station at the push of a button. Developed in the mid-thirties, this item could be attached to any existing radio. Another accessory developed by Briggs & Stratton was a headphone set, available from most dealers at prices ranging from $6 to $7.50. Also developed were rheostats (electronic resistance units), audion sockets, cat whiskers and other related items. Briggs & Stratton even attempted to re-tool the Briggs Loading Company to produce Bakelite composition moulding, a new plastic-type resin material used to produce radios, radio parts and accessories, but the plan never came to fruition.

Probably the most recognized of the radio-related products of Briggs & Stratton was the battery eliminator, introduced in the mid-twenties. Known as the Radi "A" battery eliminator, this device eliminated the need for battery power. The Radi "A" was plugged into a standard household outlet. Again Briggs & Stratton had filled a void in the industry with engineering foresight. The only problem with the Radi "A" was that it lost its charge when not in use, such as when it sat on shelves waiting to be purchased. The eliminators were eventually recalled, and research was started to correct the problem. However, the invention of the rectifier in 1927 allowed for the use of AC power in all radios, and completely eliminated the need for radio battery power. The introduction of this new technology meant the end of the Radi "A."

To compete within the industry, Briggs & Stratton developed a line of radio power units. Although the rectifier bulb eliminated the need for radio batteries on new radios, there was still a substantial market for old

Left: The Basco "B" Power Unit, a device that improved radio operation by delivering only as much power as needed.

radios and conventional power sources. In 1927, Briggs & Stratton introduced its new line of Radio Power Units, known as "A" Power, "B" Power and "AB" Power.

The "A" power unit was an exide "A" battery, with a built-in charger that operated when the radio was idle. It automatically charged the battery to peak voltage, then shut down, avoiding overcharging and possible damage. The "B" power unit was a conversion unit, with the exception that it utilized a rectifier bulb. It also employed a regulator to adapt to the specific voltage needs of the radio, improving reception and sound quality. It featured additional power-storage capacity, which improved overall operation. The two units could operate in tandem as the "AB" power unit.

The Briggs & Stratton radio lines experienced nominal success for about 15 years. Though sales were never as strong as for locks and electric specialty items, they were considered respectable. Net sales averaged more than $100,000 a year between 1922 and 1929.[8]

An advertising campaign was launched in 1927 and 1928 to market the new radio power units.

But eventually Briggs & Stratton would focus on the cost-efficient small engine business, and the Basco radio products were phased out. In 1937, the licensing rights for the Radio Tuning Device were sold to the Arcturus Radio Tube Company of New Jersey for a royalty of $7\frac{1}{2}$ cents per unit and a minimum royalty of $10,000 per year.

The 1920s marked a period of exceptional growth for Briggs & Stratton. In 1927, the corporation began another expansion at its East Plant facility. Between 1927 and 1930, eight land lots were acquired, at a cost of $375,273, and existing facilities and equipment were upgraded, at a cost of $42,197.[9]

Two advertisements for Basco radio power units. Individual dealers could customize the ad by inserting their names in the text.

By 1930, it was evident that the small engine was the future of Briggs & Stratton. By the mid-thirties, all Basco lines except automotive locks were de-emphasized or discontinued, and the Basco trademark was virtually eliminated. Other radio-related products were also phased out or sold, and by the close of World War II, Briggs & Stratton had completely abandoned the radio business.

A 1940 company postcard illustrates the pleasure of boating with a Briggs & Stratton engine.

Chapter Six

OLE EVINRUDE AND THE MARINE INDUSTRY

"I liked the outboard business better. It just had more romance. I wasn't contributing much to Briggs & Stratton and I decided I wanted to devote all my time to Outboard Marine."

— Stephen F. Briggs

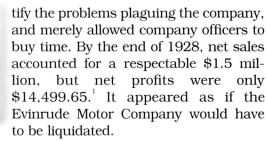

STEPHEN BRIGGS WAS a marine enthusiast who loved motor boats and took particular interest in the manufacture of marine engines. His early affiliation with Ole Evinrude, a customer of his first business venture, the Lemke-Briggs Electric Company, helped to fuel this early interest. When the Evinrude Motor Company was near bankruptcy in 1928, Briggs proposed the idea of acquiring and revitalizing the company.

The Evinrude Motor Company was incorporated October 29, 1910 with a working capital of $20,000, to manufacture detachable rowboat motors and supplies. Ole Evinrude, president of the company, had developed the principles and engineering concepts necessary for outboard motor production. Ole and his wife, Bess, with Chris J. Meyer as vice president, built the company into a successful venture in a matter of years.

A 1913 buyout displaced Ole Evinrude as president, and by 1926, the Evinrude Motor Company faced serious financial and organizational problems. In February 1926, the company undertook a total reorganization, adding substantial capital through various stocks and notes. Unfortunately, the reorganization did little to rectify the problems plaguing the company, and merely allowed company officers to buy time. By the end of 1928, net sales accounted for a respectable $1.5 million, but net profits were only $14,499.65.[1] It appeared as if the Evinrude Motor Company would have to be liquidated.

Fortunately, the company was given a chance to survive. On June 1, 1928, under the direction of Stephen Briggs, Briggs & Stratton acquired all outstanding common stock of the Evinrude Motor Company at a total cost of $94,875, and thus obtained controlling interest in the company.[2] Briggs reasoned that it made sense to add outboard motors to the Briggs & Stratton line of small engines.

By December 31, 1928, Briggs & Stratton had invested $365,759.06 in Evinrude. But the company was still in dire financial straits.[3] The manufacture of outboard motors may have been similar to the manufacture of standard small engines, but marketing, sales and promotion techniques were very different.

Above: This 2-horsepower Evinrude detachable row boat motor was first introduced around 1910.

A January 1940 advertisement that appeared in *Motor Boating* and *Yachting* magazines boasts of the quality and dependability of Briggs & Stratton inboard motors.

Harold Stratton, along with other members of the board of directors, insisted that Briggs & Stratton divest Evinrude. Briggs refused. Convinced that Evinrude was commercially viable, he took the future of the company into his own hands. Though Stratton urged the company to sell Evinrude, he had faith in the instincts of Briggs, and became an investor in the new outboard motor company.

The Outboard Marine Corporation

In early 1929, Briggs began organizing a group of investors to independently acquire Evinrude from Briggs & Stratton. Among these investors was Ole Evinrude, then president of the highly successful Elto Outboard Motor Company, an acronym for Evinrude Light Twin Outboard. The plan was to consolidate two (and later three) of the four major manufacturers in the field of outboard motors. The

1928 — Evinrude Motor Company is acquired by Briggs & Stratton.

1929 — Evinrude, the Elto Outboard Company and the Lockwood Motor Company merge to form the Outboard Marine Corporation.

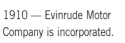

1910 — Evinrude Motor Company is incorporated.

1929 — Stephen Briggs organizes a group of investors to buy Evinrude from Briggs & Stratton.

combination of the Evinrude Motor Company, the Elto Outboard Motor Company, and the Lockwood Motor Company accounted for about half of all outboard motors manufactured in the United States. The Johnson Motor Company, which would later be added to the group, alone comprised the entire other half.

The partners in the consolidation plan were Ole Evinrude and the Elto Outboard Motor Company of Milwaukee. Elto was incorporated in 1921 by Ole and Bess Evinrude after Ole had relinquished control of the Evinrude Motor Company following the 1913 buy-out. In the six years since starting operations, Elto reported a steady profit of about $85,000 a year.[4] Though Ole Evinrude seemed to have little reason to join Briggs and the Evinrude

Company, he was eager for the opportunity to regain his namesake company and serve as president of the new organization, which was considerably larger and more influential.

The Evinrude Motor Company, already controlled by Briggs, merged with Elto on the promise that the Lockwood Motor Company would be added to the consortium. The Lockwood Motor Company, formerly Lockwood-Ash, of Jackson, Michigan, had been incorporated in 1906, and returned a modest but steady profit of $20,000 annually.[5] According to Briggs, the principal reason to include Lockwood in the consolidation was to secure the ser-

The Wagemaker Company of Grand Rapids, Michigan, manufactured a line of Wolverine Boats that used Briggs & Stratton inboard motors.

1936 — OMC acquires Johnson Motors, creating the world's largest producer of outboard motors.

1935 — Briggs moves from president to chairman of Briggs & Stratton, and becomes president of OMC. Charles Coughlin becomes president of Briggs & Stratton.

1948 — Briggs retires from the board of Briggs & Stratton to work full-time for OMC.

vices of its chief engineer, Finn T. Irgins, among the premier outboard engineers in the world.

On February 23, 1929, the Detroit broker-age firm of J.D. Currie organized the merger of the Evinrude Motor Company and the Elto Outboard Motor Company into the Outboard Marine Corporation (OMC), with Ole Evinrude as president, Jacob Stern as executive vice president and general manager, Charles Coughlin as vice president and Briggs as chair-man of the board. On March 4, Lockwood was added, and the new organization became offi-cial on April 3, 1929.[6]

The strategy was a tremendous success, and by 1931, OMC outsold Johnson Motors to claim the title of "world's largest producer of outboard motors." In 1936, OMC acquired Johnson Motors,

and has led the world in the production of out-board motors ever since.[7]

A New Role for Stephen Briggs

The organization of OMC marked the end of an era for Briggs & Stratton. As chairman of the board of OMC, Stephen Briggs could no longer devote all his attention to Briggs & Stratton. In 1935, he relinquished his position as president, and was appointed chairman of the board of the Briggs & Stratton Corporation, a position created specifically for him. He held that position while acting as president of OMC until 1948.

In 1948, Briggs left Briggs & Stratton to devote his attention to the Outboard Marine Corporation. "I liked the outboard business better," Briggs stat-

Briggs & Stratton advertised heavily in *Motor Boating* and *Yachting* magazines between 1939 and 1941.

A reliable Briggs & Stratton inboard engine made oars unneccessary on many boats throughout the world.

ed in a 1962 *Milwaukee Journal* article. "It just had more romance. I wasn't contributing much to Briggs & Stratton and I decided I wanted to devote all my time to Outboard Marine."[8]

Briggs' old college friend, Charles Coughlin, was promoted from manager of factory operations to president of Briggs & Stratton, a post he held until his death in 1972. Harold Stratton remained vice president until his death in 1962.

The Marine Industry

Although Stephen Briggs was occupied with OMC, Briggs & Stratton independently developed a successful line of inboard marine engines and related products. The most popular application of Briggs & Stratton engines was as inboard engines for rowboats. The favored engines for this use were the Model ZM in 1931, Models AM, AMT and BM in 1934, and the Model IMT in 1938. The engines ranged from $^3/_4$- to 5.6-horsepower, and ranged in retail price from $68 to $130.

Other engines were sold to boat manufacturers. One of Briggs & Stratton's largest customers was the Wagemaker Company of Grand Rapids, Michigan, which manufactured its Wolverine inboard boats with Briggs & Stratton engines. The Wolverines ranged from 14 to 16 feet, and could be equipped with either a Model AM or H engine. Prices for the complete boat and engine package ranged from $162.50 to $255.[9]

Another important customer was Marine Sales and Service Limited of Vancouver, British Columbia, which offered two boat models equipped with Briggs & Stratton engines.[10]

To complement its marine engines, Briggs & Stratton developed a specialized marine transmission. Introduced in 1940, this gear-type transmission was a vast improvement over the belt-type transmission used during the mid- to

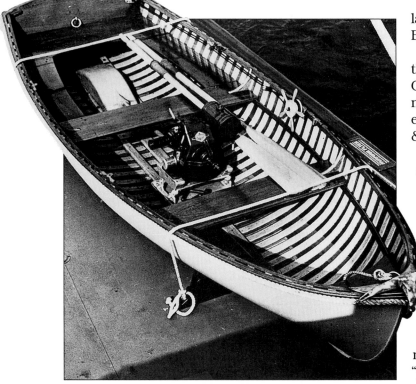

Above: A Briggs & Stratton engine engaged in a marine application. Notice the drive train running to the propeller shroud to the stern of the boat.

Below: These photos provide a working example of how a Briggs & Stratton marine inboard fits into a small rowboat.

late-thirties, and was standard on Models AMG, BMG and ZMG.[11]

Briggs & Stratton engines were also used by the United States Motors Corporation (USMC) of Oshkosh, Wisconsin. The USMC made extensive modifications to Models N, 14 and Z. The USMC even created a separate facility to convert Briggs & Stratton engines for its needs.

In the forties, Briggs & Stratton engines were also used in specialized marine vehicles. The most famous was the Sea-Scoot, a product of the Moto-Scoot Manufacturing Company of Chicago. The Sea-Scoot was constructed entirely of metal and consisted of an upper section supported by two large pontoons. Two people could sit comfortably in the cockpit, with additional passengers perched along the tops of the pontoons.[12] The main drawback of the Sea-Scoot was its steep price of $227 or $325, depending on the model, belying the advertising claims that it was "priced low enough to be within the price range of every vacationist and sports enthusiast."[13]

In the sixties, a lesser-known application of Briggs & Stratton engines was in the banca, a long, narrow fishing skiff used in Philippine fishing rigs and Thai river boats. The fishing boats had outriggers powered directly by inboard engines driving a simple forward/neutral/reverse trans-

Right: One distributor in the Philippines organized a series of races for bancas, with the finals held on Manila Bay. Most fishermen raced their bancas, but some constructed special racing boats. The name in the banner, Ang Maton refers to a cartoon character created to promote Briggs & Stratton engines.

Fred Stratton Jr. gets a firsthand demonstration of a Briggs & Stratton marine engine and transmission in a Thai river boat.

mission. The bancas were similar, but instead of outriggers, they were powered by a Briggs & Stratton engine with a propeller shaft mounted to it, which was attached on a swivel at the back of the boat. Models 243431 and 326431, the last two cast–iron models produced by Briggs & Stratton, were the most popular for this application.

A rather popular event that grew out of this application of the Briggs & Stratton inboard was an annual boat race established in 1977 between members of the local fishing community, sponsored by Briggs & Stratton, and offered the winner such prizes as cash and new automobiles.

Briggs & Stratton salesmen visited rural fairs, community gatherings and households, promoting Power Chargers with flashy demonstrations such as this display built into the trunk of a car.

CHAPTER SEVEN

POWERING RURAL AMERICA: WASHING MACHINES AND POWER CHARGERS

"Every farm woman is entitled to this economical work saver. She has earned her freedom from the scrub board."

— 1936 Promotional Booklet

IN THE 1930s, more than 85 percent of American farmers did not have electricity available.[1] The Rural Electrification Administration, which would bring electricity to nine out of 10 farms by 1950, would not be created until later in the decade. Meanwhile, vast portions of America were not wired for electricity, and had no power available for electrical appliances. While urban Americans were beginning to enjoy the benefits of electric washing machines, rural Americans were still doing the wash by hand.

If a company could develop household and farm appliances to operate on an alternative power source, or if it could manufacture a portable source of electricity, it would find a sizable market. This opportunity led Briggs & Stratton to develop a new line of products.

From the beginning, Briggs & Stratton engines were used to power farm machinery and tools. They powered tractors, water pumps, generators, saws and crop sprayers, as well as gristmills, cotton pickers, corn huskers, fruit pickers, tobacco laths and milking machines. The Briggs & Stratton "Fullpower" engines offered farmers a portable, non-electric power source

that could be used in virtually unlimited applications.[2]

To help meet the needs of the farmer and exploit this new market, Briggs & Stratton developed several portable engines specifically for use on rural tools, machinery and appliances.

In 1925, Briggs & Stratton introduced yet another application for its popular and versatile Model F-Fullpower Series engine. It was the first engine used on the new gasoline powered "farm" washing machine. The gas-powered washing machine would become the most lucrative market for Briggs & Stratton engines prior to the end of World War II.

Gas-Powered Washing Machines

The Briggs & Stratton Model FH was developed in November 1925. Like prior models in the series, the FH generated $\frac{1}{2}$ horsepower at 1,750 rpm. To meet the special requirements of the

Above: A Briggs & Stratton Model WM engine, used to power washing machines.

washing machine, it also featured a kick starter.

The washing machines were manufactured by several companies and were of fairly standardized design. Typically, they consisted of a large tub with a wringer mechanism attached to the top rear of the unit. The tub assembly was mounted on legs to accommodate the high profile of the FH engine, mounted on a carriage assembly beneath the tub. The washing machine agitator was pow-

Above: Washing machine engines. Left to right: Model Y, Model L and Model FH.

ered by a belt-drive gear system that ran from the engine to a large gear at the bottom of the tub. With the connection of an exhaust tube, the washing machine could be used inside. Later

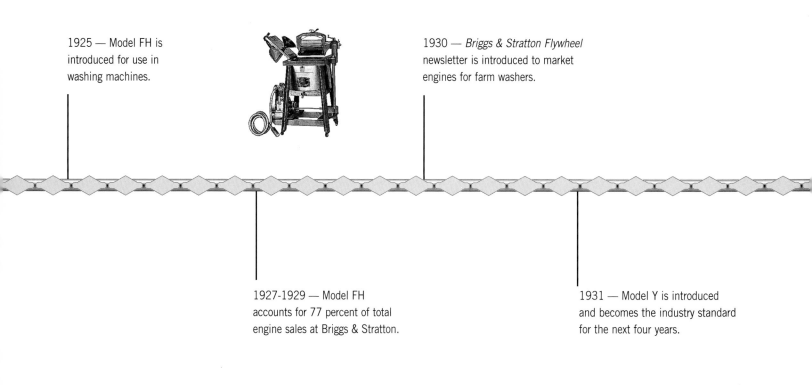

1925 — Model FH is introduced for use in washing machines.

1930 — *Briggs & Stratton Flywheel* newsletter is introduced to market engines for farm washers.

1927-1929 — Model FH accounts for 77 percent of total engine sales at Briggs & Stratton.

1931 — Model Y is introduced and becomes the industry standard for the next four years.

models of the washing machine offered double tubs (one for the rinse cycle), larger square-shaped tubs, and an enclosed engine compartment that reduced noise.

The gas-powered washing machine was an immediate success, accounting for nearly $600,000 in net sales during its first year on the market.

Several companies, realizing the vast market for gas-powered washing machines, began using Briggs & Stratton engines for their units. The company's biggest customers before 1930 were Automatic Electric Washer Company of Newton, Iowa; the Dexter Company, Fairfield, Iowa; the Haag Brothers Company, Peoria, Illinois; the Meadows Corporation, Chicago; and the Syracuse Wash Machine Company of Syracuse, New York. These companies accounted for at least $50,000 of net sales in 1927.[3] Future washing machines using Briggs & Stratton engines included such

prominent names as the Sears, Roebuck Kenmore, Peerless and Water Witch; the Montgomery Ward Washer; and models by Maytag, Barlow-Seelig (later Speed-Queen) and the 1900 Company (later Whirlpool).[4]

The Model FH engine was Briggs & Stratton's most popular engine, selling 19,053 units in 1927, 29,791 units in 1928 and 41,813 in 1929. It accounted for 77 percent of total engine sales for those three years, and 93 percent of the Model FH engines manufactured during this period were installed in washing machines.[5]

Besides the Depression, another reason sales of the Model FH fell off in 1930 was the introduction of the Model L. Introduced in January, the Model L was also an immediate success, with sales of 23,761 units, almost double the number of FH units sold. The Model L had a bore and stroke identical to the FH, but it incorporated significant improve-

Above: The Model WM engine, mounted beneath the machine. The WM, or washing machine, engine had a lower profile than previous engines.

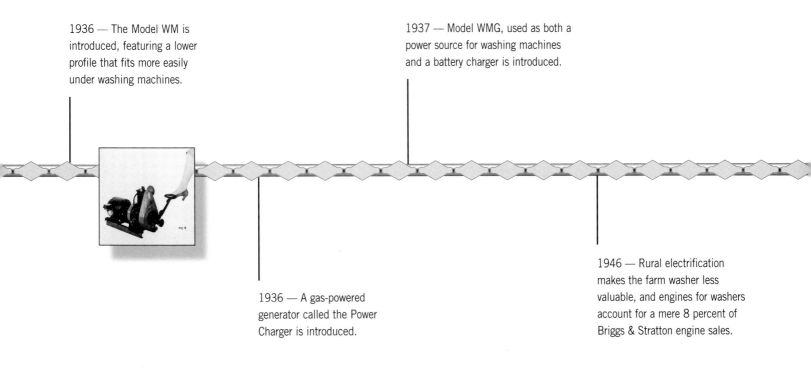

1936 — The Model WM is introduced, featuring a lower profile that fits more easily under washing machines.

1937 — Model WMG, used as both a power source for washing machines and a battery charger is introduced.

1936 — A gas-powered generator called the Power Charger is introduced.

1946 — Rural electrification makes the farm washer less valuable, and engines for washers account for a mere 8 percent of Briggs & Stratton engine sales.

ments to the engine. The new design was an "L-head," with the valves in the cylinder block rather than above it in the cylinder head, so named because the assembly resembles an upside-down L. "Flathead" is the automotive term for this design. Another common term is "side valve." The L-head was less expensive to manufacture and presented a shorter vertical profile, allowing for more clearance between the engine base and the base of the wash tub. This meant a more compact, attractive and convenient unit to the homeowner. The L-head design became the standard small engine design for many years to come, and is still in production today.[6]

The unusually high quality of the L-head was guaranteed by the rigorous three-stage testing procedure it endured before leaving the factory. First was the Block Test, in which the unit was run continuously for eight hours. Next was the Power Test, a four-stage test during which the engine was started and stopped several times to ensure ease of starting. The third stage involved the fine adjustment of the points, valves and magneto. After this, the engine was run again and inspected for defects, then cleaned and crated for shipment.[7] Although this testing process began with the Model L, it became standard for Briggs & Stratton engines.

In August 1931, another engine was developed for use in washing machines. The Model Y, which also used an L-head design, sold 10,597 units in 1932, leading Briggs & Stratton in engine model sales, and becoming the standard washing machine motor for the next four years.

In August 1936, the Model WM was introduced, offering a smaller, 2-inch, bore; a shorter, $1\frac{1}{2}$-inch-stroke. Though smaller than the Model Y, it could generate $\frac{1}{2}$ horsepower at 2,300 rpm. Sales of washing machine engines were staggering. From 1927 to the end of World War II, slightly more than half the engines manufactured by Briggs & Stratton were used to power rural washing machines. In 1935 alone, Model Y engines accounted for $1.9 million in sales, or 70 percent of the total for the year.[8]

Power Chargers

The only source of electricity available to most rural families came from a lead-acid cell battery similar to the type now used in automobiles. Though these batteries were useful, they constantly needed charging. To meet this challenge, Briggs & Stratton introduced the ingenious Model WMG engine in June 1937, a product that served as both a power source for washing machines and a battery charger.

The unit, known as the Briggs & Stratton Start-Charger, was mounted below the wash tub and could be connected to any battery while in

WASHING MACHINES

BRIGGS & STRATTON engines powered many different brands of washing machines, including, from left to right: the Prima Electric Washer, the Boss Power Washer, the Safety Washer-Dryer, the Dexter Improved Washer, the Daylight from Puffer Hubbard Manufacturing Company of Minneapolis, and the Lindsay, from Altorfer Brothers of Peoria, Illinois. These machines were all designed with enough room to accommodate the high profile of the FH engine, as was the Maytag unit pictured below.

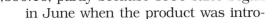

use. Best of all, it came equipped with an electric starter. The Start-Charger was only the first of many new electric-oriented products introduced by Briggs & Stratton during the period.

A gas-powered generator known as the Power Charger (PC), introduced in 1936, was a great boon to farm families. Like the Start-Charger, it was an engine that could also be used to charge batteries. The Power Charger, however, could also be used as an independent lighting plant by connection to a battery-operated lighting system.

In the summer of 1936, PC-Models 100 and 200 were introduced. Both used the Model Y engine, generated $\frac{1}{2}$ horsepower and came equipped with an electric starter. The Model 100 produced a power load of 100 watts, and sold for $33.50, while the Model 200, recommended for lighting plant applications, was priced at $59.50 and produced 200 watts.

The Model WM Power Charger, introduced in December 1936, came with a $\frac{1}{2}$-horsepower Model WM engine and generated 100 watts. The list price varied between $33.50 and $70, depending on who purchased the unit, how it would be used and whether or not installment charges were included.

By the close of 1936, 3,511 Power Chargers had been delivered, representing $118,422.36 in net sales.[9] The following year, sales nearly doubled to $217,590.16, partly because 1936 sales began in June when the product was introduced. Sales in 1938 dropped to below $100,000, and remained relatively flat for several years. Though sales were consistent, they never reached the volume of the rural washer.[10]

In 1938, the three initial models of the Power Charger were discontinued to make way for Models WBG and WMG, both at 75 watts; the WMB, at 100 watts; and the Model 300 Series, which featured a new Model I engine and produced an impressive 300 watts of power. The Model 300 also had the ability to charge both 6- and 12-volt batteries.

Production of the Power Charger continued into the early fifties, when rural electrification all but eliminated the need for portable power sources.

Briggs & Stratton had successfully targeted a previously dormant market by recognizing the specialized needs of farmers. The use of Briggs & Stratton engines offered farm families the advantage of extended work hours, the convenience of

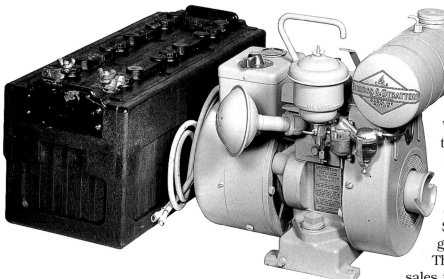

A Briggs & Stratton Power Charger with its accompanying battery.

campaign flooded state and national farm publications. The campaign included national newspapers such as *The Farm Journal, Farmer's Wife* and *Country Gentleman*, as well as state publications such as *The Dakota Farmer, Missouri Ruralist, Wallace's Farmer-Iowa Homestead* and the *Wisconsin Agriculturalist and Farmer*. In all, the farm press network boasted a circulation in excess of 10 million.[11]

Using the same marketing technique employed for the Motor Wheel, Briggs & Stratton began a newsletter in 1930 geared toward sales of Farm Washers. The *Briggs & Stratton Flywheel* included sales forecasts, service reports, product information and human interest stories.

To help promote in-person and point-of-purchase sales, sales kits were developed to provide on-site battery-charging, and the comforts of radio and reliable electric lights.

The Briggs & Stratton Power Charger was also used by urban residents as a lighting power source for vacation cottages, trailers, garages, boathouses and boats. They were deployed at industrial sites such as oil rigs, freight docks, filling stations, stores and railroad tenders. Farmers also removed their Power Chargers from the farm to use as a power source for roadside produce stands.

Awakening a New Market

The washing machine engine was heavily promoted in a campaign that introduced the product to both manufacturers and consumers, and served to orient the Briggs & Stratton sales force about the rural market. General Sales Manager Edward V. Oehler, who had orchestrated the successful Basco Radio campaign, saturated the farm community with information about the Farm Washer and Power Charger, while a print

This sales display demonstrates the usefulness of a Briggs & Stratton Power Charger.

A rare photograph of a Model 100 Power Charger using a Model Y engine.

salesmen with promotional booklets, pamphlets, posters, banners, advertising templates and even postcards. Almost all Farm Washer literature claimed that the machine would benefit the "farm woman." According to these materials, the Farm Washer was "built for a woman to operate," and, "The release of the farm woman from the wear and tear of washing aids her personal appearance." Since using the washer took a third of the time of hand washing, "More time is left the farm woman for other chores."[12]

Farm Washer literature focused on the practicality of a machine that might seem extravagant to cash-strapped farmers. "The task that was once hardest becomes a simple chore in the week's routine," noted one advertisement. "Every farm woman is entitled to this economical work saver," stated another. "She has earned her freedom from the scrub board." One ad was even more specific. "Almost every other piece of farm labor-saving equipment was built for the man. ... A power washing machine is a woman's helper. ... She deserves it."[13]

The Farm Washer began to lose popularity in the forties, as isolated rural areas grew in population and acquired electricity. By 1946, Farm Washer engines accounted for only 14 percent of engine production and 8 percent of net engine sales, and by 1959, these engines constituted a mere 0.3 percent of engine production. The Farm Washer was almost totally phased out, although it was manufactured until the late eighties for use in Third World countries and remote areas.

A Model F engine, part of a series produced in 1921 and 1922.

CHAPTER EIGHT

THE THIRTIES

"I think the combination of Mr. Charles Coughlin and Mr. Ray Griffith sure got off on the right foot. Mr. Coughlin was a great businessman. No question about it. And Ray Griffith, I think when it comes to manufacturing, he was a genius in my opinion."

— Jack Ebershoff, retired vice president of engine sales

THOUSANDS OF AMERICANS lost everything they owned in the stock market crash of October 29, 1929. But Black Tuesday was less a cause of the Great Depression than a symptom of deep problems in the American economy. Convinced that American industries would continue to grow as they had in the early part of the century, speculators bought stocks on large margins. The combination of cash infusions and technological advances caused production to soar. But consumers could not keep up with the volume of products being manufactured. As industries lost sales, they were forced to cut their payrolls. People without jobs could not afford the products being manufactured. Finally, the system collapsed and the nation plunged into economic crisis.

No segment of the population was left untouched by the Great Depression. In 1930, 1,300 banks closed. Over the next two years, 3,700 others followed. With people out of work and cut off from their savings, the economy continued to spiral downward. Agriculture also suffered because Americans simply couldn't afford food. Families stood in long bread lines and lived in cardboard slums known as "Hoovervilles."[1]

Briggs & Stratton was not immune to the financial devastation. Sales of gas-powered washing machine engines dropped from $1.25 million in 1929 to below $1 million in 1930.[2] Net sales of all gas engine models stayed well above $1 million until 1931, before falling to $882,136.16, and finally plummeting to $516,547.71 in 1932, the worst year for engine sales since the product was introduced in 1921.

As sales fell, so followed production and employment. In an effort to salvage the work force, Briggs & Stratton developed a new and inexpensive line of products. From 1931 to 1934, Briggs & Stratton received contracts to manufacture coin-operated paper-towel dispensing machines for Northern Paper Mills of Green Bay, Wisconsin, producing roughly 1,000 per year at $5.75 to $7.50 per unit. The machine did not live up to expectations, often jamming or not dispens-

Above: In 1930, Briggs & Stratton established a nationwide network of service representatives to repair its products.

ing towels at all, and it was discontinued by Northern Mills in 1934.

Several novelty items were also designed and manufactured during this period, including pen holders, lipstick cases, lamps and cigarette containers. One of the most interesting was the Dry Ice Cooler. Introduced in 1932, the unit was a bottled water dispenser cooled by dry ice instead of refrigeration. It even allowed the user to control the temperature of the water. Following extensive research, however, the unit was considered cost-prohibitive, and further development was abandoned.

A further initiative to maintain the work force levels during the period was the development of new relationships with two major retailers, Sears, Roebuck and Montgomery Ward. Beginning in the early thirties, every imaginable form of equipment or implement utilizing Briggs & Stratton engines was featured in the mail-order catalogs of these retailers. Sold under such trade names as Craftsman, Defiance, Economy, Powermaster, Kleen-Air, Cross Country and Reliant, Wardway, Waterwitch and Powerlite, these products found their way into almost every home in America.

A Shift in Direction

In the thirties, the company continued to shift its focus from automotive specialties

This scooter from the Moto-Scoot Manufacturing Company was powered by a Briggs & Stratton engine.

October 29, 1929 —
Stock market crashes and the Great Depression begins.

1931-1934 — To stay afloat, Briggs & Stratton produces a range of novelty items.

1930 — Nationwide service organization is established.

1935 — Briggs & Stratton acquires a manufacturing facility on 32nd and Center streets.

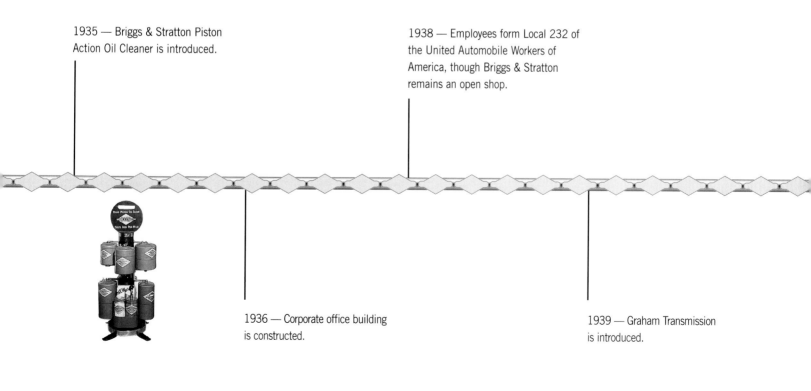

to small engines, as sales of electrical specialties continued to drop. In 1930, electrical specialties accounted for about 8 percent of net sales, compared to 35 percent in 1925. By 1940, only 6 percent of net sales were electrical specialties,[3] as automobile manufacturers were increasingly making their own specialty parts.

Locks also suffered a decline in sales, dropping from 43 percent in 1930 to 25 percent in 1940.[4] Although these numbers continued to fall, the market never disappeared, because automobile manufacturers found it more economical to purchase locks from Briggs & Stratton than to produce their own.

While sales of electrical specialties and locks declined, engine sales doubled in a single year, rising from $446,977.93 in 1926 to $1,022,726.30 in 1927.[5] In 1930, net sales of engines totaled $1.67 million, or 41 percent of total sales, and in 1940, engine sales were $2.97 million, about 48 percent of total sales.[6]

Briggs & Stratton engines were increasingly used in lawn mowers and garden cultivators, a lucrative market that accounted for $204,925.70 in net sales in 1929.[7] But washing machines were still the most popular use for Briggs & Stratton engines in the thirties, followed by generators and pumps. The United States government was among the customers, spending slightly under $3,000 a year on engines for pumps and generators between 1930 and 1940. Other uses included power compressors, rock drills, reel units, grinders, surfacing machines, road graders, spreaders, vibrators and mixers.

Scooters, Bicycles and "Midget" Automobiles

During the thirties and early forties, Briggs & Stratton engines were highly prized power sources for scooters, bicycles and "midget" automobiles.

Among the scooter manufacturers using Briggs & Stratton engines were the Moto-Scoot Manufacturing Company of Chicago and Merx Products, Inc. of Minneapolis, which offered the Commando, billed as "The Aristocrat of Light Motorcycles." The Commando was offered in two

1935 — Briggs & Stratton Piston Action Oil Cleaner is introduced.

1938 — Employees form Local 232 of the United Automobile Workers of America, though Briggs & Stratton remains an open shop.

1936 — Corporate office building is constructed.

1939 — Graham Transmission is introduced.

model versions, the 112, with a $^1/_2$-horsepower engine, and the 300, which offered a 3-horsepower engine. Both were equipped with a speedometer, head and tail lights, windshield and saddlebags, and were available in either maroon or dark blue.[8]

In 1939, sales of engines for scooters was $72,557.07, falling to $15,101.90 in 1940, and averaging less than $3,600 annually between 1942 and 1945. Sales rose dramatically during the post-war boom, as between 1946 and 1948, scooter engine sales ballooned to nearly $500,000 annually.

Briggs & Stratton motors were also used to power bicycles. Vastly improved from the Motor

Wheel of the early twenties, this item could be mounted along the cross-member on the rear fender, and was typically encased in a metal housing for cleanliness, safety and sound reduction. The Speedrive Company of Cincinnati offered such an attachment, and for $97.50, the owner could travel 100 miles on one gallon of gasoline.[9]

By far the most interesting of these applications was the midget auto, a miniaturized version of either a street car or a racing automobile. One of the most popular was the racer manufactured by Cannon Ball Baker, Inc. of Indianapolis. Never a major source of revenue, engines for this unique application accounted for less than $5,000 in net sales in 1939.[10]

To accommodate the varied demand for small engines during the thirties, Briggs & Stratton developed several new models. A total of 62 distinct engine models, in six new series, were developed between 1931 and 1940. These included the Model Z of 1931, Models A, H and K of 1933, and the Model B of 1934. Ranging from $^1/_2$ to 5 horsepower, these engines were used in a wide variety of applications. Next to Models Y and WM used for Farm Washers, the most popular engines were in the Model A series, with net sales of $181,255.29 in 1935 and $235,437.82 in 1936. Engines in this

To market its new oil cleaners, Briggs & Stratton developed displays like the ones pictured above and left.

series ranged between 1 and $1\frac{1}{2}$ horsepower, offering plenty of power for portable industrial and agricultural use. In 1935 and 1936, new models accounted for more than $100,000 in net sales.[11]

Expansion

Its facilities overburdened, by March 1930, Briggs & Stratton was producing an average of 500 engines per day.[12] To increase both capacity and efficiency, the company first improved the East Plant, adding a new carburetor test laboratory in 1934 and various interior improvements to the office annex between 1938 and 1941.[13] But the decision to add a new facility was inevitable. In 1935, Briggs & Stratton acquired the old Westinghouse Electrical Plant located at 2748 North 32nd Street, now 32nd and Center streets in Milwaukee. Purchased for $59,640,

By the 1930s, Briggs & Stratton had developed a worldwide market for its engines and engine parts. Trinidad, above, New Zealand, right, and Uraguay, below, were among the countries using Briggs & Stratton engines.

the three-story building known as the West Plant added 246,327 square feet, and soon became the primary facility for the manufacture of cast-iron engines, especially washing machine engines. Charles Graf, who was superintendent of the facility, said it assembled 900 engines a day, with only 24 operators.[14] "I didn't sit in the office. I walked around the plant and they all knew me. And if I saw something wrong, I'd tell them," he reminisced. "I had that line made all mechanical. The engine would turn around, it would tip up, and it was quite a thing. We even had an automatic gas fill and oil fill. ... I lost hearing on it. I wear a hearing aid now."[15]

The inside of a Start-Spark, which promised to start engines even on the coldest days.

In 1936, a new office building was constructed, adding 6,300 square feet to the factory structure, for a total working area of 252,627 square feet. Although the East Plant was still a working facility, it was then relegated to a support role of manufacturing locks and engine parts.

Personnel Changes

The thirties also saw important personnel changes for Briggs & Stratton. In 1934, Else Bodendorfer became treasurer, holding the post until her death in 1954. Bodendorfer, who joined the company in 1918 as secretary to Stephen Briggs, was the first woman executive at Briggs & Stratton. Briggs became chairman in 1935, and Charles Coughlin became president. Ray Griffith became vice president of manufacturing, an important position in the company.

"I think the combination of Mr. Charles Coughlin and Mr. Ray Griffith sure got off on the right foot," recalled Jack Ebershoff, an engineer who became vice president of engine sales in 1965. "Mr. Coughlin was a great businessman. No question about it. And Ray Griffith, I think when it comes to manufacturing, he was a genius in my opinion. Ray Griffith was the greatest manufacturing person I had ever heard of."[16]

In 1936, the company hired Leo Lechtenberg, a brilliant young man who would earn a mechanical engineering degree from Marquette University in 1938.[17] He was promoted to development engineer in 1945, and to assistant chief engineer in 1957.[18] Best known for his development of the aluminum block engine, Lechtenberg was promoted to vice president of engineering in 1957, a position he held until 1978.

Supporting Products

Although the manufacture of small engines had become the principal activity of Briggs & Stratton, the company was still experimenting with the acquisition, manufacture and sales of associated products. Among these items was the tractor transmission, used exclusively on Sears, Roebuck tractors with Models A and K Briggs & Stratton engines. Initially used on single speed walk-behind tractors, the line was expanded in 1938 to include Model B and WI engines to

AN IMPROVED STARTER DRIVE ASSEMBLY

Use The Quiet

CUSHION-ACTION

BRIGGS & STRATTON

STARTER DRIVE

for

Lasting Satisfaction

Part No. 80999 $3.00 LIST

Standard equipment on 1940-41 Model 85 Ford V-8, Mercury and Lincoln Zephyr.

This patented drive operates through a resilient rubber cushion which absorbs shocks and annoying noises when starting—prolongs the life of starting motor, gears and assembly.

The Briggs & Stratton Starter Drive Assembly has been tried and tested for over three years in thousands of cars under every conceivable operating condition and will render years of dependable, trouble-free service.

In addition to its cushioned-in-rubber feature, it possesses many other outstanding advantages not found in conventional styles of starter drives.

CONSTRUCTION DETAIL

- **Rugged Construction**—Special analysis steel—hardened and heat treated for corrosion and wear resistance.
- **Precision Built**—Carefully made and assembled to highest standards of quality for perfect performance.
- **Simplified Design**—Only two moving parts. No springs or clutches to break.
- **Easy to Install**—Only one set screw used to lock securely to starting motor shaft—requires no adjustments.
- **No Service Parts**—Made in one integral unit—nothing to get out of order or require adjustment.
- **Fully Guaranteed** against imperfections in workmanship and materials.

Fits all Ford V-8 Models, 1932-41 (except 60 H.P. and trucks); Mercury 8, 1938-41; Lincoln Zephyr, 1936-41.

FORM NO. 1081-99

BRIGGS & STRATTON CORP., MILWAUKEE, WIS., U. S. A.

BUILDERS OF PRECISION AUTOMOTIVE EQUIPMENT FOR OVER 30 YEARS

accommodate more powerful tractors that featured low, high and reverse gears. By 1941, sales had declined to $11,550, and the tractor transmission was discontinued.

In 1939, the 5-horsepower Model Z Series engine was introduced, designed to accommodate the first Sears, Roebuck riding type tractor. The unit retailed at Sears for $345.00, and that year 1,757 units were sold, accounting for $119,473.20 in net sales for Briggs & Stratton.[19]

Introduced in 1935 for the automotive market, the Briggs & Stratton Piston Action Oil Cleaner used wool fibers and a gravity compression system known as piston action to keep engine oil clean. Product literature claimed the use of an indestructible cleaning element, lower cost, better protection and a life of 12,000 miles. The filters were available through Briggs & Stratton, independent automotive service dealers, distributors and catalogs.

In addition to its own unit, Briggs & Stratton manufactured and distributed various other oil filters under trade names such as Diamond, Cross Country, Reliance, Jordan, Jumbo and Golden Jubilee. Oil filters experienced a lucrative, though short-lived success at Briggs & Stratton. Their first year on the market, oil cleaners accounted for $74,125.71 in sales and seemed to have a promising future. However, sales of oil cleaners and accessories never grew, and in 1936, 94,207 units were shipped, accounting for $61,439.99 in net sales.[20]

These products continued to average around $50,000 per year in sales before falling to $382.60 in 1942. The following year, these lines were discontinued, along with other automo-

Briggs & Stratton was constantly finding ways to improve engine performance. The Cushion-Action Starter Drive (above) made the engine easier to start, and the Variable Venturi Vacuum Control Carburetor (right) increased automobile performance.

Though lawn mowers did not provide the dominant business for Briggs & Stratton until after World War II, the company's engines powered lawn mowers in the thirties. Pictured here are three early reel-type mowers, all using engines in the P Series.

tive products developed under the Basco trade name, all casualties of defense re-tooling.

Another short-lived product was the Lawn Mower Pusher, the predecessor of the modern self-propelled lawn mower. Introduced in 1938, the Lawn Mower Pusher was powered by a Model H engine, but was discontinued only six months later, in October 1938.

Also introduced in the late thirties was the Air-Saver, an air compressor valve to regulate the flow of compressed air in manufacturing machinery. The primary function of the Air-Saver, which initially sold for $12.50, was to keep air lines from leaking compressed air, which could be costly. Although successful, it became a casualty of defense production and was sold off in 1949. The Air-Saver was reintroduced in the seventies by the Air-Saver Valve Company of Birmingham, Michigan, with the advertisement, "Today's Air-Saver valves are the result of numerous improvements made to the basic valve, which was designed and built by Briggs & Stratton over forty years ago."[21] The Air-

Saver was later constructed of nylon and manufactured as a fuel valve by the Fastex Company of Des Plains, Illinois.[22]

Among the more innovative products introduced by Briggs & Stratton in the thirties was the Graham transmission. Developed in Europe by Viennese engineer Alain Madle several years earlier, the variable-speed transmission never reached its potential because of problems with speed augmentation and reduction. Full licensing rights to the transmission were granted to Briggs & Stratton in 1939, and the company immediately began developing a new variable-speed device that employed "metallic traction and modern steels."

Available in three different models, the Graham transmission offered non-slip torque-responsive loading, full-speed range and variability with full motor power throughout a 4:1 speed range. These units were used in conjunction with just about any device using an electric motor, including blueprint copiers, pumps, printers and power tools. During World War II, it was also used for the drive mechanisms on American anti-aircraft guns. In 1939, Graham transmissions accounted for $85,083.45 in net sales, peaking at $450,739.85 in 1943, before falling to $1,240.28 by 1946.[23] In 1947, Briggs & Stratton sold the rights to the Graham transmission to the Graham Company, Inc., of Milwaukee.

Automotive products developed during the thirties included the Start-Spark, a sort of battery booster that made it easier to start engines in the winter by increasing the heat, voltage and frequency of the spark. Another product was the Variable Venturi Vacuum Control Carburetor, acquired in 1931 from Rolland D. Koenitzer of Milwaukee. This automatic pressure control device increased available horsepower in automobile engines by modifying the size of the carburetor venturi. Initially designed for use with Ford automobiles, it never went into production, and in November 1939, it was decided that Briggs & Stratton, through an agreement with Koenitzer and the Koenitzer Engineering Corporation, would

sell the unit for use in trucks, tractors, marine and industrial applications. The product realized absolutely no success, and the agreement with Briggs & Stratton was terminated in 1940.

Another product developed in 1938 was the Cushion Action Starter, an automobile "self-starter" that utilized a new type of hard rubber starting mechanism instead of the traditional metal spring. This unit saw limited success between 1939 and 1942, becoming standard equipment on Ford, Mercury and Lincoln automobiles, averaging $108,000 per year in sales

during that time. In 1943, sales dropped below $50. The product experienced a brief rally over the next few years, but was discontinued in 1950.[24]

Nationwide Service

From the inception of the company, spare parts and service for their electrical specialty products were offered by the company through its Milwaukee Street facility. After the move to the East Plant, a local service station system was established. More service stations popped up in the form of car service centers that worked in conjunction with Briggs & Stratton. By the late twenties, business had grown so dramatically that a more organized system was necessary to get replacement parts and information into the field, which by then covered the entire United States and sections of Canada.

In 1930, Briggs & Stratton established a nationwide service organization using independent authorized central service distributors. Located strategically throughout the United States and Canada, these distribution centers were operated by a factory-trained manager and staff. These centers provided replacement parts, special tools and engine repair service in a mod-

ern shop under the official factory policies of the Briggs & Stratton Corporation. The centers would also honor one-year factory guarantees to replace any defective parts.

The first of these service centers were opened in June 1930 in Wichita, Kansas; Kansas City, Missouri; Minneapolis and Omaha, Nebraska. In July, stations were opened in Chicago, Philadelphia and Baltimore, as well as the Canadian cities of Toronto and Winnipeg. By 1931,

Though sales of automotive keys and locks declined in the thirties, Briggs & Stratton continued production.

Briggs & Stratton improved customer service by establishing a network of authorized service and sales distributors.

there were stations in 26 cities throughout the United States and Canada.[25]

This system was soon refined to include Authorized Service Distributors and Registered Service Dealers. By the end of the thirties, Central Service Distributors included warehouse storage and distribution centers for smaller distributors and dealers. These centers created a relationship of trust with customers, and generated a sizable income averaging $352,066 in sales, representing about 10 percent of overall sales.[26]

Owing to the ingenuity and industry of Briggs & Stratton executives and employees, the corporation survived the thirties. Sales were booming, people were working, and the company was still growing to meet increasing demand for its products. One event, however, became the most significant to have risen out of the ashes of the Great Depression — the development of the labor union.

The Labor Union

In 1935, the Roosevelt administration passed the National Labor Relations Act, which granted workers the right to form labor unions. The Wagner Act of 1935 authorized the formation of the National Labor Relations Board (NLRB), a legislative body developed to regulate labor activities.

The workers at Briggs & Stratton, like workers at many industrial concerns, saw an opportunity to win increased wages and better working conditions. Beginning in the summer of 1935, efforts began in earnest to organize Briggs & Stratton employees.

One of the more interesting organization efforts was publication of a pro-union newsletter,

The tools recommended by Briggs & Stratton for use by factory certified servicemen trained in repairing Briggs & Stratton engines.

The Key, issued by the self-proclaimed Young Communists Group of Briggs & Stratton. *The Key* called for complete unionization of the plant with a local branch of the American Federation of Labor, as well as increased wages and a 30-hour work week. It also called attention to exploitation of workers and warned against strike-breaking. The newsletter, not known for subtlety or equanimity, suggested that employees were driven like slaves and attacked management with such incendiary labels as "Hitlerite." Typical articles were "Organize — Prepare to Strike Against Wage Cuts," and "Portrait of a Briggs Slave." The adversarial relationship between labor and management established at Briggs & Stratton was unfortunately common to many manufacturing organizations.

On May 16, 1938, employees of the Briggs & Stratton Corporation, by secret ballot, unanimously approved and signed a labor agreement with the management of the Briggs & Stratton Corporation. This agreement recognized the United Automobile Workers of America, Local 232, as the exclusive representative of all hourly employees working at Briggs & Stratton. It allowed representatives of each side to collectively bargain on issues of seniority, wages, hours, vacations and other issues. The most significant improvement was the increase in wages, which increased the overall average by $.10 per hour. At the time, the starting wage for men was $.55 per hour, while the starting wage for women was $.40 per hour.

Established by Clifford Matchey, who also served as its first president, Local 232 represented 800 of the 1,066 workers at Briggs & Stratton. An open shop was established, meaning each worker could decide if he or she wanted to join the union.

Briggs & Stratton supported the war effort through production of ordnance fuse caps. The absence of women in this photograph indicates that the photograph was taken around 1940, before the United States entered World War II.

Chapter Nine

WORLD WAR II

"The beauty of it was that you could go from full reverse to full forward without any interruption. The further you moved the lever to one side, the faster it would go. We built a lot of those."

— Engineer Leo Lechtenberg,
on the Graham transmission

IN SEPTEMBER 1939, Nazi Germany launched its Blitzkrieg into Poland, occupying that country in a mere three weeks. By the following summer, the German Army occupied most of Europe and was turning its guns toward the Soviet Union. In the Pacific, Japan had overrun most of Southeast Asia and China, and was plotting to take over the entire island population of the region.

As early as 1940, Briggs & Stratton had begun the production of defense matériel. The first defense products produced were ordnance fuse caps for use in aerial bombs and artillery shells. The M-108 Model was introduced in 1940, followed by the M-103 and M-57 in 1941. These fuses ranged in cost to the government from $.33 to $3.75 per unit, and were used primarily for aerial ordnance. The M-57, however, was also used for the detonation of 75mm artillery shells. In 1940, 2,000 M-108 fuses were produced. With the escalation of the war and introduction of the M-57 and M-103, fuse production rose dramatically in 1941, with shipments of 1,020,000 fuses. Briggs & Stratton Factory Tour Representative Ed Mueller, who retired in 1984 after 51 years with the company,

used a cut-away model of a bomb to explain the safety features of the fuses.

"That little fuse has an aluminum firing pin. The reason is centrifugal force. When the shell was fired, it would kind of want to detonate, but the safety features were on, so it wouldn't blow up a gun. ... See this little brass piece that goes in here on the side? That locked the firing pin off the explosive charge for firing. As the shell was spinning through the air, centrifugal force would force that brass piece away and allow the firing pin to strike the charge when the shell hit the target. That was the safety feature. If the gunner missed a safety hold, it would just pop the cap, and it wouldn't kill anybody. It wouldn't even hurt anybody." [1]

The December 7, 1941 Japanese attack on Pearl Harbor was the catalyst that plunged America into the fury of world war. More than

Above: This airplane magneto was designed during World War II to withstand the extreme cold associated with high-altitude flying.

2,000 United States Navy personnel and 400 civilians were killed in the pre-dawn attack. Within four days, the United States declared war on Japan and her Axis partners, Italy and Germany.

"When the war came along, we were already very close to the war effort," said Jack Ebershoff, an engineer who became vice president of engine sales in 1965.[2]

Wartime Defense Production

By the summer of 1942, Briggs & Stratton was at full defense production. The company increased fuse production, shipping 5.3 million fuses around the world, accounting for $8.8 million in net sales. The following years, fuse production was reduced, replaced by other products,

December 7, 1941 — Japanese attack on Pearl Harbor plunges America into World War II.

1940 — Briggs & Stratton produces ordnance fuse caps.

Above: A Model ZZ powers a generator that lights an airfield in Europe.

particularly engines. However, fuses continued to be a significant defense product, accounting for more than 17 percent of production and $10 million in net sales between 1940 and 1945.[3]

To produce these fuses, Briggs & Stratton acquired a vertical milling machine from the Davis & Thomas Company for $20,000, a device that could turn out 550 fuse cap pieces per hour.

During the war years, Briggs & Stratton also manufactured an airplane magneto, specially designed for the extreme cold associated with flight above 35,000 feet. Initially developed by General Electric, production of the magneto was transferred to Briggs & Stratton in 1943. The magneto, manufactured at the East Plant facility, was used aboard the P-47 Thunderbolt, the P-61 Black Widow and the A-26 Invader. Shipments totaled 6,097 in 1943, increasing to 47,124 in 1944, and 33,979 in 1945.[4] Priced between $113 and $250 each, magnetos accounted for more than $15 million in net sales,

A Briggs & Stratton Model ZZ powers a generator that runs a field communications center.

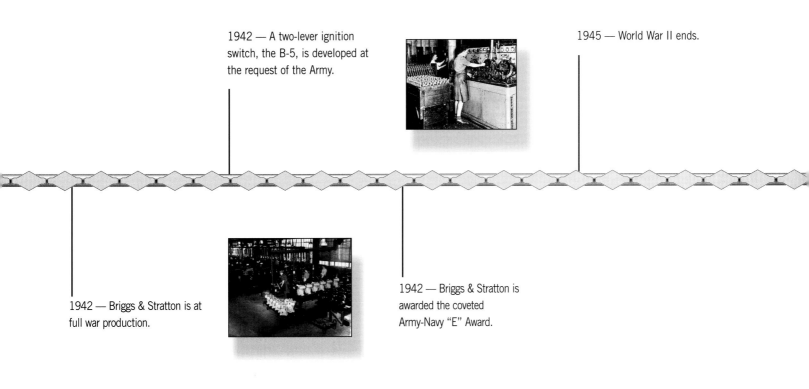

1942 — A two-lever ignition switch, the B-5, is developed at the request of the Army.

1945 — World War II ends.

1942 — Briggs & Stratton is at full war production.

1942 — Briggs & Stratton is awarded the coveted Army-Navy "E" Award.

A Briggs & Stratton engine heats the interior of a plane during World War II.

and 25 percent of total war production, between 1942 and 1945.[5]

As significant as these specialty defense products were to the war effort, the bulk of war matériel manufactured by Briggs & Stratton lay in its civilian product lines. Electrical specialties, engines, spare engine parts, Graham variable speed transmissions and Air-Saver valves accounted for nearly 60 percent of production between 1942 and 1945.[6]

The Graham transmission was especially useful as a power drive for anti-aircraft gun installations because of its remarkable agility. "The beauty of it was that you could go from full reverse to full forward without any interruption," recalled engineer Leo Lechtenberg. "The further you moved the lever to one side, the faster it would go. We built a lot of those."[7] The Graham transmission accounted for more than $1 million in net sales between 1942 and 1945.

Air-Saver valves, used to regulate the flow of air on compressors, were used predominantly for tire inflation, lubrication and other applications in mobile repair facilities. The Air-Saver did not enter into war production until 1945 and accounted for only $2,642 in net sales.[8]

Electrical switches, one of the first products developed by Briggs & Stratton during its formative years, became an important product of war production, proving invaluable in military aircraft. First developed for aircraft use in 1929, single-lever electrical switches were used in single-engine aircraft in France, Spain, China and Great Britain. American manufacturers used these switches on trainers, fighters, bombers and liaison planes. The switches, designated by the Army as Model A-7 and Model A-8, were also used on the PT-17 Primary Trainer, AT-6 Advanced Trainer, P-51 Mustang, P-40 Curtiss Warhawk, P-47 Thunderbolt and A-35 Dive Bomber.

Another switch developed during the thirties was the Model C-2B Gun Control Switch, used exclusively in the A-30 dive bomber to operate machine guns located in the nose and wings. In order to meet an emergency shortage of ignition switches for aircraft in 1942, a total of 24,393 single lever switches were manufactured and shipped to aircraft manufacturers around the country. The following year, Briggs & Stratton produced 45,243 switches.

Bicycles became primary sources of transportation, due to critical gas shortages and rationing during World War II. Consequently, sales of bicycle attachments increased from about $1,700 in 1939-40, to more than $12,000 in 1943. Briggs & Stratton developed its own power attachment for bicycles in 1946, featuring a Briggs & Stratton engine mounted on the rear assembly of the bicycle.

The B-5

At the request of the Army, Briggs & Stratton experimented with a two-lever ignition switch known as the B-5. Introduced in November 1942, it was used in multi-engine aircraft, such as two- and four-engine medium to heavy bombers. Briggs & Stratton delivered 11,911 B-5 switches delivered in 1942, 17,818 in 1943, and 29,506 by May 1944. Priced between $7.25 and $8.65, the switches accounted for $1,437,032 in net sales.[9]

The B-5 switch was used on such famous aircraft as the Boeing B-17 Flying Fortress and B-29 Super Fortress, the B-24 Liberator, the Lockheed P-38 Lightning and the C-45 and C-46 transports. Between January 1942 and May 1944, approximately 164,671 single- and double-lever switches were delivered to the government.[10]

Although not documented as well as those used in aircraft, several Briggs & Stratton switches were used in military ground vehicles. Similar to those used in civilian automobiles, these switches

A Briggs & Stratton Model U with its standard vacuum supply fuel tank.

were used for ignition and lighting in jeeps, trucks, tanks and other vehicles.

The sale of automotive and aircraft switches by Briggs & Stratton was somewhat serendipitous. In early 1942, a government ban was placed on the manufacture of automobiles, adversely affecting not only the automotive industry, but all of its support industries, including electrical switches and locks. Supplying switches to the military allowed Briggs & Stratton to replace a temporarily vacant market with another, more lucrative one, helping to keep its 1,600-person work force intact.

Energy in the Field

The most utilized of all war production manufactured by Briggs & Stratton was the small gasoline engine used by all branches of the service. Most of the engines "drafted" for military service were Models AP, I, N, U and ZZ, all introduced in 1940. The most common use was for power generators that provided lighting to troops in the field. Power Units developed by the U.S. Army Signal Corps were Models PE-43, PE-75,

Above and right: Women working in the West Plant in 1944. During World War II, women formed the backbone of industrial production across the country.

defense camps to power air-raid sirens, purify water and for general lighting.

The Army Signal Corps also relied on Briggs & Stratton power units for the important task of keeping troops entertained, using them to power loudspeakers at United Service Organization (USO) shows, and operate movie projectors.

The Ordnance Department used the engines to power "combat cars," vehicles that were essentially crosses between large "go-karts," small jeeps and artillery gun mounts.

Briggs & Stratton discovered certain challenges associated with producing engines for the U.S. government. The most serious problem was the corrosive effect of extended storage and sea water on certain engine parts. To solve this problem, engineers at Briggs & Stratton devised a

PE-77, all manufactured by the Climax Engineering Company of Clinton, Iowa, and Leach Brothers, Inc., of Oshkosh, Wisconsin. The PE-75 was also manufactured by the Penn Boiler & Burner Manufacturing Corporation of Lancaster, Pennsylvania, and U.S. Motors Corp., Oshkosh. Also extensively used was the Power Charger, the self-sufficient power and lighting plant made popular in rural America by Briggs & Stratton.

The Signal Corps used these units to power equipment such as radios and radars. The Quartermaster's Corps used them to power bread machines, cooking equipment and lights in mobile kitchens, and to pump and heat water for field sanitation purposes. The Medical Corps relied on Briggs & Stratton power units to pump and purify water in the South Pacific and keep field hospitals well-lit during surgery. The Army Air Corps used them for aircraft engine heaters, refueling pumps and emergency landing lights at airstrips. The Coast Guard and Navy used them for portable fire control pumps. Briggs & Stratton engines were also used in civilian

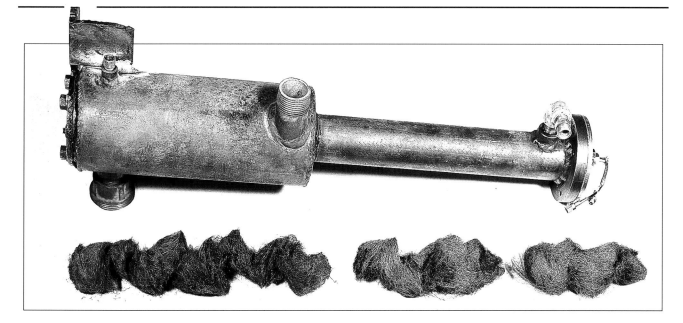

A military Anti-Spark Muffler used in World War II.

coating of 95 percent carbon tetrachloride and 5 percent lanolin that proved effective.[11] Engineers found that a simple lacquer coating prevented the disintegration of rubber ignition wires. Carburetors, choke levers, throttles, governor vanes and spark plug shields all required a plating of cadmium instead of zinc to protect against premature breakdown.[12]

More Power for the Cause

Between 1942 and 1945, engines and spare parts made up 53 percent of the war production manufactured by Briggs & Stratton. Engines and spare parts brought in $32 million in net sales, with just under 250,000 engines shipped per year.

By 1943, Briggs & Stratton had completely retooled its East Plant for fuse cap and magneto production, at a total cost of $2,115,046.29.[13] From this point forward to the end of the war, Briggs & Stratton was in full production, with three full shifts working the factory 24 hours a day.

A new challenge faced by Briggs & Stratton was in the employment of women defense workers. By law, women could not work between 6 p.m. and 6 a.m., and this restriction made it difficult to fill the night shift. As the war progressed, women were given permission to work the necessary hours.

Between 1940 and 1945, wages increased at Briggs & Stratton from about $.85 per hour to $1.20 for men ($.70 to $.96 per hour for women), employment almost doubled, from 1,023 to 1,732, and engine production rose from 145,814 to 246,336 units annually.[14] Sales of defense products totaled $51,242,378 in net sales, accounting for 75 percent of net sales during that four year period.[15] Although actual "war product sales" only began to be recorded as such in 1942, following the American entry into the war, several products, including switches and engines, were being sold to the U.S. government as defense products as early as 1939. As early as February 1941, Briggs & Stratton was listed in *Financial World*'s "200 Companies with Biggest Arms Orders," with $2.5 million in defense contracts.[16]

Briggs & Stratton was judged so successful with war production, that in August 1942, the company received the prestigious Army-Navy "E" Flag, awarded to defense manufacturers by the United States War Department in recognition of outstanding performance in wartime production. The flag was proudly flown on the company flagpole, below the American flag, outside of the West Plant. Every employee was also awarded an "E" pin in appreciation of their diligence and hard work.

Following the declaration of V-E Day in April 1945 and V-J Day in August later that year, Briggs & Stratton entered a new era as a leading small engine manufacturer, and began the development of innovative engine designs that would hurl the company to the cutting edge of industry.

Registered Service Dealers were usually lawn and garden equipment dealerships that were authorized to sell and service Briggs & Stratton engines.

Chapter Ten

POST-WAR AMERICA

"After World War II, the market for lawn and garden equipment grew tremendously with the growth of suburbia. All these people were coming back from the war and starting families and living in houses with lawns. As the lawn and garden business grew, Briggs & Stratton grew along with it."

— Harold Stratton II

WHEN WORLD WAR II ended, a booming economy and the mobility of automobiles encouraged city-dwellers to move into the serenity of the suburbs. This pilgrimage provided new opportunities for American business, and Briggs & Stratton was prepared to capture it. Briggs & Stratton engines were perfectly suited for the lawn mowers that would become an integral part of suburban life.

The company's main technical contribution was the aluminum alloy engine, which was a perfect match for the rotary lawn mower. Between 1954 and 1977, Briggs & Stratton introduced a series of aluminum engines of higher horsepower, which made the old cast-iron engines virtually obsolete. This line of aluminum engines, and the inexpensive lawn and garden equipment it made possible, created a large and growing market. Briggs & Stratton became a large and successful company in the era following World War II.

The only surviving product from the pre-engine days was the automotive lock. Although these locks accounted for less than 20 percent of total sales throughout the fifties, Briggs & Stratton supplied roughly 75 percent of the automotive locks in America. In a recent interview, Harold Stratton II discussed the transition to a post-war economy.

"When World War II started, 50 percent of sales came from the automotive side and 50 percent from the engine side. ... After World War II there were a couple of things that happened of significance in the engine business. First of all, the market for lawn and garden equipment grew tremendously with the growth of suburbia. All these people were coming back from the war and starting families and living in houses with lawns.

"Secondly, the development by Briggs of the all-aluminum engine had a very positive impact on the size, weight and cost of the engines offered for this market. This development helped make powered lawn and garden equipment more attractive to customers. As the lawn and garden business grew, Briggs & Stratton grew along with it."[1]

Between 1930 and 1945, sales of lawn mower engines averaged just over $338,000, or 4 percent of total sales. But in 1946, sales of these engines

Above: This nuclear engine could power a luxury garden tractor, including its air conditioner, heater, cigarette lighter, radio, telephone, lights and radar system, on one capsule of uranium a year. Apparently a prank item, it was featured in the August 24, 1959 issue of *Product Engineering.*

On December 18, 1952, Briggs & Stratton produced its 1 millionth engine of the year. From left to right, Vice President of Production Gordon Bell, President Charles Coughlin and Vice President of Manufacturing Ray Griffith, examine the landmark engine, a 5-horsepower Model 14. Briggs & Stratton was praised in the manufacturing world for achieving an unprecedented level of productivity.

soared to almost $3 million, and suddenly 31 percent of all engines produced at Briggs & Stratton were sold to lawn mower companies.[2] Over the next several years, lawn mowers became the largest market for Briggs & Stratton engines since the Farm Washer.

Stephen Briggs Leaves the Company

In 1948, Stephen Briggs resigned from the board of Briggs & Stratton to work full-time for OMC. Briggs, whose engineering brilliance and business acumen had created an industrial giant, gracefully left the company he had created 30 years earlier.

Briggs loved to experiment, and during his time at Briggs & Stratton, the company dabbled in many markets. During his tenure, the company sold automobiles, Motor Wheels, Frigerators and radios. After Briggs left in 1948, the experi-

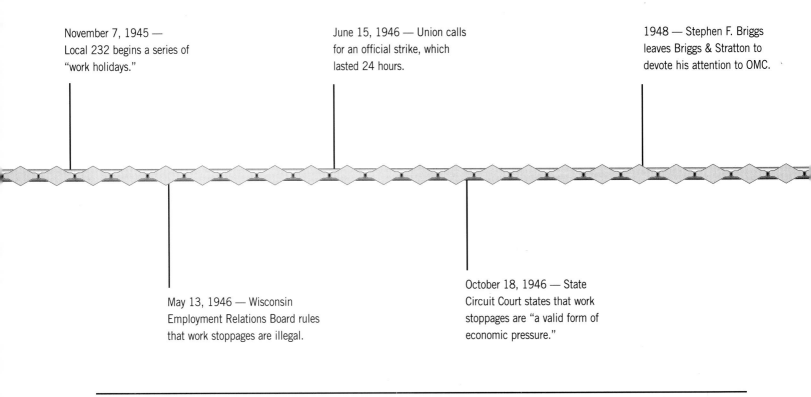

November 7, 1945 — Local 232 begins a series of "work holidays."

June 15, 1946 — Union calls for an official strike, which lasted 24 hours.

1948 — Stephen F. Briggs leaves Briggs & Stratton to devote his attention to OMC.

May 13, 1946 — Wisconsin Employment Relations Board rules that work stoppages are illegal.

October 18, 1946 — State Circuit Court states that work stoppages are "a valid form of economic pressure."

The West Plant assembly line where the millionth engine was produced. Audrey Mollner, now retired, worked on the milestone engine.

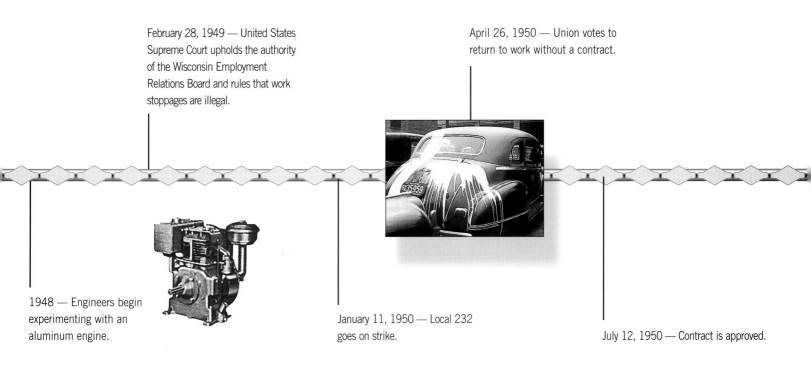

February 28, 1949 — United States Supreme Court upholds the authority of the Wisconsin Employment Relations Board and rules that work stoppages are illegal.

April 26, 1950 — Union votes to return to work without a contract.

1948 — Engineers begin experimenting with an aluminum engine.

January 11, 1950 — Local 232 goes on strike.

July 12, 1950 — Contract is approved.

mentation stopped, and the company focused on two things — producing small engines, and supplying automotive locks and accessories.

Harold M. Stratton remained vice president of Briggs & Stratton until his death in 1962. Charles Coughlin remained president until his death in 1972. "He was a marvelous guy," recalled President John Shiely, whose father, Vincent Shiely, succeeded Coughlin as president.

"He always had a story or a song. He was not only an exceptional industrialist, but quite a person to be around. He was a little older by the time I met him, but there was still a remarkable spark and aura about him. My whole family made a holiday visit to his house every year. I know my father always considered him a strong mentor and talked about how much he learned from Charlie Coughlin about how to run a successful manufacturing business."[3]

Few people probably recognized it at the time, but Coughlin was a pioneer in the successful implementation of the cost leadership discipline in a manufacturing environment. This achievement

was later recognized by Harvard Business School Professor Michael Porter in the definitive corporate strategy book, *Competitive Strategy.*[4] Coughlin's daughter, Colet Coughlin, remembers that her father had a down-to-earth quality. "He was accepted by all of society, but he never forgot that he was a boy from South Dakota. He had no pretense, which was unusual."[5]

"He didn't believe in putting money into luxury living. His office was unreal. You went up a freight elevator and you went in and he had two desks with a swivel chair in between them and then straight chairs all around. It was just the most austere place in the world. But he said, 'This is a place to work. It isn't a place to lounge around.' He had a policy that the door was always open to anyone who worked there. He always felt that a fellow who worked on a machine and worked there a long time knew best how to improve that machine. He knew all the men by name. He spent a lot of time down in the shop. When I was a kid, when I went to town, invariably I would run into somebody whose whole family worked at Briggs & Stratton. It was one of those things where year after year, generation after

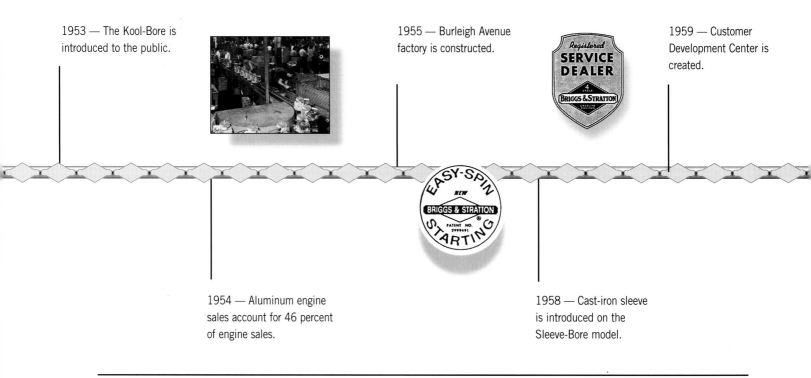

1953 — The Kool-Bore is introduced to the public.

1955 — Burleigh Avenue factory is constructed.

1959 — Customer Development Center is created.

1954 — Aluminum engine sales account for 46 percent of engine sales.

1958 — Cast-iron sleeve is introduced on the Sleeve-Bore model.

generation, they worked there. There was a real feeling of camaraderie.[6]

Though Coughlin did not believe in spending money on himself, he was extremely generous when it came to helping others. In 1929, he personally donated $75,000 to SDSC for the construction of the Campanile, an impressive tower-like structure located near the center of campus. The donation included money for sidewalks, a chimney, beacon lights and a tubular bell chime system similar to that used in London's famous Big Ben Tower. In 1962, he donated $50,000 to aid in the construction of a new football stadium, after a fund-raising drive begun by college regents failed to raise sufficient revenue.[7]

Coughlin had always been a generous man, said Colet Coughlin. "I heard a lot at his funeral from men who told me he paid for their wives' cancer operation. But you never knew any of this. He never attached his name to anything."[8] Ed Mueller, who retired as manager of inventory audit in 1984, described Coughlin as "one of the nicest people you would ever want to meet."

"He was great. You could talk to him. He would go around and walk through the plant and talk to the employees and see someone all alone and slip them a $10 bill. He backed our bowling league. I really can't praise him enough. He was a great man."[9]

The Aluminum Engine

The most significant development in lawn and garden care was the invention of the rotary lawn mower, which replaced the reel-type mower in the late forties. The lightweight, low-cost engine was a perfect match for the rotary lawn mower, and the main technical contribution of Briggs & Stratton.

The reel-type mower used a belt or chain, and had a horizontal crankshaft engine, which sat atop the reel-cutting assembly and powered it by a belt running from the crankshaft gear to the reel gear. The rotary mower employs a vertical crankshaft engine mounted directed to the deck assembly of the mower, with a rotary cutting blade attached beneath the deck, directly to the crankshaft. The rotary mower could cut grass more evenly, especially on irregular ground, and its small size made it easier to store. However, the cast-iron engines used to power the mowers weighed

Charles L. Coughlin was president of Briggs & Stratton from 1935 to 1972. He guided the company through World War II, labor difficulties, and the incredible growth of the post-war years. A brilliant industrialist who never forgot his humble South Dakota roots, Coughlin was respected by all who knew him.

as much as 40 pounds, making the units difficult to push. Also, at first the engine was not equipped to endure the dirt and stress of lawn-mowing.

In the late forties, it was evident that the future for Briggs & Stratton small engines lay in residential applications. The company's managers and engineers set out to design an engine specifically suited to the needs of a rotary lawn mower. This new engine should be able to withstand the heat and dirt associated with lawn mowing, and it should be lightweight.

The company had already experienced success with aluminum alloys in engine models FJ-1 and FJ-2, so engineers pursued the possibility of creating an engine cylinder entirely of aluminum alloy. This lightweight material disperses heat well, and reduces cylinder wear by actually "healing" scoring along the cylinder wall caused by dirt that entered the cylinder through the intake system. Another advantage was that aluminum, as a raw material, actually costs less than cast iron.

Development Engineer Leo Lechtenberg and his staff began working on an aluminum engine in 1948. The largest problem was that the same alloy could not be used in both the piston and the cylinder bore, or galling would result. To prevent galling, one material must be harder than the other. Lechtenberg examined the work of Porsche, a company that was successfully using an aluminum piston in a chromium plated cylinder. Lechtenberg and his engineers reversed the materials and put a chromium plated piston in an aluminum cylinder. The decision was due primarily to problems associated with a chrome-plated cylinder. Overhauling a chrome-plated cylinder would require replating it, a prohibitively expensive process.

Putting the Engine to the Test

On August 4, 1950, a Model N engine with an aluminum liner in the cylinder and a chrome-plated piston was ready for testing. Engineers ran the engine at a "wide-open" throttle setting of 3,600 rpm for 1,436 hours. The piston experienced only nominal wear, and the cylinder wall had worn a mere .0003 inches. With this success as a guide, Lechtenberg in 1951 undertook the design for an all-aluminum engine.

"I went to the drawing board and made several designs. In fact, two important ones. In one, the crank case was split right through the center, the actual crank shaft. In the other one, which is the design we use today, the sump fits into the crank case. By having a different cover on the crank case, you can have a horizontal-shaft engine or vertical-shaft engine, basically with the same tooling. Die casts were expensive, and the idea was that you could make both kinds with one die. Actually, the way it developed from there was that we had many, many sets of dies that sold and the feature wasn't as important as it started out. But the important thing was we brought the weight down to 19¹/₂ pounds."[10]

Details such as the placement of breaker points and blower, and size and arrangement of the cooling fins were perfected. The only remaining problem was the weakness of the cylinder caused by the sand-casting process. In December 1951, engineers experimented with aluminum cylinder

In 1950, Briggs & Stratton established its Service Distribution Warehouse and Headquarters in this 27,000-square-foot building it had purchased from Harley Davidson.

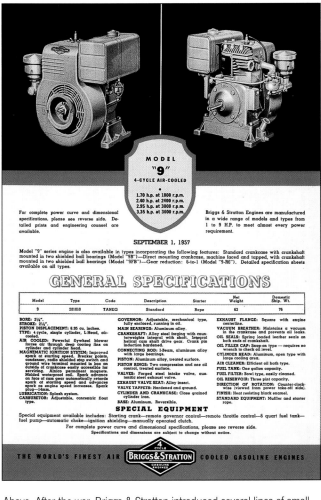

Above: After the war, Briggs & Stratton introduced several lines of small, efficient engines that were less than 3 horsepower.

suction feed carburetor. Soon after the aluminum engine was introduced, the model names became five or six digits long, with each digit describing an engine feature. The first digit or two continued to describe the displacement in cubic inches.

More than 100,000 hours of testing ensued on the 6B-H, included the "shake test," to simulate long hours of use; and the "dust bowl" test, to simulate long hours of exposure to dirt and flying debris. To further reduce weight and ensure proper balance and firing, J.R. Harkness, an engineer who had joined Briggs & Stratton in 1949, designed a special ignition system utilizing an Alnico magnet and a lightweight aluminum flywheel. The Magnematic was an automatic magneto ignition that offered tremendous improvements

Below: Engines of more than 3 horsepower, used in heavy industrial applications, became more common after the war. Engines in the 9 and 14 series were introduced in 1948 and remained in production well into the sixties.

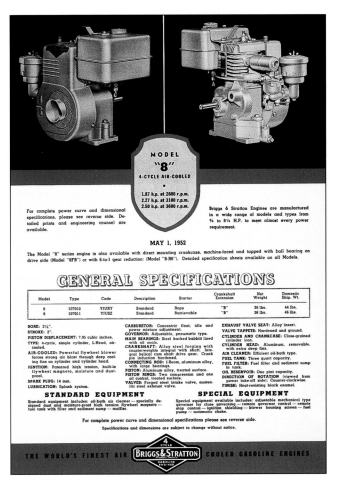

sleeves that were die-cast and tested in sand-casted aluminum engines. The results were excellent. On March 11, 1952, Lechtenberg's assistant, Paul Ebert, assembled and started the first all-aluminum engine manufactured by Briggs & Stratton. This was a Model 6B, a ½-horsepower vertical-cylinder, horizontal-crankshaft engine, with a $2^5/_{16}$-inch bore and a $1^1/_2$-inch stroke. On May 15, the Model 6B became the Model 6B-H for application to the rotary lawn mower.

The old cast-iron engines had letter designations, such as F, Y and WM. But sometime after World War II, the company switched to numerical designations, with the numbers representing the engine's displacement in cubic inches. The 6B-H, then, was a 6-cubic-inch engine. The letter H described the horizontal cylinder. Other letters described other engine features, such as S for a

over both the existing flywheel and external magneto systems used at the time. It featured a more efficient firing system, a waterproof coil and breaker points, and a condenser mounted outside the crankcase for better accessibility and easier maintenance. "Personally, I think that's the best small ignition system ever built," said engineer Jack Ebershoff, who retired in 1970.[11]

Aluminum Engine Production

The first aluminum engine released by Briggs & Stratton for the general public was the Model 6B-H, introduced in May 1953. Initial sales were disappointing, accounting for only 16 percent of all engines shipped in 1953.[12] Apparently, the public was skeptical about the reliability and durability of an engine constructed primarily of aluminum. Customers, especially dealers, were afraid that the new design would be too soft. "Many of our customers didn't want a soft-bore engine," recalled Ebershoff. "But the fact that it worked as well as it did sold other people on the idea. And of course, it was a little less costly, too."[13]

There were several obstacles still to be overcome in the aluminum engine design, since an aluminum alloy was different than the familiar

Field training schools were established throughout the United States to teach distributors and dealers about Briggs & Stratton products and policies. The above lesson was conducted at Bill Grindle's auto shop in Texas, while the class below took place in 1949 at the Savage Brothers Electric Company in Roswell, New Mexico.

cast iron. Determining the precise amount of silicon necessary to properly disburse the alloy

through the cylinder was an unexpected problem. Engineers also needed to find the proper cleaning procedure for the piston prior to the plating process, to ensure adequate cohesion.

Within a few years, metallurgy skills and application techniques for both the alloy and chrome plating were perfected. Tempered aluminum alloys were chosen which best suited the design of the engine, and a new chromium plating process involving 18 separate steps was selected for the best coverage and durability of the piston. For the most durability, cast Arma Steel was chosen to build the crankshaft.

By 1954, sales of the aluminum engine took off, and the 683,725 units sold accounted for 46 percent of the engines shipped that year. In 1955, rotary lawn mower sales increased to 946,822 and reel-type mower engines dropped to 313,615. From that year forward, aluminum engines dominated engine production and sales at Briggs & Stratton. From 1955 to 1960,

Above: Until 1954, the West Plant was the company's primary manufacturing facility. This dealer advertisement illustrates several aspects of production at the facility.

Left: Point-of-purchase promotions helped dealers sell Briggs & Stratton products.

sales of Briggs & Stratton aluminum engines averaged over 2 million units per year, $45 million in net sales, and 74 percent of total engines shipped and sold.[14] By 1957, aluminum engine sales represented about 80 percent of total engine sales. Aluminum engines made it possible to produce low-cost lawn and garden equipment, creating a large and growing market for Briggs & Stratton.

A Decade of Prosperity

The growth of sales for Briggs & Stratton following World War II was dramatic. Sales in 1946 reached

The testing of Briggs & Stratton engines was, as a rule, incredibly intensive, but even more so for the new aluminum engines. Here the "dust bowl" test, conducted in a small building in the West Plant, tested both the air cleaner and the durability of the engine.

$15.7 million, jumped to $21 million the following year, and increased to $27 million by 1950. Between 1951 and 1959, net sales averaged just under $50 million annually, reaching $89 million in 1959.[15] The most important reason for this success was the introduction of the aluminum-alloy engine.

Another reason for this increase in volume was the start of the Korean War. In 1950, Communist-backed forces in North Korea invaded South Korea. The United States, in association with countries allied after World War II under the North Atlantic Treaty Organization (NATO), went to the aid of South Korea, with the intent of containing Communist influence in Southeast Asia.

As in World War II, Briggs & Stratton was awarded numerous government contracts for war matériel. This time, however, production was limited to supplying small engines for equipment such as battery chargers, generators and reel

units. Most of these contracts were received in 1952, the height of hostilities in Korea, and accounted for $828,000 in net engine sales, a small figure compared to World War II sales.[16] By the summer of 1953, the war had ended.

On December 18, 1952, a significant milestone was reached when the one-millionth engine produced that year rolled off the assembly line at the West Plant. The production of that engine, a Model 14, marked the first time a manufacturer of small engines had reached that level of production. The event was recorded by still and motion picture photography and was heralded by both labor and management. The year ended with a total engine production of 1,015,700.

It had taken 16 years, from 1924 to 1939, for Briggs & Stratton to produce its first million engines, and five years, from 1940 to 1945, to produce its second. However, between 1946 and

Above and right: As demand for aluminum engines skyrocketed, Briggs & Stratton built a state-of-the-art manufacturing facility on 82 acres along 124th and Burleigh streets in Wauwatosa, Wisconsin. Construction of the $5 million, 474,919-square-foot plant began in 1954.

applications of Briggs & Stratton engines, or researched improvements to existing applications.

Expansion to Meet Demand

Briggs & Stratton had increasing difficulty meeting the exploding demands for its products. Between 1945 and 1960, both the East and West plants were expanded and improved. In 1945, the office annex was constructed along Center Street, adding 6,500 square feet of work space to the East Plant. In 1948, an additional parcel of land was purchased for $35,000 to use as an employee parking lot at the East Plant. More purchases and additions during this period pro-

1952, the company shipped, on average, 500,000 engines per year. Throughout the remainder of the fifties, Briggs & Stratton produced a remarkable average of 2,079,889 engines per year.[17]

The Briggs & Stratton Foundation

Briggs & Stratton demonstrated its corporate benevolence by establishing the Briggs & Stratton Foundation, Inc. in 1953. Though the company had supported a variety of charitable causes since before World War II, the foundation offered scholarships to the children of Briggs & Stratton employees, and contributed to a number of tax-exempt and non-profit organizations in Milwaukee and elsewhere. Since its founding in 1953, the foundation has donated more than $10 million. The largest recipient over the years has been United Way.

As well as financial contributions, Briggs & Stratton donated engines, replacement parts, tools, manuals, charts and repairman's handbooks to high schools, trade schools and other institutions of learning.[18] The company also donated engines and parts to inventors who experimented with new

Above: Briggs & Stratton touted its modern manufacturing methods in several trade magazine advertisements.

But the most significant expansion was an all-new, state-of-the-art facility on Burleigh Street in Wauwatosa. Briggs & Stratton had purchased the 82-acre site in 1951 for $210,240, and construction began in 1954. Completed in 1955, the facility became the exclusive site for the manufacturer of the new Kool-Bore aluminum block engine. The new plant contained 474,919 square feet covering more than 10 acres, with an additional 7 acres for parking as many as 1,000 cars.[20] The plant included five separate assembly lines, a dedicated die-casting facility, and a water collection system for use in manufacturing, boiler operation and state-of-the-art fire protection. In 1955, *Factory Management & Maintenance* magazine selected the new plant as one of the 10 most significant manufacturing facilities in the country.[21]

In 1958, a new production and service warehouse was completed on the southeast corner of the new Burleigh Street property, behind the plant constructed in 1954. The service parts dis-

vided the company an additional 40,530 square feet of space, and by 1960, the East Plant contained a total square footage of 164,973 feet.[19]

The West Plant was expanded several times during the post-war period. The most substantial addition related to the West Plant was the former Harley Davidson Factory at 3212 West Center Street, purchased in May 1950. This building, which became known as West Plant No. 2, cost $166,078 and brought an additional 36,216 square feet of work space to the existing 293,157, for a total of 329,373 square feet. West Plant No. 2 became Briggs & Stratton's service distribution facility, one of the first of its kind in the country. A highly modernized warehouse, it was used for stocking, packaging and shipping replacement parts.

Advertising in the fifties focused on the company's reputation for quality and durability.

The warehouse area of the service building. To give a relative idea of the massive size and capacity of the facility, each box holds one engine.

tribution function was moved to the new facility from the older facility on the West Plant site. The warehouse featured IBM computer cards for identification of parts, and a conveyer line system to carry parts from inventory shelves to shipping.

Patent Problems

In early 1951, a patent infringement lawsuit was filed by Heza Packwood, claiming that Briggs & Stratton and the Savage Arms Company (a co-defendant not affiliated with Briggs & Stratton) infringed on Packwood's patent for a clipper screen to filter debris sucked into the air intake of the carburetor during lawn-mowing. After less than a week, the jury decided in favor of Packwood. Briggs & Stratton paid $7,500 to Packwood, and Savage Arms paid $750.[22] Though a minor case, it was the

beginning of a series of legal difficulties for Briggs & Stratton later in the decade.

In December 1954, Briggs & Stratton filed a patent infringement suit against the Clinton Engine Corporation of Maquoketa, Iowa, alleging that Clinton had infringed on three aluminum engine patents, including two by Leo Lechtenberg. The Clinton Corporation retaliated by filing a $15 million anti-trust lawsuit against Briggs & Stratton, alleging illegal and monopolistic practices, and accusing the company of placing undue pressure on the patent officers who awarded the patent to Briggs & Stratton. The Clinton Corporation specifically accused Briggs & Stratton of lowering prices to undercut competition, and spreading rumors that the Clinton Corporation was in financial trouble.

The patent infringement case began April 19, 1955 in the Federal District Court in Dubuque,

The aluminum engine, introduced in 1953, revolutionized the small engine business. Left and below are two views of the first aluminum engine, the $1^1/_2$ horsepower Model 6B, which used a chrome-plated piston against an aluminum cylinder and featured a vertical cylinder and horizontal crankshaft.

Clinton, the company in turn decided it was in the best interest of the industry to drop its suit against Briggs & Stratton as of February 16, 1960.[25]

The Kool-Bore and the Sleeve-Bore

Some dealers remained skeptical that aluminum could withstand extreme levels of heat and stress. To silence these objections, Briggs & Stratton began, in 1958, to insert cast-iron sleeves into the existing aluminum engines. Although these modified models sold well, they had distinct disadvantages over the all-aluminum engines. The cast-iron disturbed the superior heat dissipation of the aluminum case by forming an effective heat barrier. The problem was solved, and the cast-iron bore "sleeved" engine became a standard product, as well as a heavy-duty complement to the all-aluminum engine.

In 1958, the new aluminum engine was introduced as the "air age" engine, a play on "space age" that suggested the light weight of the product. All-aluminum engines were called Kool-Bore to reflect their superior heat dissipation, and engines with the cast-iron sleeves were called Sleeve-Bore. The first Kool-Bore engine was Model 60100, introduced in June 1958, and the first Sleeve-Bore engine, Model 61100, was introduced the following month.

Organized Opposition

Not confined to Briggs & Stratton, labor unrest was thought to be the result of a post-war

Iowa. After nearly one year of testimony and cross examination, Judge Henry Gaven ruled in favor of Briggs & Stratton, stating that the patents were indeed valid and infringed by Clinton. Immediately, a motion was given for appeal, and less than a month after the initial decision, on April 12, 1956, the case was reopened by Judge Gaven. A new trial began on June 4, 1956, and after almost another year of litigation, Judge Gaven reversed his initial ruling on January 2, 1957, stating that there had been no patent infringement. In his decision, Gaven stated that there was "... a great difference between invention and technology," and that "techniques are a matter of artisanship and consequently not patentable."[23]

"Actually, I was amazed," recalled Lechtenberg. "The three federal judges just plain did not understand the engineering."[24] Briggs & Stratton filed an appeal, but it was refused by the United States Supreme Court a year later. Litigation on the anti-trust suit filed by Clinton against Briggs & Stratton was the only matter left to decide, and since the patent suit had been decided in favor of

BRIGGS & STRATTON®

prosperity in which everybody wanted a share. Employees demanded higher wages and more control over working conditions, while management often implemented procedures in violation of fair labor standards.

On November 7, 1945, Local 232 of the United Automobile Workers of America began a series of "work holidays." Under the leadership of Anthony Doria, secretary-treasurer of Local 232, these unannounced work stoppages and subsequent walkouts, were called under the pretense of meeting at a local union hall to discuss union issues during work hours. Specifically under discussion was the refusal of Briggs & Stratton to comply with a National War Labor Board directive requiring retroactive wage increases and vacations. Briggs & Stratton management considered the work-hour meetings a method of disrupting production for the purpose of putting economic pressure on the company. Relations soon deteriorated to the point that management accused union leaders of unfair labor practices, and union leaders accused management of intimidation tactics and threats of job losses to those who walked off the job. "I've always been against the unions at our plants," said retired engineer Jack Ebershoff. "At least ever since the day they wouldn't let me into work."[26]

"After all the years I was at Briggs & Stratton, to have some people that I knew quite well, a couple of whom were really nice fellows, decide that I shouldn't go to work that morning, well, I'll never forget that. ... That was the big strike in 1950."[27]

But Ebershoff said he went to work despite the strike.

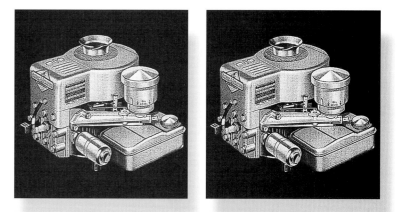

Above: These lightweight aluminum engines were introduced in July 1958. Engine 60501, left, weighs less than 19 pounds and features a rope starter, while Model 60502, on the right, features a rewind starter and weighs less than 21 pounds.

"I just told them, 'Now listen, you know it's my job to deal with these customers. They're expecting to hear from me periodically. They know we're in trouble here and they're waiting for a telephone call from me. And I'm going to make that call.' I pushed them aside and walked in and it was nothing great. But that hurt a great deal because they were friends of mine."[28]

The conflicts also strained relationships between workers. Briggs & Stratton ran an "open shop," and factions soon developed between union workers and non-union workers. Intimidation and threats of violence became common on the work floor, especially directed to workers who refused to participate in the "work holidays." One incident in 1946 involved name calling and vandalism between two women, culminating in a $20,000 civil lawsuit for slander.[29]

The "work holidays" instituted by Local 232 were so effective that they caught the attention of labor organizations nation-wide. The union's labor "weapon" soon became a favored protest method in Wisconsin and throughout the country.

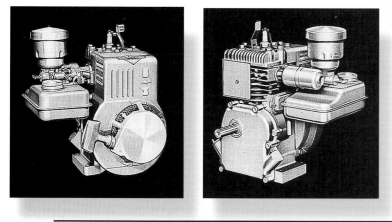

Left: In 1958, the aluminum engine was given the name Kool-Bore because of its ability to dissipate heat. The 2-horsepower Model 60100 engine was the first engine known as the Kool-Bore. It was also offered in a Sleeve-Bore design that featured a cast-iron cylinder and aluminum piston.

Above: Vertical crankshaft engines for rotary lawn mowers are assembled at one of five new assembly lines at the Burleigh Plant.

Management filed a complaint of unfair labor practices with the Wisconsin Employment Relations Board (WERB). On May 13, 1946, the WERB ruled that the work stoppages were illegal under Wisconsin law, equating them to the "sitdown strike," that had been ruled illegal some years earlier. The board's decision stated that Local 232 was not implementing a strike, but instead using a new labor tactic to keep members working while placing extreme economic pressure on the company. The decision ordered:

> "The respondents to cease and desist from engaging in any further work stoppages by arbitrarily calling union meetings during regularly scheduled working hours or by any other con certed effort to interfere with production of the complainant except by strike ... also ... to refrain from further coercion or intimidation of employees in the plant who may refuse to take part in such work stoppages."[30]

WERB also noted that the tactic was in violation of the union's collective bargaining agreement, which stated:

> "The company agrees that there will be no lockout of its employees, and the union agrees that there will be no strike, slow-down or stoppage of work, until all peaceable means of reaching a ... decision ... have been tried."[31]

After an unsuccessful attempt to appeal the ruling, Local 232 called for an official strike on June 15. Like the walkouts, it lasted only 24

In 1948, Local 232 of the United Automobile Workers of America would meet at Jefferson Hall at 27th Street and Fond du Lac Avenue during work hours, ostensibly to discuss union issues. This strategy, developed by Secretary-Treasurer Anthony Doria, was eventually ruled illegal.

hours. In a further attempt to gain management concessions, Doria even sent a telegram to President Harry S. Truman, asking him to seize the two Briggs & Stratton plants, as he had done when coal workers went on strike the prior year.

After another month of tenuous negotiations, work practices and 44 work stoppages, Briggs & Stratton management and Local 232 agreed to a settlement on August 30, 1946. The settlement included, among other things, a wage increase of 18½ cents per hour, or 18.7 percent, whichever was higher.[32] Though it seemed as though problems between the two sides might come to an end, in truth they were just beginning.

On October 18, 1946, the state circuit court of Wisconsin overturned the WERB decision, stating that, "Work stoppages to hold union meetings were a valid form of economic pressure," and that "walkouts were a form of strike and therefore a legal labor practice."[33] This decision led to further unrest over the following three years. To exacerbate the situation, Doria called for an additional wage hike in February 1947, only six months after the August 1946 settlement. On June 11, Briggs & Stratton won a legal victory when the circuit court's decision was overturned by the Wisconsin State Supreme Court, which ruled that the walkouts "were not strikes because no strike vote by secret ballot had been conducted."[34] News of this decision quickly spread throughout the nation as Local 232 geared up for yet another appeal.

While awaiting judicial review, an incident occurred at Briggs & Stratton that further deteriorated labor relations. On August 12, 1947, an explosion ripped through the East Plant injuring seven workers, one seriously. The union immediately accused management of negligence, charging that Briggs & Stratton had violated safety rules, and had not provided workers with basic first aid. Strikes were once again called at both plants.

Doria himself called for a formal investigation into the accident, and demanded that charges be filed against any Briggs & Stratton official found negligent. As tensions continued to escalate, a union plan for more stoppages was again instituted in 1948. This time, the stoppages were so-called legalized versions referred to as "short-strikes." Local 232 even demanded retroactive "strike time" pay for time lost during their own work stoppages.

After another year of negotiations, stoppages and tensions, a final legal opinion was issued regarding the legality of the work stoppages. On February 28, 1949, the United States Supreme Court, in a 5-4 decision, upheld the authority of the WERB to govern state labor practices, thus upholding the original decision that sporadic work stoppages were illegal. The order was similar to the ruling handed down by the WERB in 1946, and merely reinforced the authority of the board to rule on such matters within its own jurisdiction.

During the 15-week strike, people were assaulted and paint was thrown on cars, houses and workers. Acts of vandalism, such as the paint spattered on the car, became all too common.

The First Major Strike

The Supreme Court decisions only served to increase tension between Local 232 and management. When the court refused to rehear the argument in May 1949, Briggs & Stratton endured another six months of futile negotiations and "short strikes." Finally, Local 232 announced it had enough. After working since September 11, 1947 without a contract, and after 56 work stoppages, the union voted on January 11, 1950, to undertake its first major strike.

Separated by differences on some 117 issues, each side immediately began its own strategy for a long and drawn-out strike.[35] Doria and Local 232 immediately began demanding strike wages, while President Charles Coughlin and management made plans to hire replacement workers. "We hired a bunch of people from outside and we just kept going," recalled Charles Graf, manager of the plant on 32nd Street, who retired in 1980.[36] Picket lines sprang up at both plants, and later at local businesses, including the Sears, Roebuck store at 21st and North avenues, a highly visible distributor of products powered by Briggs & Stratton engines.

Emotions ran high on all sides, and intimidation became the new tactic of labor, as non-striking workers and replacement workers were threatened and even attacked as they crossed picket lines. Some workers were even attacked in their homes, and two had their wedding interrupted by strikers who picketed and shouted insults at the couple during the ceremony and reception. One man had a beer bottle hurled through the window of his 4-year-old son's bedroom, narrowly missing the boy. Threatening phone calls and vandalism were widespread. Paint was thrown on houses, cars and even people; windows were smashed and tires slashed. One man, upon leaving work at the East Plant, found that the wheels on his car had been loosened.[37] A worker pulled a knife on a striker standing in a picket line, and a fight erupted between a striker and a worker on a Center Street trolley bus.[38]

Colet Coughlin, the daughter of Charles Coughlin, remembers the strike and the impact it had on her father.

"It was vicious. It was as if [the union] was pelting anyone who worked at Briggs & Stratton.

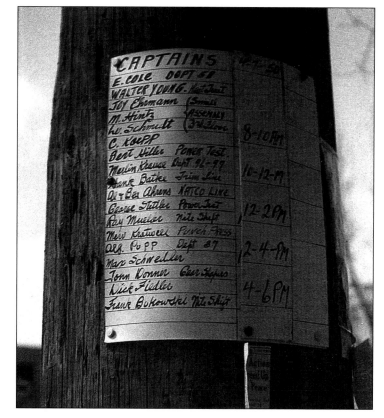

During the 1950 strike, union leadership kept the picket lines organized. A schedule of captains indicated who would be in charge at different times.

Their children were pelted with stones and rocks, their houses were painted. It was a nasty strike. They got so they were sending registered letters from 11 at night until 7 in the morning, every hour on the hour. I slept downstairs on the couch the whole time, and I never gave him one of those letters. ... There was no truth in them. They said things like, 'You were born with a silver spoon in your mouth.'

"I remember he sent out something to everybody in the plant, telling them how much they were losing, each hour, each day, each week and each month, and how long it would take to make it up.

"It was bad news all the way through and it went on for a long time."[39]

But despite the strike, Coughlin said her father felt a strong kinship with the employees at Briggs & Stratton.

"During that strike, we had just come home from Mass on Christmas Day and the phone rang. Somebody wanted to talk to Dad and I put him on. It was one of the strikers, and he said, 'We're over at such and such a tavern and we just wanted to call you, Charlie, and wish you a Merry Christmas.' Dad said, 'Well, where are you? How many are there?' And he told them, and Dad said, 'Stay there.'

"He grabbed me and the two of us went down and he brought up a case of champagne and went in the car, over to the tavern, near the plant, and all these men were there. We stayed the entire day. My mother was ready to kill us. But he was so thrilled the men had called. They absolutely loved him. He was one of them."[40]

Several arrests were made, but labor waited until March to call for order and gain control over the unruliest strikers.[41] By then, management had hired some 1,100 replacement workers in an attempt to keep production levels near normal.

To further aggravate the situation, the local newspaper began printing a series of editorials accusing union members of illegal harassment, intimidation and pettiness related to their demands. One editorial said the strikers' actions were similar to Hitler's and Stalin's persecution of Jews and Catholics.[42]

The Strike Ends

On April 2, 1950, the National Labor Relations Board officially charged Briggs & Stratton with 10 counts of unfair labor practices, including refusal to meet contractual obligations, and threatening striking employees with job loss. Hoping to avoid the formal hearing scheduled for April 24, (later rescheduled for May 9), Briggs & Stratton delivered an offer to the union on April 14. Although the offer was initially rejected, it was responsible for finally ending the strike. On April 26, 1950, the union voted to return to work without a contract if "all strikers will go back to their status quo positions existing before the strike and that no striker will be denied employment just because providing

such employment might require the release of employees hired to replace strikers"[43]

To accommodate this union demand, as well provide fairness to the new workers, Coughlin added a third shift to both plants. Meanwhile, negotiations continued between union and management, with the primary stumbling block being payment of retroactive wages to all strikers dating back to September 11, 1947.

In early June, union members voted to strike if a contract could not be completed in two weeks. Though it took more than the allotted time, a settlement was reached without a strike on July 12. In a 4-to-1 secret ballot, 1,800 striking members of Local 232 voted to accept the new contract.

The new contract was for a five-year period, and included a retroactive pay increase of 10 cents per hour from September 11, 1947. The contract also called for an across-the-board wage increase

Dick Zerniak, president of Local 232 of the Allied Industrial Workers meets with Charles Coughlin, president of Briggs & Stratton.

Above: The label on a Briggs & Stratton Model 5S engine.

Over the next decade, labor and management relations seemed to improve, with relatively painless contract and wage negotiations arbitrated by officials on both sides. During this period, the American Federation of Labor (AFL) merged with the Congress of Industrial Organizations (CIO) in 1955. Consequently, Local 232 changed its name to the International Union, Allied Industrial Workers (AIW), AFL-CIO, Local 232 on May 1, 1956.

Improvements to the Aluminum Engine

The gas-powered rotary lawn mower, unlike most farm equipment, was viewed as more of a

of 10 cents per hour, a closed union shop, the right to open wage negotiations on a yearly basis, and several revamped procedures regarding seniority, layoffs, job transfers and arbitration. The contract also included a pension plan that cost 15 cents an hour, as well as a health care package that cost 4 cents per hour.[44]

The package cost Briggs & Stratton $800,000 in back wages alone to union employees.[45] The company, however, seemed pleased with the contract, and a spokesman stated that, "The company has made the type of offer it has in the hope of obtaining a long period of industrial peace. We have the union's assurance that it will give its full cooperation to this end."[46]

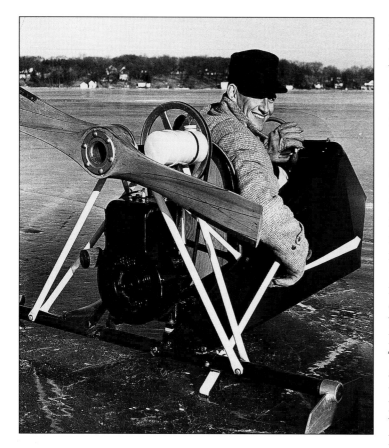

A Model 23, altered to power this ice sled on Pewaukee Lake in Wisconsin.

maintain than the more complex float-type carburetor. Complementing the Pulsa-Jet was the Vacu-Jet, a suction-type carburetor that utilized a single mixture adjustment, and the Flo-Jet, a concentric float carburetor that provided both an idle and power mixture adjustment.

These new carburetors required clean, high-quality gasoline in order to operate properly. Gas stored in gas tanks for long periods of time could deteriorate the inside of the tank. To overcome this problem, Briggs & Stratton developed a new fuel tank that utilized an epoxy sealant for the inside of the tank, and nylon tubing to transfer fuel to the carburetor.

In the fifties, Briggs & Stratton began exploring alternative energy sources for its small engines. In 1958, the company introduced a carburetion system for converting engines from gasoline to use liquified petroleum (LP) gas for fuel. Though this system had been used in industrial applications since World War II, it was the first time it had been introduced to the general marketplace. A fuel comparable to gasoline in combustion efficiency, horsepower output and octane levels, the primary advantage of LP gas was that it burned cleaner. Although the LP gas system was an engineering success, it never ignited the marketplace. However, it is still employed today in limited and specialized applications.

Filtering the carburetor intake air in often extreme environments is crucial to proper engine operation, leading to the development of the Oil-Foam, "No-Spill" air cleaner during this period. Called No-Spill because of the heavy retention qualities of the filter element, this system used a polyurethene element soaked in engine oil and encased in a metal housing attached to the air intake of the carburetor. The use of oil in a tightly meshed filter element allowed for an efficient filtering system that could be cleaned on a regular basis with dish soap or kerosene. Variations of the Oil-Foam air cleaner are still in use today.

During the late fifties, an electric starter was also developed for use on larger Briggs & Stratton engines. First introduced in 1956, the 110-volt electric starter offered safe starts for industrial engines by simply plugging the unit into a standard polarized wall outlet. A clutch was automatically engaged upon initial cranking and disengaged once the engine started.

luxury item, used only periodically. Owners demanded low maintenance and ease of operation. It became the mission of Briggs & Stratton to develop an engine to precisely meet these customer needs. "I went around with [future President Vincent] Shiely to every one of the lawn mower manufacturers, and we sketched their mowers to determine the engine space that was available," Lechtenberg recalled. "We needed to design an engine that would fit between the rails as the deck moved up and down."[47]

A new Choke-A-Matic remote choking system was developed in 1959. This system made it possible to choke the carburetor from a remote switch located on or near the push handle of the lawn mower, making it easier to start the engine.

To improve overall engine performance, a new Pulsa-Jet carburetor was introduced in 1960, which was more durable and easier to

Also developed during this period was the Starter-Generator. Reminiscent of the Power Charger so popular during the 1930s and 1940s, the Starter-Generator could start the engine, recharge a battery, and even generate 6 amperes for lights and other electrical equipment.

By 1959, sales had topped $89 million, a substantial increase from 1955 sales of $58 million.[48] The aluminum engine had catapulted Briggs & Stratton into a new level of success. "No question about it," said Lechtenberg. "I came up with a good design."[49]

A New Level of Service

West Plant No. 2 became the first authorized facility for training field service representatives. Upon completion of training, graduates would work in one of the many service distributors or dealerships around the country. For $25, service dealers, shop owners, service managers and mechanics would learn engine disassembly, bearing replacement, refacing of valves and valve seats, resizing cylinders, and the theory and operation of small engines. Also available was training in shop layout, customer service and the administration of warranty claims.[50]

Briggs & Stratton also established Field Training Schools throughout America and Canada, where individuals could learn factory service procedures from factory-trained instructors, using factory-designed methods and tools. These courses were popular not only with new recruits, but with established dealers and distributors eager to maintain skills within the ever-changing industry.

By 1960, Briggs & Stratton had more than 12,000 service outlets around the world, or, in the words of one advertisement, "From Reykjavik to Buenos Aires ... Bombay to Stockholm and in all principal trade centers in between you will find an authorized Briggs & Stratton service organization."[51]

A toy train in Pennsylvania powered by a Model ZZ engine. The fifties saw an increase in leisure time, creating new markets for Briggs & Stratton engines.

These flywheels are among the items manufactured at the Grey Iron Foundry, purchased by Briggs & Stratton in 1969. After expansions in 1978 and 1980, the foundry now contains 118,650 square feet of work space.

Chapter Eleven
TECHNOLOGY & INNOVATION

*"In that time and place, there were very few
companies that were better managed."*

— President John Shiely

I N THE SIXTIES AND SEVENTIES, the Briggs & Stratton Corporation focused on two goals — improving the small engine, and finding ways to produce as many of these engines as humanly possible. With the exception of automobile locks, the company no longer produced electrical specialties, automobile gadgetry, or such novelty items as paper towel cabinets or metal gift boxes. The creation of the aluminum engine provided the company with a commanding lead in the small engine industry.

In a 1973 speech, President Vincent Shiely pointed out that Briggs & Stratton "makes only two products: single-cylinder, air-cooled four-cycle engines and automotive locks." Shiely further noted that "about 90 percent of Briggs & Stratton total sales volume is represented by small, single-cylinder air-cooled engines, 2 horsepower through 16 horsepower." The company was already the largest producer of these engines in the world. The challenge would become one of continuing technological improvement.[1]

Customer Development Center

In 1959, Briggs & Stratton had created the Customer Development Center for the exclusive role of meeting customer demands for noise reduction, safety and increased reliability. Originally an offshoot of the sound laboratory created during development of the Sonoduct engine, the Customer Development Center was located at the Burleigh Plant. The facility housed seven distinct areas, including a sound laboratory for noise-reduction research, a cold room for improving cold-weather starting, and a tractor dynamometer room to study engine vibration reduction.

One of the biggest complaints from small engine owners was that the engines were difficult to start. Beginning in the early sixties, innovative systems were developed to cure this problem. In 1960, the company introduced the Briggs & Stratton Shock-Free Wind-Up starter, a manual starting system for use on small engines. This unit implemented a hand-cranking starter system with a heavy starter spring. To start the lawn mower, all that was needed was a quick crank of the starter handle. The Shock-Free starter eliminated jerky starts and kick-

---

Above: The Sonoduct engine cut noise dramatically by fitting into a fully enclosed housing under the lawn mower deck.

Opposite page, and above: The Briggs & Stratton Corporate Service Center distributed products to local distributors and dealerships.

backs that were frustrating and uncomfortable to consumers. Fred Stratton Jr. described the wind-up starter as "a good idea with a flaw."

"The good idea: To start the lawn mower, all that was needed was to crank the start handle to wind up the spring, and then turn a lever to put the spring-powered starter into motion. The flaw: On the retail sales floor, a potential customer could crank up the spring and leave it in that state. Later, another customer, oblivious to the danger from the wound-up spring, could turn the lever, bringing the spring-powered starter to life — a danger if the customer's hand or foot was near the blade. It was this flaw that killed the wind-up starter."[2]

But the Shock-Free starter was not the last word in engine-starting. In 1961, Briggs & Stratton introduced the Easy-Spin starting system, which cut the effort of manually starting an engine in half. The breakthrough design of Easy-Spin was actually fairly simple. When a small engine is engaged as it is during the starting process, a compression load is built up within the cylinders, requiring considerable strength to overcome. The solution was to

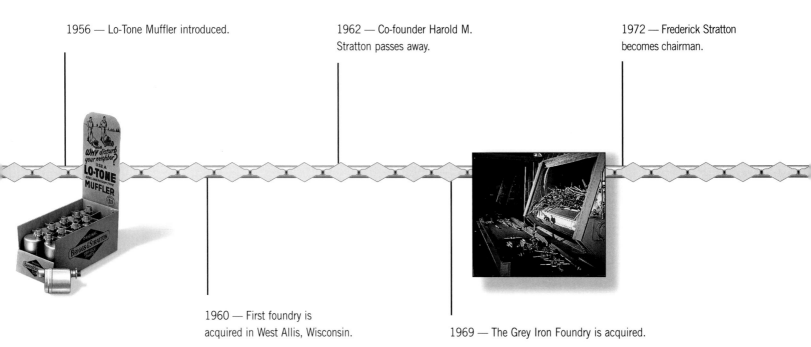

1956 — Lo-Tone Muffler introduced.

1962 — Co-founder Harold M. Stratton passes away.

1972 — Frederick Stratton becomes chairman.

1960 — First foundry is acquired in West Allis, Wisconsin.

1969 — The Grey Iron Foundry is acquired.

momentarily reduce compression during the starting process without decreasing engine performance during normal operation. Briggs & Stratton engineers designed a special lobed cam which articulated the intake valve, momentarily opening the valve $1/100$ of an inch to allow a substantial reduction in compression only during the starting pull-cycle. The Easy-Spin was a revolutionary innovation, replacing all but electric starting systems. When new federal safety regulations in 1982 required all small engine manufacturers to add emergency shut-off switches, company engineers discovered that engines with the Easy-Spin intake valve were unacceptably difficult to restart when hot. The Easy-Spin was moved to the exhaust valve, but this move resulted in some power loss. Where horsepower was an issue, a mechanical compression release was used. The intake valve Easy-Spin is still used on Briggs & Stratton's larger engines, but it will be eliminated by emission regulations in 1997.[3]

Another complaint from customers was engine vibration. This was especially prevalent aboard riding lawn mowers when using the larger 7- and 12-horsepower engines. In response, Briggs & Stratton

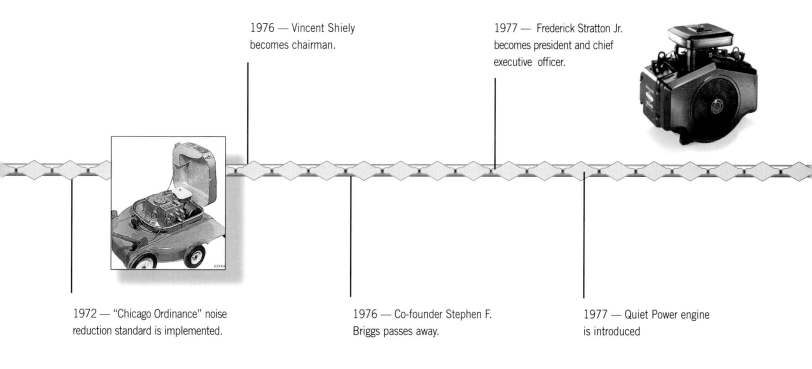

1976 — Vincent Shiely becomes chairman.

1977 — Frederick Stratton Jr. becomes president and chief executive officer.

1972 — "Chicago Ordinance" noise reduction standard is implemented.

1976 — Co-founder Stephen F. Briggs passes away.

1977 — Quiet Power engine is introduced

developed the Synchro-Balanced engine, which utilized a series of strategically located crankshaft
weights. This technique created a precise balance
along the crankshaft, where engine torque and thus
vibration are created, significantly reducing the
vibrations conducted to the equipment and rider.

Mowing lawns is dirty work, and grass and flying dirt particles could still make their way into the
engine. "The rotary screen was a big development to
keep the grass out of the engines," recalled engineer
Leo Lechtenberg. "If you didn't have these screens,
the grass would just clog the [cooling] fin and the
flywheel. The engine would be short-lived."[4]

The Snowblower

Although lawn mowers were the primary
application for Briggs & Stratton engines, a winter
application was emerging in the form of the Snowblower. Although the engine was similar to that of
a lawn mower, cold tem-
peratures, snow and
moisture created a new

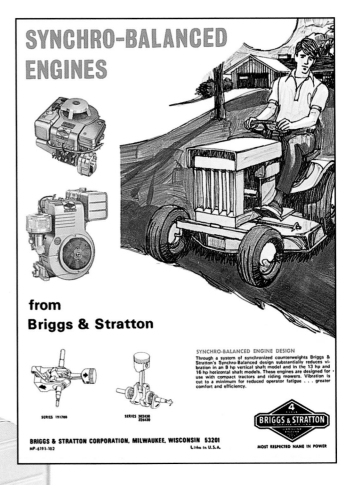

In order to reduce the vibrations caused by the high rpm
and torque of lawn mower engines, especially in riding lawn
mowers, Briggs & Stratton developed the Synchro-balanced
engine, which utilized an intricate design of counterweights
placed along the engine's crankshaft. This ad demonstrates
the basic philosophy of the design.

In the mid-sixties, snowblowers became a new market for
Briggs & Stratton engines. The Sno-Gard engine shown here
was designed specifically for winter conditions.

set of problems for engineers. Briggs & Stratton
engineers developed an engine especially adapted for use on snowblowers. Called the Sno-Gard,
it was equipped with a combination of refine-
ments that protected the more sensitive portions of
the engine from the winter elements, including an
air-intake shield, a starter clutch shield, and a special housing to cover the spark plug and carburetor, as well as heat the carburetor.

The End of an Era

On March 10, 1972, Charles L. Coughlin,
president of Briggs & Stratton from 1935 to 1971,

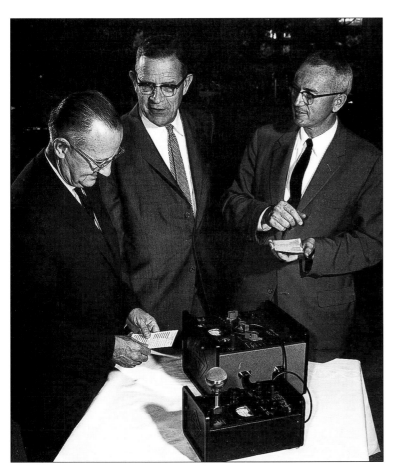

Left: Jack Ebershoff, Hugh Brown and Bob Harkness examine a printout showing the noise levels of a new engine. Briggs & Stratton was a pioneer in the development of quieter engines, and this device from General Radio allowed engineers to measure the noise of mufflers and blades before and after alterations were made.

Below: The quiet, enclosed Sonoduct engine was still in the experimental stage in 1958 when it was examined by Briggs & Stratton executives. Left to right: Ed Oehler, vice president of sales; Hugh Brown, vice president of engineering; Bob Harkness, vice president of research; and Jack Ebershoff, vice president of engine sales.

I think he was also a very outstanding people person. A good motivator. He was a person that people wanted to be around. He was capable of making hard decisions. The essence of leadership is the ability to take people where they don't want to go, and at that time there were a lot of challenges. He was able to direct the company and motivate people to do the things that had to be done to solidify Briggs & Stratton's position as a cost leader in the industry.

"He always said, 'I'm not in this for a popularity contest.' He had the leadership qualities and charisma to drive those things through without alienating anybody."[5]

and chief executive officer and chairman of the board since 1970, died at the age of 86. He had served Briggs & Stratton for a remarkable 56 years. A fighter to the end, it was a surprise to nobody that Coughlin continued to perform his duties as chairman right up to the day of his death.

Vincent R. Shiely became chief executive officer. A graduate of Notre Dame and the Harvard Business School, Shiely had been an executive at the Toro Company, one of Briggs & Stratton's biggest customers, when he had been hired by Coughlin. Shiely was vice president from 1959 to 1963, executive vice president from 1963 to 1971, and president from 1971 to 1977.

Shiely's son, John Shiely, himself president and chief operating officer of Briggs & Stratton since August 1994, recalled his father's many leadership qualities.

"As one of the first generation of schooled professional managers, he referred to himself as a 'hired hand.' He recognized his obligations to the shareholder constituency. He was very outgoing.

This advertisement from the seventies emphasized the power of the 16-horsepower Quiet Power twin.

The new chairman of the board was Frederick P. Stratton, the son of co-founder Harold M. Stratton. Stratton had been with the company since 1935, moving up through the ranks to the position of vice president of sales. "When [Stratton] came into a room, he just lit it up," remembered Colet Coughlin, the daughter of Charles Coughlin.

"He was the loveliest man and the most fun, the sweetest guy you could ever meet in your life. He was a great businessman. He loved being in advertising. He didn't want to be in anything else. Everybody loved him. I can't say enough good things about Fred."[6]

President John Shiely, the son of Vincent Shiely, agreed with Coughlin's assessment. "He

was an exceptional sales guy and a wonderful human being. He was just a superb person and always a lot of fun to talk to. I have some very fond memories of the time we spent with him on his sailboat out on Lake Michigan."[7] Shiely said Coughlin, Vincent Shiely and Frederick Stratton worked together to make Briggs & Stratton a remarkable company.

"An extraordinary operations guy, a good financial guy and professional manager, and a top sales and people person. It obviously worked, because the company achieved extraordinary things in terms of shareholder returns. A lot of our focus now is on creating shareholder value. These guys were very highly focused early practitioners of the cost leadership discipline. In that time and place, there were very few companies that were better managed. In 1972, the company achieved a return on equity of 25.3 percent, ranking seventh in the entire Fortune 500 — a remarkable achievement in value creation."[8]

A Quieter Engine

Briggs & Stratton engineers found ways to reduce engine noise, so peaceful suburban mornings would not be shattered by the roar of a neighbor's lawn mower or snowblower. The first attempt to lessen the noise of the engines was the Lo-Tone Muffler, introduced in 1956. The muffler utilized a

Above and opposite page: The Quiet Power engine, introduced in 1977, was developed to compete with other manufacturers, particularly Japanese companies that were cutting into traditional Briggs & Stratton turf by producing lawn mower engines.

system of carefully placed baffles that controlled noise levels without compromising engine performance. This new system produced a "six-point" noise reduction level that was said to have the same effect on the human ear as doubling the distance a person stood from the engine.[9]

One of the most unique approaches to the sound-abatement problem was the Sonoduct engine, developed in 1958. The Sonoduct reduced the noise of a lawn mower by literally flipping the engine over, and encasing it within a metal shroud. Though not exactly an upside-down engine, the flywheel was mounted on the underside of the engine to allow the deck of the mower

A point-of-purchase display for the Lo-Tone Muffler, one of many technological advances from Briggs & Stratton in the fifties and sixties.

to function as a natural muffler. In association with the engine shroud and Lo-Tone Muffler, engine noise was reduced substantially.

Although an engineering marvel, the Sonoduct met with mixed reviews and never caught on as well as expected. It was manufactured on a limited basis, and discontinued in 1960. The main problem with the Sonoduct was that it posed certain impracticalities for original equipment manufacturers. In order to mount this engine on a rotary lawn mower, a special mower deck had to be designed and manufactured, an expense the manufacturers were not willing to incur. Although a commercial failure, the Sonoduct engine led to further innovations in sound-reduction technology.

An advanced Lo-Tone Muffler, introduced in the early seventies, was an improvement over its 1956 namesake because it contained twice as many baffles and reduced noise levels from 77 to 68 decibels.[10] A second initiative, for use on smaller engines, was the Super Lo-Tone muffler created in the new sound-abatement laboratory in 1972. The laboratory, built adjacent to the Customer Development Center at a cost of $300,000, was the first of its kind to be used by a small engine manufacturer. The Super Lo-Tone muffler also reduced noise to 68 decibels, six decibels

GO KARTS

In the late seventies and early eighties, Briggs & Stratton supplied engines to several experimental and sport vehicles, especially ones designed by engineering students.

Briggs & Stratton in 1979 created a riding lawn mower to promote its new 18-horsepower twin-cylinder engine. Known also as the "attack" lawn mower, the Grand Prix Lawn Mower was designed to resemble a miniature Grand Prix race car with a conventional rotary lawn mower deck assembly mounted beneath the body. The vehicle was able to reach a top speed of between 80 and 90 miles per hour

road course. In addition to national recognition, winners received financial support for college.

Though Briggs & Stratton moved away from motor sport participation in the eighties, the company responded to public demand in 1993 and re-entered the field of kart racing with the new Briggs & Stratton Motorsports Division. Located at the Corporate Office Building in the Burleigh Plant, the division provides engines, parts, racing gear and information through a network of about 100 Briggs & Stratton Motorsports Centers in the United States and Canada.

The Motorsports Division also provides support to such organizations as the World Karting Association, International Karting Federation, Quarter Midgets of America and National Hot Rod Association.

"Our 5-horsepower engine in the racing side is used by the World Karting Association," said Curt Larson, vice president and general manager of the Industrial Division. "They kind of promote us as their baseline model. That's helped to pull in a lot of this business."[12]

as well as mow the lawn, though not necessarily at the same time.[11]

Mini-Baja and Mini-Indy events, held at different track facilities around the United States, used 8-horsepower engines donated by Briggs & Stratton. The events, which began in 1974, required engineering students to build their own racing vehicles. The Baja event used off-road vehicles, while the Indy event, of course, used Indy-style vehicles. Each vehicle was judged on aesthetics, durability, soundness of design, and of course, its ability to complete the

Above: The Motorsports Division sponsors several racing events for younger racers, including those sanctioned by the World Karting Assoication, Quarter Midgets of America and the National Hot Rod Association's Jr. Dragster.

Above, left: University of Texas-Austin engineering students proudly pose with their vehicles and their trophies after winning the 1982 Mini-Baja.

below the "Chicago Ordinance," a noise reduction standard mandated on January 1, 1972.[13]

In 1973, President Vincent Shiely spoke optimistically about the company's plans to further reduce noise in lawn mower engines.

"The most widely known noise code has been adopted by the City of Chicago. It calls for an acceptable noise level, measured in decibels at 50 feet. Progressive standards have been established for 1972, 1975 and 1978. It is our belief that practically all walk-type mowers are meeting the 1972 code today, and some are already meeting the 1975 code. We are optimistic about meeting the 1978 codes by a combination of reducing internal engine noise and the use of enclosures."[14]

In 1977, Briggs & Stratton unveiled a truly revolutionary design in small engines — the 16-horsepower twin-cylinder engine. The result of four years of research and design, the twin was built to replace the company's line of heavy cast-iron engines. The new engine, called the Quiet Power twin, provided more power, lower fuel consumption, less vibration and quieter operation, all at a substantially lower cost to the company and the customer.

Production of Quiet Power twin engines began in 1977. The engine was used primarily in riding lawn mowers and small tractors, and helped Briggs & Stratton reach new industrial mar-

Wisconsin Governor Warren Knowles and Briggs & Stratton Chairman Fred Stratton admire a photograph of co-founder Harold M. Stratton in the corporate board room at the Burleigh Plant.

kets. Briggs & Stratton offered the twin at $228, a price $70 lower than the competition. The company even beat the price of its own 16-horsepower cast-iron model, selling the twin for $40 less.[15]

A new Solid State Ignition System, introduced by Briggs & Stratton in late 1976, eliminated the use of the standard ignition condenser, points and plunger, and instead utilized a coil, transistor and trigger coil, which supplied a voltage pulse to fire the spark plug. The new system provided smoother firing and easier starting, and eliminated the need to replace and adjust ignition components during routine maintenance.

From the fifties to the seventies, Briggs & Stratton significantly improved its small engines, making them quieter, easier to start, and easier to maintain and operate. Lawn and garden care was no longer the chore it had once been.

New Facilities

Among Briggs & Stratton's ongoing challenges was to expand its production of crankshafts, camshafts, flywheels and other parts that

Briggs & Stratton engines have long been a familiar sight on Craftsman lawn mowers made famous through Sears, Roebuck. This model however features a Briggs & Stratton electric motor, not so common to the consumer, but quieter and kinder to the environment.

The Burleigh Plant. The lighter area is the North Addition, which, when completed in 1967, more than doubled the size of the plant.

required specialized casting. In 1960, the company acquired its first foundry, the Le Roi Division facility of the Westinghouse Air Brake Company in West Allis, Wisconsin, a southwest suburb of Milwaukee, for more than $1 million.[16] In 1965, the foundry was expanded, and in 1975 a water treatment building was added. In 1980, the Crichton Building was added, bringing the total work space to 327,576 square feet.

In 1984, the West Allis Foundry underwent a $13 million renovation, which completely automated the plant. Disamatic automatic molding equipment was installed, and new computers controlled all foundry operations, making West Allis one of the most advanced facilities of its kind in the country.

In 1969, the company purchased a second foundry, located at 1501 South 83rd Street, from the Zenith Foundry Company for $800,000.[17] The new acquisition was named the Grey Iron Foundry, reflecting the type of castings to be made. It manufactured flywheels and other components. In 1978, the Grey Iron Foundry was remodeled and expanded, and in 1980, it was expanded again, creating a total work area of

118,650 square feet. The principal reason Briggs & Stratton acquired the Grey Iron foundry was that it gave the company the ability to manufacture its own flywheels. Grey iron flywheels were relatively expensive to manufacture because they included the fins that drive cooling air over the cylinder and cylinder head.

These two foundries continued efforts towards vertical integration of industrial production. Since Briggs & Stratton could substantially supply its own parts, it could manufacture more economically. This vertical integration allowed Briggs & Stratton to reduce costs. By 1975, Briggs & Stratton made all engine components except piston rings, spark plugs and valves.

The most significant expansion in the Milwaukee area during this period was at the Burleigh Plant in Wauwatosa. In 1967, with annual net sales up to $126, million and the company producing more than 5 million engines per year,[18] the North Addition was constructed, providing an additional 637,800 square feet of work space. The addition actually doubled the size of the plant, at a cost of more than $6 million. A new parking lot provided spaces for an additional 1,500 cars.[19] The facility now housed additional manufacturing capabilities with equipment transferred there from both the East and West plants. It was hailed as "the most modern and efficient single-cylinder engine plant in the United

Wisconsin Governor Warren Knowles visits the new North Addition. From left to right: Lawrence Regner, Vincent Shiely, Knowles, Wauwatosa Mayor Ervin Meier and Fred Stratton.

States," capable of producing 25,000-30,000 engines per day.[20] Briggs & Stratton moved its corporate offices from the East Plant to the Burleigh Plant. So impressive was this new facility that it warranted a tour by several state and local government officials, including Wisconsin Governor Warren Knowles.

Less than a year after the massive expansion at the Burleigh Plant, company officials acquired a 55-acre site in Menomonee Falls, a Northwestern suburb of Milwaukee. The land, located near the new and growing Menomonee Falls Industrial Park, was appraised at $472,855 and owned by Coughlin, then president of Briggs & Stratton. Since the sale raised concerns over conflict of interest, it was not until company stockholders approved the sale by an overwhelming 3,048,370 to 130,598 in September 1968, that Briggs & Stratton concluded the transaction, providing Coughlin with a significant profit.[21] The land was not developed until the late seventies, when Briggs & Stratton constructed a new components plant, as well as a manufacturing and distribution center.

In 1970, Briggs & Stratton produced almost 6 million engines, accounting for nearly $164 million in sales.[22] In 1973, with annual sales of $261 million,[23] the Burleigh Plant expanded again. Construction of the two-story South Addition began in the spring, and added 338,800 square feet at a cost of approximately $21 million.[24]

In 1973, President Vincent Shiely could boast that capital improvements had actually reduced the price of horsepower from $13.99 per horsepower in 1953 to $8.05 in 1972.

"We have a highly integrated manufacturing operation and produce every major component in our engines," he said. *"We purchase only a few parts, mainly spark plugs, valves, and small hardware such as nuts and bolts. ... Cost reduction has also been accomplished through design. Three years ago, we replaced our 8-horsepower cast-iron engine, selling for $89, with an 8-horsepower aluminum model, selling for $50. This fall,*

THE HYBRID

One of the most unusual uses for Briggs and Stratton engines was the Gasoline/Electric Hybrid automobile, introduced in 1980. The fuel shortages of the seventies, combined with increasing environmental concerns, prompted automobile manufactures to search for alternative power sources. The concept of an electric-powered car gained popularity, but the prototypes were extremely limited in speed and range. Since they had to be recharged often, they were not considered practical. The public's primary concern was that the vehicle would run out of battery power before reaching its destination.

Engineers at Briggs & Stratton decided to solve this problem by supplementing an electric car with a small, twin-cylinder, 4-cycle engine. The result was the Hybrid.

The Hybrid gasoline/electric car consisted of a coupe-type automobile body, designed by Kip Stevens of Brooks Stevens Design in Mequon, Wisconsin, which rested on a standard automotive tubular frame and suspension. The Hybrid was 4 feet high, 5 feet wide and 14½ feet long. It weighed about 3,200 pounds. It was powered by an electric motor that used 12 six-volt batteries, and a Briggs and Stratton 18-horesepower twin-cylinder engine under the hood.

The two power sources could be used independently or in tandem, according to the needs of the user. With electric power alone, the driver could reach a top speed of 40 miles per hour and travel between 30 and 60 miles. The gas engine could carry the car between 175 and 280 miles at about 45 miles per hour, depending on driving and road conditions. Each power source could be switched on or off at will, to produce added power or replace the other. Although the car could reach a viable speed, it took 33 seconds to reach 40 miles per hour when powered by the engine.

The real benefit of the car was fuel economy, which ranged from 25 miles per gallon with the gas engine to 150 miles per gallon using only the electric motor.

Initially, automakers, including engineers at Ford, showed interest in the Hybrid, but the limited range and inconvenience of recharging the batteries made it too much of a risk for manufacturers. The Hybrid faded into obscurity by 1983.

Above: The Glendale Plant was acquired in 1972 to replace the antiquated East Plant, and automotive lock assembly operations were substantially modernized. Two such assembly operations are shown here.

Above, right: An aerial view of the facility in Glendale, Wisconsin.

Briggs & Stratton will introduce a new 10-horsepower aluminum engine that will sell for $75, in contrast to our current cast-iron model, which sells for $100."[25]

In 1974, annual sales topped $300 million. A 3,000-square-foot addition was constructed at the Customer Development Center, and it was converted to a state-of-the-art Engine Application Center, which included a sound lab, dynometer rooms, and other areas for testing and improving engines. After 1979, the center would be used primarily to help customers appy Briggs & Stratton engines to their equipment.

In August 1976, Briggs & Stratton purchased the Levitz Furniture Company's 155,000-square-foot warehouse located on 11 acres of land just to the north of the Briggs & Stratton North Addition. The building included a warehouse and a showroom. The company continued to use the warehouse, but converted the showroom into an office building that housed the accounting department, a new data processing center and an auditorium. It also housed the service training school, which was moved from the ductile iron foundry building in West Allis.

Scrap metal, a basic foundry raw material, being received at the West Allis foundry. Scrap metal has been recycled since 1981, when an incinerator was built along the south end of the facility.

In 1984, Briggs & Stratton remodeled a portion of the building, moving the service school to the Menomonee Falls distribution center and moving the auditorium into a portion of the warehouse. The same year, a new corporate office building and lobby was constructed at 12301 West Wirth Street, to the south of the Research and Development Center where company operations are currently housed. In all, from initial construction in 1954, through all of the additions up to 1980, the Burleigh Plant had accumulated just under 2 million square feet of work space.

Christian Haugen pours molten metal at a Briggs & Stratton foundry.

Frederick P. Stratton Sr., chairman of the board at Briggs & Stratton from 1972 until his untimely death in June 1976.

Although small engines were the core of Briggs & Stratton business, automotive locks and keys still accounted for 10 percent of annual sales. By the early seventies, production reached 135,000 locks and keys per day, supplying 40 percent of a $50 million market. The East Plant, by then an aging facility, could no longer maintain production levels necessary to stay competi-

tive in the field, and upgrading the facility was determined not to be cost-effective. So in 1973, a new facility was acquired for the manufacture and distribution of automotive locks. This facility was purchased from the Square D Company at an approximate cost of $2.7 million, and was located on 27 acres in Glendale, a northeast suburb of Milwaukee.[26] Known as the Glendale Plant, this 200,000-square-foot building included a cafeteria and administrative offices. Following expansions in both 1974 and 1979, the facility provided 367,200 square feet.

New facilities eliminated the need for the East Plant buildings that had housed original operations as early as 1915. By the late sixties, these early Briggs & Stratton properties were eliminated. By 1967, production of engine components had been moved to Wauwatosa, and after 1974, when lock production was moved to the Glendale plant, the East Plant facilities were empty. Two years later, the buildings were demolished and the land traded to the Reliance Boiler Works in exchange for its buildings near the Briggs & Stratton West Plant.

The West Plant, constructed in 1936 at 32nd and Center streets, still had some life left in it. Primarily responsible for the manufacture of cast-iron engines, this facility, even with expansion in the seventies, could not produce fast enough. In 1972, Briggs & Stratton purchased the Milsco Manufacturing Company building, located across 32nd Street from the main plant, and in 1977, the Reliance Boiler Works was purchased. Together, these buildings added almost 500,000 square feet to the West Plant.

In 1986, following the automation of the Burleigh Plant and a joint-venture project with Puling Machinery Company in China to manufacture cast-iron engines, this facility also produced electric starter motors and other components for aluminum engines. But, with the growing acceptance of aluminum engines, the domestic market for cast-iron engines was disappearing. The West Plant had become obsolete. Cast-iron engine production equipment was moved to the Wauwatosa plant and to a joint-venture plant in China, and the production of aluminum engine components was moved to Wauwatosa and Menomonee Falls. On August 1, 1986, the West Plant, acquired in 1936 to mass-produce washing machine engines, was closed. It was subsequently sold for $350,000 in April 1987 to a Milwaukee Realtor.

A Series of Tragedies

On June 1, 1976, tragedy struck as Board Chairman Frederick Stratton died of a heart attack at the age of 62. His son, Frederick Stratton Jr., became a member of the board of directors, while Vincent Shiely assumed the chairmanship. But within a year, in May 1977, Shiely fell ill to a malignant brain tumor, and following surgery, died in August. Fred Stratton at the age of 38, became president and chief executive officer of Briggs & Stratton. Lawrence G. Regner, who had been with the company since 1934, became chairman of the board, remaining in that position until his 1984 retirement.

On October 16, 1976, Stephen F. Briggs, the mechanical genius who co-founded Briggs & Stratton, died at the age of 90 at his home in Naples, Florida.

Briggs had been a generous man who established a company policy of charitable donation in the thirties, and was responsible for major contributions to his alma mater, South Dakota State College, which later became South Dakota State University. In 1952, Briggs, an accomplished amateur motion picture photographer and director of nature films, donated $10,000 worth of photographic equipment to the SDSC photo lab. "Briggs has made available to us equipment the college could not afford to purchase," stated the head of the SDSC Audio-Visual Department. "This equipment gives us the opportunity to undertake projects that would have been impossible before."[27]

In 1957, Briggs established the Briggs Scholarship at South Dakota State College, which, by 1976, had awarded some 800 students about $800,000 in scholarships. Following his death, his sons, John and James, established the Briggs Foundation at SDSC, which offers a $1,250 scholarship to 40 students per academic year who might otherwise be financially unable to pursue a college education.

In addition to his incredible engineering talents, Briggs was a gifted motion picture photographer. He produced eight short films by 1952

Stratton was succeeded by Vincent R. Shiely, who was chairman until August 1977, when he also suffered an untimely death, caused by a brain tumor.

about tropical water birds and other wildlife, the life and culture of the Caribbean, as well as promotional films for the Outboard Marine Corporation. Several of his films were purchased by Walt Disney, including *Water Birds* and *The Life of a Gooney Bird*, a film that is considered a classic in the field of bird photography.

CEOs, a remarkable testament to the stability of the company. Charles Coughlin was CEO from 1935 to 1972, Vincent Shiely, from 1972 to 1977, and Fred Stratton from 1977 to the present. With few exceptions, changes in top management ranks have been evolutionary. The company's top executives are usually promoted from within, having spent years, and even decades, working for Briggs & Stratton.

A New Generation

Fred Stratton Jr. recalled that his first job, in 1958, was "in the tabulating department, as we called it in those days."[29] Stratton said he had always been fascinated by engines. "I always liked anything powered by engines. Cars, boats and airplanes."[30] He continued to work summers at Briggs & Stratton while attending Yale University. After receiving an MBA from Stanford University, he worked at Arthur Andersen for two years, and Robert W. Baird & Company for eight years. "I wanted to work somewhere else to get the experience and gain a little self-confidence. So I would know that I could do things on my own, and not because of my name," he said.[31] He joined Briggs & Stratton in 1973, when his father was chairman and Vincent Shiely was president.

"Young Fred had worked for me a couple of summers while he was still going to school," recalled engineer Leo Lechtenberg.

"They had been grooming him for a while. I'm sure he never expected to be thrust into the position when he was. We never predicted, of course, after Coughlin died, that Fred [Sr.] would suddenly have a heart attack, much less that Vince would end up with his problems."[32]

Lechtenberg, then vice president of engineering, said he never doubted that Stratton was the right person to lead the company. "I didn't see anybody else we could spare from their present job that would make a strong leader without disrupting a lot of other management," he said. "As far as I was concerned, Fred was the way to go."[33]

Jack Ebershoff, vice president of engine sales from 1965 to 1970, also praised Stratton. "This young fellow had done a great job," he said. "He's

Stephen F. Briggs established a policy of charitable donations at Briggs & Stratton in the thirties, and continued this tradition of generosity throughout his life.

Miscellaneous footage shot during his various excursions were used in the Warner Brothers film *Drugs Along the Mohawk*, starring Gary Cooper. All proceeds from the sales of these projects were donated to the Audubon Society.[28]

The deaths of Coughlin and Briggs, along with the death of Harold M. Stratton in 1962, marked the end of an era. The company founders had passed on, and a new generation had taken the helm of Briggs & Stratton. In the past 60 years, Briggs & Stratton has had only three the only guy I know that could follow the people that preceded him."[34]

Stratton quickly grew into the job. "At first it was 90 percent panic and 10 percent fun," he said in a 1978 interview. "But I'm happy to say it now seems the other way around."[35]

Stratton's brother, Harold Stratton II, joined the company in 1977. He is president and chief executive officer of STRATTEC Security Corporation, a spin-off of the company's automotive lock business. Stratton graduated from St. Lawrence University and received an MBA at Notre Dame. He worked at American Motors between 1973 and 1977, before joining the family business. Harold Stratton said two things prompted him to join Briggs & Stratton.

"One thing was I really didn't have much of a personal life in Detroit. I never got into any major social groups, probably because I was working pretty hard. Milwaukee is basically a nice place to live, a lot nicer than Detroit, so I was looking forward to coming back. Another reason was there were so many changes going on at Briggs & Stratton, with my father passing away in '76 and Vince passing away in '77."[36]

Stratton recalled being a young boy and going to the office with his father.

"At a relatively young age, my father tried to explain to me that he worked for a company of which we were part owners. That led to a discussion of how we were part owners. He tried to explain stock and those kinds of things. I was fairly confused. He explained that it's like having a small piece of the company. In those days, he would go to work on Saturday sometimes, and drag one or two of us along. Whenever I was there with him, I would look for the piece that I owned. It was like, 'Which corner is it? Is it a chair? What do I own here?' I didn't quite get it."[37]

The Model 92908 was one of several standard engine models developed in the early eighties. Though they were suitable for many applications, the primary use was to power lawn and garden equipment such as mowers, edgers, tillers and snowblowers.

Chapter Twelve
MOVING SOUTH

"In Murray [Kentucky] we had a real opportunity to incorporate the best technology that we had for making engines, along with some real different management practices. It allowed us to get away from some of the encumbrances we had with trying to manage our operations effectively, and to provide better jobs for the folks that were part of it."

—Dick Fotsch, vice president and general manager of the Small Engine Division

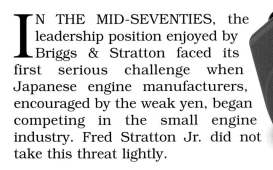

IN THE MID-SEVENTIES, the leadership position enjoyed by Briggs & Stratton faced its first serious challenge when Japanese engine manufacturers, encouraged by the weak yen, began competing in the small engine industry. Fred Stratton Jr. did not take this threat lightly.

"Although we are the world's leading producer of small engines, we are the smallest engine company in the business. The reason, of course, is that all our competitors have other businesses that are bigger than their engine businesses. Tecumseh's main business is compressors. Kohler's main business is plumbing. Honda's main business is automobiles. Kawasaki, Suzuki, Yamaha, Fuji, Mitsubishi, Kubota and Yanmar all have other businesses. Engines are our principal business. We take it very seriously. We couldn't let Japanese competitors take it away from us."[1]

Briggs & Stratton responded in several ways to this threat, and some of the responses worked better than others. The actions of Briggs & Stratton, as well as the strengthening yen,

allowed Briggs & Stratton to triumph. By the end of the decade, the tide had been stemmed. Among the most significant assets held by Briggs & Stratton was Stratton himself, newly appointed as president and chief executive officer. Not long after he became president and CEO, the old conservative company image began to give way to a new and bolder management approach.

Stratton was forced to make decisions that were unpopular with Briggs & Stratton employees. Success depended on a three-pronged strategy of quality improvement, increased efficiencies in the manufacturing process and improvements in the design and performance of the engines.

The First Southern Facility

In 1977, Briggs & Stratton, for the first time, established a facility outside of Wisconsin. After careful consideration, the company acquired a

The popular Vanguard V-Twin engine, introduced in 1987.

262,800-square-foot plant in Perry, Georgia, from the Magee Carpet Company. Located 100 miles south of Atlanta, the facility in this small town manufactured locks and lock parts.

The decision, viewed with suspicion by Local 232, was influenced largely by General Motors. In 1977, Briggs & Stratton signed a contract to supply 50 percent of all of the locks and lock parts used by General Motors. In 1979 and 1980, it was increased to 100 percent. As part of the contract, General Motors insisted that Briggs & Stratton build or acquire a second facility. The acquisition of the Perry plant cost Briggs & Stratton $7 million, but it meant a 75 percent increase of business to the automotive lock division. Since the General Motors production occupied only part of the new facility, Briggs & Stratton could pursue further expansion business from other automobile manufacturers, including Volkswagen and Japanese automakers.

The new plant was warmly welcomed in the economically depressed town of Perry, providing 300 jobs to a community that had suffered several plant closings. But the move from Wisconsin was something of an omen for the Briggs & Stratton work force.

A World of Opportunity

In the late seventies, Briggs & Stratton resolved to expand its once lucrative, but then diminishing, foreign markets. In a bold initiative launched in 1979, the company made its first foreign acquisition, Farymann Diesel GmbH & Company of Lampertheim, near Frankfurt, West Germany. The established company was purchased to function as a base for European as well as American distribution of small diesel engines, as well as a manufacturing facility. With the massive increase in energy and fossil fuel costs during the period, Briggs & Stratton elected to break into the diesel engine market, with the hope that Briggs & Stratton could establish a greater presence and credibility in European industrial markets.

Beginning with 123,433 of original square footage, Briggs & Stratton-Farymann Division expanded in 1981 to include a new test house, a warehouse and an office for international distribution and sales, known as Briggs & Stratton-International. Although this venture showed promise, the energy crisis soon subsided, and sales of small diesel engines were extremely poor.

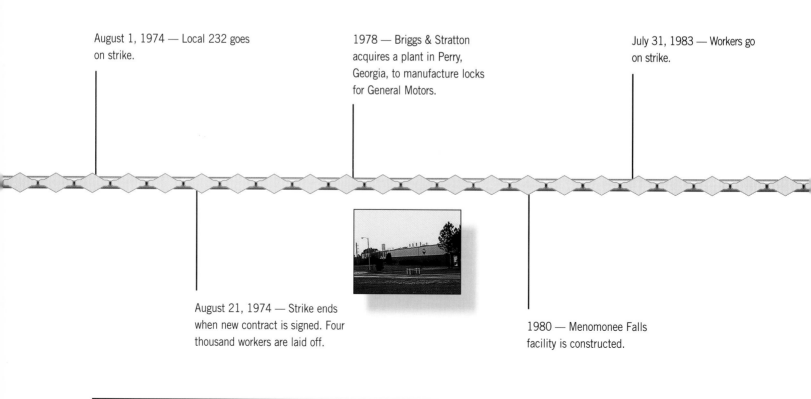

August 1, 1974 — Local 232 goes on strike.

1978 — Briggs & Stratton acquires a plant in Perry, Georgia, to manufacture locks for General Motors.

July 31, 1983 — Workers go on strike.

August 21, 1974 — Strike ends when new contract is signed. Four thousand workers are laid off.

1980 — Menomonee Falls facility is constructed.

Briggs & Stratton reluctantly decided to divest the entire operation. "Farymann has never made money for Briggs" stated Stratton in 1984, "Their annual unit production is less than our daily unit production."[2]

Hugo Keltz noted that Farymann was one of the smallest diesel manufacturers in the world. "The volume was small, maximum 20,000 engines a year," he said. "And Briggs & Stratton being the largest manufacturer in the world for small gasoline engines, I guess we felt we could perhaps run this small company like we run the big Briggs & Stratton company. It really didn't work very well."[3]

In a 1995 interview, Stratton said the company had miscalculated.

"We got caught up in it because it was the time of the energy crisis when the price of fuel went up, so the fuel efficiency of diesel became more valuable. The fuel savings had a greater dollar value relative to the price of the engine. A diesel

Briggs & Stratton purchased Farymann Diesel of Laperthiem, West Germany, in 1979 to distribute and manufacture diesel engines.

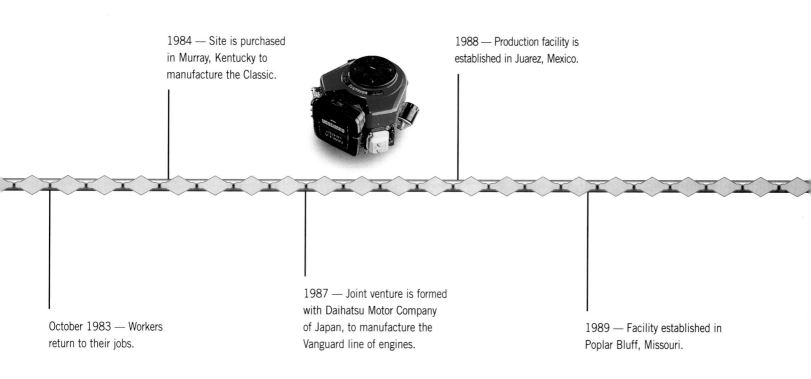

1984 — Site is purchased in Murray, Kentucky to manufacture the Classic.

1988 — Production facility is established in Juarez, Mexico.

October 1983 — Workers return to their jobs.

1987 — Joint venture is formed with Daihatsu Motor Company of Japan, to manufacture the Vanguard line of engines.

1989 — Facility established in Poplar Bluff, Missouri.

engine is a more expensive engine. It has to withstand a much higher compression ratio. ... At that time, everybody expected the energy crisis to last a long time, for the price of fuel to rise steadily. ... It was not a good bit of business."[4]

Meanwhile, Briggs & Stratton pursued another European partner for the purpose of distributing foreign-made diesel engines in the United States. In 1982, Briggs & Stratton entered into a joint venture with Lombardini Fabbrica Italiana Motori S.p.A. in Reggio Emilia, Italy. This venture formed Briggs & Stratton Lombardini Diesel, Inc., with a distribution facility located in Atlanta, Georgia. The partnership was intended to market diesel engines in the United States, with the hope that it could build enough volume to justify a manufacturing plant in the U.S. But in 1984, Briggs & Stratton ended its involvement in the air-cooled diesel engine business and sold Farymann to a German investor.

The Menomonee Falls Plant

In 1980, Briggs & Stratton constructed a new facility located at the intersection of Highway 41 and Pilgrim Road in Menomonee Falls, on the land sold to the company by Charles Coughlin in 1968. This new plant, of which one-third was devoted to distribution and two-thirds to manufacturing, cost $35 million, measured almost 790,960 square feet, employed about 600 people, and had its own highway exit ramp. The new plant featured an innovative energy-efficient insulation system, part of a strategy to capture waste and process it as heat. The plant was quite attractive, constructed on a sloping hill and incorporating a man-made, lighted pond.[5]

In 1986, the Menomonee Falls Plant began production of the Vanguard engines, developed to compete with engines made by Japanese manufacturers. Japanese production focused on premium-line overhead-valve engines used mainly for commercial applications, and in 1987 Briggs & Stratton introduced an overhead valve engine of its own to directly challenge Japan. Ranging from 5- to 15-horsepower, the Vanguard was designed to run quieter, last longer, and operate more efficiently than other models. Development of the Vanguard took more than three years, and involved hundreds of visits to equipment manufacturers and dealers.

New Products

The principal market for Briggs & Stratton engines was lawn and garden equipment manufacturers. However, the emerging threat for engine sales came from the Japanese encroachment of industrial and commercial application markets. To counter this threat, Briggs & Stratton introduced Industrial/ Commercial (I/C) engines in 1979. Jim Wier, executive vice president of operations, explained the logic behind the decision.

"At that time, lawn and garden was such a big and important part, that unless you focused on the smaller parts they would get lost in the

One of several diesel engines manufactured by Farymann Diesel.

The Menomonee Falls Plant was built in 1980 to accommodate the expanding worldwide market of Briggs & Stratton.

shuffle. Probably more importantly, the Japanese at that time were coming and attacking our market. The Japanese attack was on the industrial side. We didn't want to allow them to get a firm foothold or take our industrial business, so that was why we decided to focus on the industrial side."[6]

In 1982, Briggs & Stratton designed a fully electronic ignition, which was considered among the most important technological improvements since the aluminum engine was developed in the early fifties. Called Magnetron, this electronic system replaced the traditional condenser and break-

Although Briggs & Stratton sold Farymann Diesel in 1984, it still owns this warehouse, which now functions as the European Distribution Center.

er point system that required regular maintenance. For years, Briggs & Stratton had been trying to perfect a maintenance-free electro-mechanical system called Magnevac, Stratton recalled.

"We spent 13 years and $15 million developing the Magnevac ignition system, an electro–mechanical system based on a magnetic reed switch enclosed in a vacuum. By the time we got the Magnevac system ready for production, solid state technology had passed us by, and solid state systems — such as our Magnetron system — were less expensive to manufacture. I remember saying to our friends at Toro, 'We may have made a stunning breakthrough in an obsolete technology.' (One of my favorite quotes). I was right. Eventually, the Magnetron ignition was (and is) used on all Briggs & Stratton engines."[7]

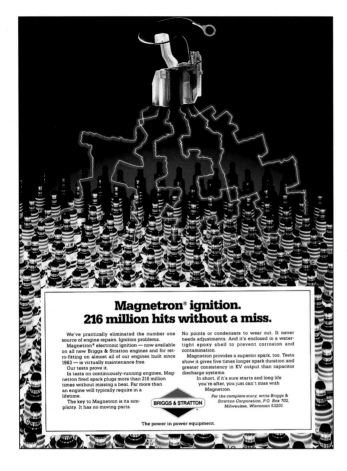

**Magnetron® ignition.
216 million hits without a miss.**

We've practically eliminated the number one source of engine repairs. Ignition problems.
Magnetron® electronic ignition — now available on all new Briggs & Stratton engines and for retro-fitting on almost all of our engines built since 1963 — is virtually maintenance free.
Our tests prove it.
In tests on continuously-running engines, Magnetron fired spark plugs more than 216 million times without missing a beat. Far more than an engine will typically require in a lifetime.
The key to Magnetron is its simplicity. It has no moving parts.

No points or condensers to wear out. It never needs adjustments. And it's enclosed in a water-tight epoxy shell to prevent corrosion and contamination.
Magnetron provides a superior spark, too. Tests show it gives five times longer spark duration and greater consistency in KV output than capacitor discharge systems.
In short, if it's sure starts and long life you're after, you just can't miss with Magnetron.

For the complete story, write Briggs & Stratton Corporation, P.O. Box 702, Milwaukee, Wisconsin 53201.

BRIGGS & STRATTON

The power in power equipment.

In 1982, Briggs & Stratton developed a sealed transistor ignition system called the Magnetron electronic ignition, which was waterproof and maintenance-free.

Labor Difficulties

Between 1950 and the early seventies, organized labor in America enjoyed great influence, and industry executives throughout the country found themselves meeting increasingly difficult demands from union leaders. The AIW, Local 232, was, by the early seventies, more than 10,000 strong, making it the largest and most powerful union in Milwaukee. On July 31, 1971, only hours from the deadline of a threatened strike, Local 232 voted, by a nearly 2-to-1 margin, to accept a new three-year contract. This contract represented a typical victory, granting union members substantial pay raises totaling 25 percent, or $.75 to $1.40 per hour for each of the three years, in addition to more holidays, increased medical benefits and a plan for early retirement.

In 1973, President Vincent Shiely commented on labor relations at Briggs & Stratton.

"This has been an excellent labor market for producing our product. There are a lot of skills here that are required. There is an ample supply of what we consider high-quality factory employment. Under our base rate and incentive system, they can earn very good money. Our average time rate is $4.80 an hour. About half of our employees are women. A very high percentage of them are married and have husbands working. We are talking about an employee working in our plant that might have a combined family income of $15,000 to $20,000 a year.

"So far as any union problems are concerned, the union is going to seek its objectives. We are going to seek ours. We don't always agree. You just can't come into agreement on some of these things. I think, in having participated in a couple of negotiations with our employees, they are a fairly responsible group of people. They have an awful lot at stake, in their pension funds, benefits and so on. We find them generally cooperative."[8]

It was no surprise to Briggs & Stratton management when Local 232 demanded higher wages, raises tied to the cost of living, a larger pension and more benefits as the 1971 contract neared expiration. Management refused to acquiesce to all of these demands, and on August 1, 1974, Local 232 voted 2,962 to 747 in favor of a strike. For the second time since the organization of Local 232, Briggs & Stratton workers went on strike, completely shutting down the company. According to a federal mediator, it was "an impossible situation. ... The company has given about as much as it can."[9] After 21 days of the strike, Local 232 accepted one of the largest wage settlements negotiated in the city of Milwaukee, totaling a remarkable 32.5 percent over three years. Additional holidays, more vacation time, an increase in benefits and improved retirement plans were also included. "They got pretty much everything they asked for," said Paul Neylon, who is now vice president and general manager of the Vanguard Engine Division.[10] Neylon said a union group called Concerned Workers actually helped his career by complaining about him in printed hand-outs.

"I used to tell them, 'The guys don't know what I'm doing out here on the plant floor, and here you

are putting it in black and white, telling them I'm actually getting people to work and getting them away from the clock before quitting time. Chasing them out of locker rooms. You're accusing me of doing my job.'"[11]

Although Local 232 had won at the bargaining table, the union could not beat the economy. The recession, the strike and subsequent union gains forced Briggs & Stratton to lay off some 4,000 workers, dropping the total work force almost in half to 4,200. Although 3,000 workers returned in later years, layoffs would continue into the eighties.

When this contract was ready for renewal in 1977, Briggs & Stratton could only assume that union officials would tone down their demands, fearing additional layoffs. However, Local 232

Right: Production in all six Milwaukee plants ground to a halt when 7,600 workers went on strike in 1983. The three-month strike prompted the company to open facilities in the South.

Below: Striking union workers prevent a roofing company vehicle from leaving Briggs & Stratton property because the company used non-union labor.

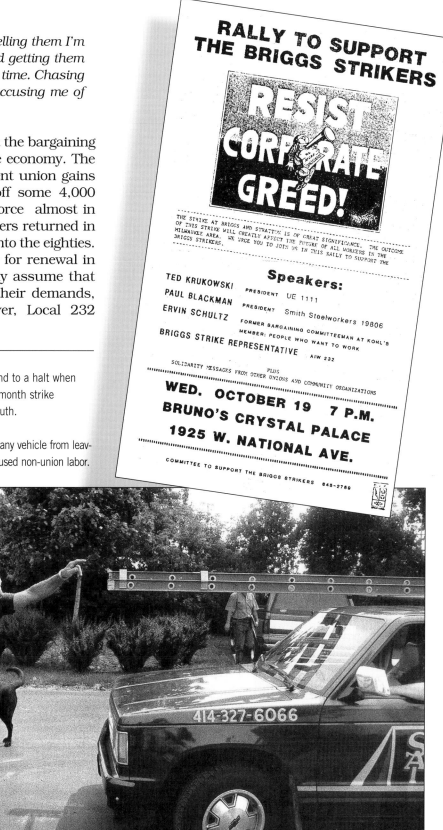

again demanded substantial wage increases, and management, unable to finance yet another shutdown, gave in.

Two years later, Local 2090 of the UAW shut down the Perry, Georgia, facility for nine weeks, severely affecting the lock production contracted by General Motors in 1977.

The Strike of 1983

By the early eighties, labor was costing Briggs & Stratton about 44 cents of every dollar, which, according to a 1984 *Business Journal* article, was "about 25 percent more than its domestic competitors and as much as 50 percent more than foreign companies."[12]

Foreign competition, particularly from Japan, was squeezing Briggs & Stratton in markets that it had traditionally dominated. By 1983, Honda Motors was not only producing and selling engines for lawn and garden equipment, it had started production of a complete lawn mower.[13]

Yet another variable squeezing Briggs & Stratton was the switch of customers from dealerships to mass merchandisers. Unlike dealers that purchase high-quality, expensive engines, mass merchandisers and discount stores like K mart, Target and Wal-Mart buy less expensive items in very large quantities and pass the savings on to customers. It was a dramatic change from the early days when outdoor power equipment was sold mostly by dealers. After the intro-

Striking Briggs & Stratton workers shout as a motorist passes through the plant gate in Wauwatosa on October 3, 1983.

duction of the aluminum engine, which made lower-priced lawn and garden equipment possible, sales began to move to mass merchandisers. The trend has continued, and today, approximately 80 percent of outdoor power equipment is sold by mass merchandisers. This trend has placed tremendous price pressure on equipment and engine manufacturers. The mass merchandisers are playing from a position of strength because their buying power is substantially higher than that of an individual dealer. Since profits are smaller when selling to these outlets, production costs became even more critical to success.

Stratton pointed out that the mass merchandisers fall into five important sub-categories: general merchandisers, such as Sears, Roebuck and Montgomery Ward; discount stores like Wal-Mart, K mart and Target; home improvement stores like Home Depot, Lowe's and Builders Square; warehouse clubs such as Sam's and Costco; and hardware chains including Ace and True Value. "Among all the mass merchandisers, Sears has the largest share, and thus is the world's largest retailer of outdoor power equipment," he explained.

Striking Briggs & Stratton workers meet with John Henkes, an aide to Governor Tommy Thompson.

"Because mass merchandisers sell 80 percent of the lawn and garden equipment sold in the United States, Briggs' largest customers are manufacturers who sell to that distribution channel: American Yard Products, MTD Products and Murray, names with which most people are not familiar. The names with which most people are familiar, Toro, John Deere and Snapper, for example, are smaller customers, because these companies sell to dealer channels."[14]

In 1983, the frustrating relations between labor and management came to a head. Management could no longer afford wage increases of 25 to 30 percent over three years. In order to survive in an increasingly competitive marketplace, the company needed concessions. Management asked for a three-year wage freeze, and a two-tier wage system for new hires.

Two assembly operations in the Perry facility. The cancellation of the General Motors contract prompted Briggs & Stratton to close the facility in the late eighties and move the assembly operations to Glendale.

Local 232 refused. In the summer of 1983, with its contract up for negotiation, the union threatened to strike for the fourth time in 10 years. On July 31, 7,600 workers walked off their jobs, shutting in all six plants within the Milwaukee area. It was a vote that many members of Local 232 would live to regret.

Though salaried employees took up the task of making engines, the strike of 1983 could not have occurred at a worse time for Briggs & Stratton. When the union walked out, some power equipment distributors turned to Japanese competitors such as Honda. "Once we get started with those Japanese and German engines, there's no going back to Briggs,"[15] stated Tony Malizia of Snapper Power Equipment.

That year, Briggs & Stratton ended a quarter without making a profit, having lost $4.8 million.[16] To help salvage production, Briggs & Stratton moved more than 250 lock assembly jobs from the Glendale Plant to the Perry Plant, many of which were never brought back.

In late October, Briggs & Stratton management informed the union that if an agreement could not be reached, strikers would be replaced with non-union workers. With a vote of 4,398 to 2,068, Local 232 went back to work, accepting a 2-percent wage increase over three years, a two-tier wage structure for new hires and allowing management the latitude to subcontract work. Amidst angry shouts of "Sabotage!!" and "Sold Out!!"[17] union members returned to work November 1.

Moving out of Wisconsin

The strike of 1983 triggered major changes at both the corporate and manufacturing levels of Briggs & Stratton. Most significantly, the strike persuaded Stratton to move Briggs & Stratton facilities out of Milwaukee. "I decided during that strike that it was ridiculous to have all our manufacturing operations shut down by a strike. I decided somewhere in the middle of that strike that it would be the last time it would happen."[18]

In 1984, Briggs & Stratton purchased the old Tappan Company Plant at 110 Main Street in the small community of Murray, Kentucky. Beginning in 1985, the 225,000-square-foot facility manufactured a line of standard lawn mower engines. One of the most attractive features of the building was the fact that it had been given to the city of Murray by

The Murray, Kentucky, plant, constructed in 1986, manufactures engines for walk-behind mowers.

of the Small Engine Division, said opening a new plant gave Briggs & Stratton the opportunity to start with something of a blank slate.

"In Murray we had a real opportunity to incorporate the best technology that we had for making engines, along with some real different management practices. It allowed us to get away from some of the encumbrances we had with trying to manage our operations effectively, and to provide better jobs for the folks that were part of it. In Milwaukee, we dealt with 50 years of evolved labor relations junk, and it's hard to unravel that in a short period of time."[19]

The Murray plant, which eventually employed 700 people, was a non-union facility. Wages were lower in Murray because the cost of living was less in this economically depressed area.

The Murray plant manufactured the Classic engine, long the high-volume, low-cost industry standard for walk-behind lawn mowers.

At the plant, Fotsch said college students hired to do seasonal work are an important part of the facility's success. Students staff the second shift, an innovation that keeps layoffs to a minimum because student turnover is naturally high. "In fact," Fotsch said. "We've never had a layoff in Murray."[20]

"By and large, they're a little less experienced, but they more than make up for it with their willingness to work, and to work hard. I've said it before and I stand by it. Our second shift, our student shift, makes the Murray plant what it is

Tappan, who in turn gave it to Briggs & Stratton, along with a $1 million community development grant as an incentive to move there. Briggs & Stratton invested $20 million for renovation, and agreed to return money to the community over the 15-year period of the grant.

Briggs & Stratton was also able to incorporate several new cost reduction strategies in Murray. Dick Fotsch, vice president and general manager

BRIGGS & STRATTON

The power in power equipment

Meeting Higher Safety Standards

In 1982, the Consumer Product Safety Act required that lawn mowers come equipped with a safety switch that would automatically shut off the engine when the handles of a walk-behind mower are released. The Consumer Public Safety Commission argued that this device would prevent some 77,000 injuries and save $253 million in medical costs. But supplying the device, popularly known as a deadman's switch, would force the price of walk-behind mowers past $100 per unit. There were four ways to meet the standard. In order of increasing expense, they were: a manual restart system, in which the deadman control would shut off the ignition system; a system that allows the engine to continue running while the blade stops; an engine stop with an electric start; and, for electric motors, a system that would shut off power. The Consumer Public Safety Commission wanted the more expensive options, but Briggs & Stratton wanted to give consumers the least-expensive option as well. Fred Stratton Jr. successfully lobbied Congress to modify the standard to include that option, which today is the most popular one.

To meet the standard, Briggs & Stratton introduced four engines designed to accommodate the operator safety-control level on the mower handle and handle the frequent stops and starts caused by the safety switch. The System 2 manual-restart engine, the System 4 electric-start engine, the 1,000-watt electric engine, and the Blade/Brake/Clutch Compliance engine all exceeded the demands placed on engines by compliance with the new standard.

Above right: The Blade/Brake/Clutch engines were designed to accommodate a separate brake mechanism known as the deadman's switch, which shuts off the blade while allowing the engine to continue running. Above left: This lawn mower is equipped with a deadman's switch and a System 4 electric-start system, which uses an electrical starting system powered by a 6-volt battery.

today, and the Murray plant is a great, competitive plant. The kids come to work. Nobody's taught them that you don't work all day for a day's pay, which other people learn as they go through life. So they worked hard and worked the whole period of time and set the standards of production."[21]

Also in 1984, Briggs & Stratton purchased a permanent testing facility in St. Lucie County, Florida, which became known as the Ft. Pierce Test Site. The warm climate meant that the facility could be used throughout the year, and also provided a chance to test equipment on grass that differed from the varieties found in the upper Midwest. The facility included a 5,000-square-foot structure for the rigorous testing of Briggs & Stratton engines in original equipment applications. The site was also used to test experimental engines and equipment, as well as experimental applications of existing equipment and engines.

The company's move to Murray had an immediate impact on union leaders. Fearful of further plant relocations, Local 232 immediately began efforts to smooth out any remaining acrimony from the previous strike. In 1985, 16 months before the contract expired, Local 232 overwhelmingly approved a three-year contract that offered a profit-sharing plan, improved health benefits and a promise to keep jobs in Milwaukee. There was no wage increase.

By 1988, the hourly labor force at Briggs & Stratton had been reduced from 10,000 workers to about 6,300. The union claimed that the eliminations only increased profit, while management argued that the cuts were needed to keep the company profitable at all. "We couldn't keep passing these price increases on to our customers," Paul Neylon said.[22]

"Our competition domestically and in Japan was getting stronger and stronger.

In 1984, Briggs & Stratton developed the Quantum engine, which boasted higher performance, quieter operation and easier starting. It remains one of the company's most popular engines.

So we finally had to dig in our heels and say, 'Enough is enough.' A lot of the folks made a darned good living. A lot of them had houses up north and snowmobiles and the rest of it. They thought there was more and more and more, but there just wasn't any more."[23]

Stephen H. Rugg, vice president for sales and marketing, said Briggs & Stratton had little choice but to move to the South.

"We got stuck up here with an intransigent labor union who seemed to have their own agenda, which wasn't an agenda that benefited their members. And that's too bad, because there are successful companies operating out of the North."[24]

George Thompson, vice president for communication, agreed.

"The union is excellent when it comes to protecting the rights of the workers when their rights

have been violated. But after a certain point, unions can, and very often do, hurt workers. You see that more and more."[25]

Daihatsu Briggs & Stratton

In an effort to stave off Japanese competition, Briggs & Stratton entered a 50-50 joint venture with the Daihatsu Motor Company. The result was known as Daihatsu Briggs & Stratton, or DBS. Located in Shiga Prefecture, 50 miles from Osaka, Japan, construction on the 57,000-square-foot plant began in December 1986 and was completed in April 1987.

The highly automated facility, run by Daihatsu, employed only 38 workers on a single shift and specialized in the manufacture $12\frac{1}{2}$- and 15-horsepower versions of the Vanguard V-Twin overhead valve (OHV) engines and engine parts. Today, it employs about 100 people on two shifts and manufactures Vanguard V-twin engines ranging from 16 to 20 horsepower. "Daihatsu is an ideal partner," said Michael Hamilton, executive vice president for sales and service.

"Daihatsu began in the small delivery-truck business. ... They have a long lineage as a company, but they never really made automobile, until fairly recently. They'd always made these little vans and pick-ups. They understood smaller engines rather than the big, pure automotive stuff. The reason it was of interest to us is we were looking for a premium line of engines that we could position with premium original equipment manufacturers looking for something better than our consumer-type engine. And this filled the bill."[26]

The Mitsubishi Agreement

The Vanguard line originally consisted of three single-cylinder engines and one twin engine. The twin engine, manufactured by DBS, did very well. But the single-cylinder engines, made at the Menomonee Falls plant, did not do as well. Briggs & Stratton needed to solve this problem, so it entered an agreement with Mitsubishi Heavy Industries, Ltd. of Tokyo, Japan, to produce all single-cylinder Vanguard engines. Briggs & Stratton produces only certain parts for the engines, while Mitsubishi is

Protecting the Environment

Since the sixties, industrial pollution had become a public concern, and Congress enacted rigorous laws to protect the nation's natural resources. In 1973, concern over these regulations prompted Briggs & Stratton to elect Igor Kamlukin to the new position of vice president of environmental product engineering. Kamulkin, a veteran of both the manufacturing and compliance fields, was responsible for making sure new engines met all safety and environmental requirements.[28]

The company also took steps to reduce the wastes associated with the manufacture of engines. Briggs & Stratton dramatically cut its solid waste disposal, which had reached a peak of 20 tons a day. During the seventies, this was reduced to about 2 tons of sterile ash deposited in area landfills. The company later developed methods to dispose of these materials through solid waste incinerators, a process that created steam that could be used at area plants.

Materials too hazardous for disposal are taken to a facility in Illinois for proper storage. About 25,000 tons of damp dirt, sand and slag

Members of the Briggs & Stratton team accept the Wisconsin Business Friend of the Environment Award.

were delivered to Future Parkland, a site in Muskego, Wisconsin, purchased by Briggs & Stratton in 1985, which is licensed to operate for 15 years, and tested regularly for toxic contamination. "Since this isn't hazardous waste, there's no reason why it can't be used," said Kassandra Preston, who is in charge of corporate compliance.[29]

Briggs & Stratton has taken a bold approach to recycling. All the aluminum used in the manufacture of Briggs & Stratton engines come from recycled aluminum. In 1981, an incinerator was built along the south end of the facility to smelt scrap aluminum. Items such as metal slugs, copper wire, punchings and turnings, accounting for some 50 to 65 million pounds per year, are sold to

scrap metal dealers. Also recycled are scrap oil, plastic spools used to coil wire, and various plastic regrind material from all plants.

Recently the corporate offices have begun recycling paper products, some 250,000 pounds per year, as well as beverage cans and bottles.

Briggs & Stratton also showed concern for the environment by improving the environmental friendliness of its paint. The company reduced volatile organic compounds and installed fume incinerators, all at a cost of $1.8 million. In addition, Briggs & Stratton switched to high-solid paints, which reduce paint consumption up to 300 percent. High-solid paints resist corrosion, contain reduced levels of formaldehyde, and are free of lead and chrome. Between 1987 and 1988, Briggs & Stratton reduced its air pollution by 23 percent, and continues to improve these levels.

Briggs & Stratton's commitment to protecting the environment can be seen in the company's efforts to reduce its use of toxic materials. Incorporating non-toxic materials in casting, cleaning, plating and painting, has helped Briggs & Stratton reduce its emission of toxic contaminants by more than 40 percent.

Briggs & Stratton also installed in-house wastewater treatment facilities at all its plants. These facilities treat oils, grease, solvents and other hazardous liquid waste caused by procedures such as electroplating.

In 1986, the company spent $100,000 to install a chromium recovery system that reduced the loss of chromium during plating. By reducing the discharge of chromic acid and other toxic chemicals by 60 percent, the system actually paid for itself in six months.[30]

Also in 1986, Briggs & Stratton was fined $30,000 for releasing high levels of polychlorinated biphenyls, or responsible for overall production and shipping the completed Vanguards to the United States.

Fred Stratton noted that it might seem unusual for an engine manufacturer to hire another company to manufacture its engines.

"We saw ourselves as an engine manufacturer. People might assume we can make any engine, and we probably thought we could make any engine. But the fact is, we were really good at one particular thing. One niche. One part of the market. Fortunately, it's a very large part of the market. We're good at making low-cost, good value engines. We don't make the cheapest product and we don't make the engines with the most features. What we're good at is building the best value for the broad middle of the market. Now, to go back to the early eighties, we saw that the Japanese challenge was moving toward the premium end. In retrospect, the rise of the premium engine occurred as a result of the yen-to-dollar relationship, which brought down the price of the premium engine enough to be an attractive alternative. We ended up designing a very good premium engine line, but when it came time to manufacture it, we tooled it inappropriately. We were losing money, and we didn't see enough profit opportunity in the premium line to justify retooling it in a more appropriate fashion."[27]

James Wier, executive vice president of operations, recalled that the Vanguard was at first an engineering success but a financial failure.

"We over-designed, over-engineered and under-tooled those first engines. We didn't have a very good manufacturing concept for those, so when we were the primary producer of the Vanguard engine, it was a financial failure. So the product wasn't wrong. We just weren't able to produce them as a financial success."[31]

Stratton explained that the Vanguard was a different kind of engine than Briggs & Stratton was accustomed to building. "If we had to do it over again, I think we would do the same thing," he said.

PCBs, caused by a solvent used to clean engine parts. The fine was later reduced to $6,000, but Briggs & Stratton got the message and replaced the solvents with a water-based, non-toxic cleaner by 1990.

These efforts have earned Briggs & Stratton recognition from government and environmental agencies in Wisconsin. In 1986, 1990 and 1991, Briggs & Stratton received the Wisconsin Business Friend of the Environment Award and the Governor's Award for Excellence in Hazardous Waste Reduction.

Briggs & Stratton accepts the Governor's Award for Excellence in Hazardous Waste Reduction.

"That is, we would admit we really don't know how to make those kinds of engines. It's not our thing. It wasn't the engineering part necessarily. I mean, we could design a great fully-featured engine. But we couldn't make it make money. We bought the wrong kind of equipment and then to correct that, there wasn't enough return to justify re-tooling. So the best solution seemed to be to find somebody who could make it for us."[32]

Stratton said the decision to outsource production of the Vanguard was painful, but necessary. "It's always painful to admit a mistake, but it was fairly obvious in the numbers that it was a mistake, and we didn't want to compound it by investing more money for an inadequate return."[33]

Paul O. Farny, president and general manager of Briggs & Stratton Daihatsu, a recently formed North American marketing joint venture, said the relationship with Daihatsu has been successful. "They specialize in small cars, and our engine size is very close to what they do for their autos. So we didn't ask someone in the big engine business to make our size product."[34]

Neylon explained that working with Mitsubishi solved several challenges for Briggs & Stratton.

"We bought the wrong equipment to do the job — a lot of programmable stuff that belonged in a model shop, not in the production environment. That was compounded by buying the first of this kind of machines. Nobody else had purchased one. ... We had a lot of problems with them. They didn't like the heat in summertime. We came out with new engines, and they weren't perfect when we came out with them. Even if they ran perfectly, they weren't the right machines for what we wanted them to do.

"But we still wanted to be a part of that market segment. We couldn't very well come out with those kinds of engines and then back away and just leave them. So we were looking for somebody we could partner with. Mitsubishi came along and had an engine very similar to ours and ultimately we signed a licensing agreement for single–cylinder overhead-valve engines."[35]

Farny, then general manager of the Industrial Division, said working with Mitsubishi allowed Briggs & Stratton to extend its Vanguard line. "It took us six years, but we are firmly re-established in the premium engine business," he said. "First [the] V-Twin, and now the Mitsubishi Vanguard line, allowed us to reinforce our presence in that market."[36] Farny explained how the relationship with Mitsubishi was established.

"When we tried to establish Vanguard manufacturing in Milwaukee, we finally realized that among others, all Japanese motorcycle manufacturers had

Briggs & Stratton Daihatsu gasoline engine, left, and diesel engine, right.

Above: V-Twin Vanguard engines being manufactured at the Daihatsu Briggs & Stratton factory in Shiga Prefecture, Japan.

Right: The Vanguard 5½ hp was extensively redesigned by Briggs & Stratton but continues to be manufactured by Mitsubishi.

established such a huge capacity for premium single-cylinder engines that it was pure nonsense to add additional capacity in Milwaukee. Competition was very fierce because everyone had made their own factory. We decided to see if one of these guys would cooperate with us. We finally found Mitsubishi, which had designed a line with very nice engines, but had done a very poor job in marketing and sales, and they were willing to work with us. We redesigned jointly and found, interestingly enough, that we could teach Mitsubishi quite a lot of things.[37]

Other Ventures

In May 1987, Briggs & Stratton entered into an agreement with another Japanese company,

executing a 10-year contract with the Komatsu Zenoah Company of Tachikawa, Japan. Under terms of the contract, Komatsu Zenoah would manufacture a two–cycle, 4-horsepower lawn mower engine, which Briggs & Stratton would purchase and distribute in the United States. This venture was not successful, Stratton said, because the rising price of the yen made the engine too expensive in the United States.[38]

In August 1986, Briggs & Stratton established a joint venture with the Chongqing Puling Machinery Works in Chongqing, China, forming Puling-Briggs & Stratton Engine Corporation. This joint venture manufactures 10- and 16-horsepower cast-iron engines for sale to China, the Philippines and Southeast Asia. The Puling-B&S Company began as an assembly plant with 50 employees, assembling components sent by Briggs & Stratton. But by 1991, a new facility was constructed and outfitted with machinery relocated from the defunct West Plant. The refurbished Puling-B&S established a work force of 150 employees, with a capacity of 50,000 engines per year. "We were the only American company looking around China that showed the slightest interest in Chongqing," said Michael Hamilton, former vice president of the International Division, and currently executive vice president of sales and service.[39]

In 1992, the company moved production of all cast-iron engines to the Puling-Briggs Plant in China. This was viewed as especially cost-effective since Southeast Asia was one of the few large markets remaining for those types of engines. Briggs & Stratton still supplies about 20 percent of the parts for assembly. Hamilton explained the reasons for the popularity of this style of engine in the region.

"They still make the old cast-iron engines, which are selling like hot cakes in Southeast Asia and are still used for fishing boats and river boats and other developing country applications. People in that part of the world prefer the old cast-iron engines because they can be frequently rebuilt and last a long time in saltwater applications."[40]

The Southern Strategy Continues

In 1985, Briggs & Stratton moved the entire production of the Perry, Georgia, facility back to the Glendale plant in Milwaukee. The Perry plant, sold for $2.75 million, was closed as a result of the loss of some significant contracts with Ford and General Motors. In 1988, a 47,000-square-foot facility in Juarez, Mexico, would be opened to begin transferring certain lock assembly work out of the Glendale plant.

Encouraged by the success in Murray, Briggs & Stratton continued its southern strategy. In 1989, a 235,554-square-foot plant was constructed in Poplar Bluff, Missouri, 150 miles south of St. Louis. The facility would manufacture Quantum engines, incorporating a highly automated facility in conjunction with a non-union work force in an economically depressed area.

Introduced in 1986, the Quantum was developed to start easier, last longer and run quieter than previous engines. It was the first engine around which an entire marketing campaign was launched. The Quantum was introduced at the Louisville Lawn and Garden Expo under the flash of laser light, multi-screen movie images, and live appearances by Air Force test pilot Chuck Yeager and guitarist Chuck Berry. Following this stellar introduction was a $500,000 advertising campaign designed by the Cramer-Krasselt firm of Milwaukee, focusing on consumer rather than commercial markets.

Briggs & Stratton achieved high productivity, low production costs, and a contented labor force. With two non-union plants in the south and one in Mexico, Briggs & Stratton was no longer vulnerable to the intimidation of the union. "It was a success in several ways," Fred Stratton said of the company's expansion out of Wisconsin.

"The principal benefit was that we could make engines at a lower cost. And the interesting thing to me was that only half the lower cost was due to the wage and benefit difference. We hear a lot about how productive our Milwaukee work force is. They work hard. But they work hard under the structure of a code of rules and regulations that are the result of 50 years of negotiating with the union. Those restrictions are out of date and they inhibit people from doing their best. ... Because we established facilities in Murray and Poplar Bluff, we're in very competitive shape."[41]

Stratton explained that archaic union rules include strict job classifications that impede production and job satisfaction. "A person whose job is classified as X, can't do work that's classification Y," he said. "The person might be fully capable of doing it, but he or she is restricted by the rules. In the new plants, if a person is capable of doing it, the person just does it."[42]

A New Way of Working

The southern strategy had the additional benefit of allowing Briggs & Stratton to construct new facilities to take advantage of the latest in production technology. Among the more significant innovations are the focused factory and cell production methods, which put teams to work on specific products instead of dividing labor into general production work. An automated cell has the ability to reduce the number of employees needed for a specific series of assembly operation from 20 to three. Though this method displaced hundreds of jobs, it created more skilled jobs, which led to increased individual job security.[43]

Further, reduction of shipping and delivery costs were achieved by locating Briggs & Stratton production facilities closer to their primary customer bases, many of which were located in the Southeast.

New initiatives were also undertaken to streamline production at the Burleigh Plant. Automated production lines, computer-based design innovations, and inventory reduction strategies helped Briggs & Stratton to further reduce costs. One of the more successful approaches is known as just-in-time, a system used by Toyota that reduced both inventory and waste. Just-in-time refers to the delivery of inventory just before it is required, avoiding storage costs and reducing clutter on the assembly line.

Similar to just-in-time is material requirements planning, a computer-based method of inventory control that delivers the right components, in the right quantity, to the right locations, at the right time, with little wasted time, effort or inventory. An offshoot of both of these systems is

In May 1987, Briggs & Stratton formed a 10-year agreement with the Komatsu Zenoah Company of Tachikawa, Japan. Here, workers assemble two-cycle engines for walk-behind mowers sold in the United States.

Chuck Fricke, vice president of service, stands in front of a display showroom of Briggs & Stratton engines in Chongqing, China.

and Development Center, constructed in 1979 along Wirth Avenue. In the mid-eighties, management effectively doubled the research and engineering budget, increasing it from 1.25 percent to 3 percent of annual sales, to over $12 million.[45] The staff was increased, and a new computer-aided design and manufacturing system (CAD/CAM) linked engineers in the laboratories directly to those working on the production floor. According to Charles Brown, vice president of engineering and quality assurance, this tool has become indispensable at Briggs & Stratton.

"I would say you won't find a drafting board in the organization anymore. You just don't find draftsmen. There are things being done certain-

Fred Stratton signs a joint venture agreement with Puling Machinery Works of Chongqing, China, in 1986. Left to right: Han Jing, project department manager of the Chongqing Corporation; George Senn, executive vice president of Briggs & Stratton; William Thomas, area counsel general; Fred Stratton Jr.; Xiao Yang, mayor of Chongqing; and Yan Jia Yu, deputy director of the Chongqing Machine Building Bureau.

the inventory reduction program, which concentrates on inventory reductions by planned deliveries and manufacturing process improvements.

Another method to streamline production costs is statistical process control, a method of finding defective parts and procedures by using graphs to visualize problems in the manufacturing process. It is also used as a method to assist inspection and quality assurance personnel in the design and operation of production machinery.

President John Shiely said these changes have yielded substantial benefits. "Things that our operating people have done in the past few years, like focus factories and cell manufacturing, provide a much higher value opportunity than pounding an enormous amount of capital into automation of outdated processes."[44]

Briggs & Stratton adopted another strategy to compete with the Japanese in the design and development of new engines. Traditionally, Briggs & Stratton refined existing engine designs, developing a new design every two years or so. A new strategy emerged to develop three or four new models every year, in different price ranges for specific applications.

To accelerate the development of new engine designs, Briggs & Stratton relies on the Research

ly in the Small Engine Division and I believe also in the Large Engine Division, where they are designing wire mesh prototypes, three-dimensional types of things on CAD/CAM. They're making parts and the physical drawing doesn't even exist. ... It's become an extremely valuable tool as more and more of our young engineers and designers have sort of grown up with it. Some of the older fellows, who were not brought up that way, it has taken them a little longer. But it's definitely a big part of the equation."[46]

New Marketing Techniques

Beginning in 1982, Briggs & Stratton more than doubled its advertising budget to $4 million, and retained the highly acclaimed Cramer-Krasselt Agency of Milwaukee to develop a new ad campaign geared toward a younger audience, aged 18 to 35, through more consumer-oriented media. Briggs & Stratton kicked off this new strategy with a $400,000, 30-second spot during Super Bowl XVII in

Service and dealer facilities in (top to bottom) Greece, South Africa and the Netherlands are a few of the many Briggs & Stratton distributorships around the world.

1983. Print advertisements in *Time*, *Sports Illustrated*, and *People* magazines followed.[47]

Briggs & Stratton began to sponsor major sporting events, including the 1988 United States Olympic Team. The company also supported the Milwaukee Brewers by purchasing blocks of tickets and advertising on a rotating panel behind home plate.

To help focus its advertising initiative, Briggs & Stratton began market research that divided its customers into the categories of industrial users, lawn and garden users, and international customers. As a result, the Industrial Division serves some 800 original equipment manufacturers throughout the United States, who use the engines for generators, pumps, compressors, sprayers and construction equipment. Engines for these customers include the Vanguard, Industrial/ Commercial, Industrial/Commercial Rental and Industrial PLUS engines.

The Domestic Lawn and Garden Division was developed primarily to serve the equipment manufacturers who supply mass merchandisers such as Sears, Roebuck, K mart and Target, which com-

prise about 80 percent of this market. The other 20 percent consists of lawn and garden specialty dealers, including Toro, Snapper and Club Cadet. Briggs & Stratton also consults original equipment manufacturers regarding the design and implementation of a Briggs & Stratton engine to existing or envisioned lawn and garden products.

To help define these mass markets, Briggs & Stratton marketing representatives divided them into four segments: Basic, for customers looking for basic lawn mowers; Value, for mass merchandise customers seeking the most value for their money; quality, for dealership customers; and Premium, for customers seeking a top-of-the-line engine.

Basic customers tend to be young people with little time, money and need for lawn care. Briggs & Stratton engines such as Sprint and Max were designed for this group. The primary selling point of the Max Series was that it was offered with an unprecedented number of options to meet the needs of many applications. These options include choice of engine color, starting options, muffler and an Industrial/Commercial package to accommodate heavier-than-average use.

Value and Quality customers, representing 60 percent of the market, tend to be older and have more money to spend on lawn care. The Quantum was built with this group in mind. The Premium customer, older and more affluent still, is even more concerned with correct lawn care. These customers are more likely to purchase lawn equipment from a dealer. The Vanguard engine was designed for this group.

Market research on Premium customers prompted Briggs & Stratton to pay closer attention to the aesthetics of engines. The company increased its use of Brooks Stevens and Associates, a renowned industrial design organization in Mequon, Wisconsin, to design the housings and exterior parts for the Vanguard and other engines.

The final component of focus marketing was the International Division, formed in 1960 from the

In the late eighties, Briggs & Stratton adopted a cell production technique that gave teams of workers responsibility for specific products. Pictured here is a cell in the Burleigh Plant, with each member working on a specific task. The man with the clipboard is the cell manager, responsible for the overall quality and efficiency of the cell's work.

virtually ignored Export Department that Briggs & Stratton had formed in the forties. The company had been exporting Motor Wheels as early as 1920, and before World War II, Briggs & Stratton had served customers in South America, Europe and New Zealand. Exports fell off dramatically during World War II, but after it ended, a Briggs & Stratton manager named John Ray established the Export Department. By 1950, the Export Department had a staff of three. By 1960 there were four, and by 1970 the staff had increased to 12. At this point, engine exports "began to skyrocket."[49] In 1971, Briggs & Stratton's first foreign regional office was established in Basel, Switzerland, and in 1974, a second was established in Manila. By 1977, Briggs

& Stratton-International had representatives in 74 countries, and published catalogs and manuals in dozens of languages. International sales accounted for 20 percent of Briggs & Stratton revenues, or $60 million.

By 1988, it became apparent that Briggs & Stratton's new, focused marketing techniques were working. Sales approached $1 billion, and the company successfully maintained its leadership of the small engine market. "It was a very difficult period," recalled Stratton. "But the Japanese threat and our response to it ended up making us a much better company, a more competitive manufacturer. It was not without missteps, but it made us a much stronger company."[50]

Briggs & Stratton engines power a wide range of construction equipment. Here, an Industrial/Commerical engine powers a roller.

Chapter Thirteen

REORGANIZATION & THE 1990S

"I think what happened to us was that we were so good at the old way of doing things that we weren't alert and responsive to new techniques. It took a shock to get us out of our complacency."

— Fred Stratton Jr.

IN 1989, BRIGGS & STRATTON lost money. The devastating loss of $20.2 million was a rude awakening for company officials, who scrambled to identify the cause of the loss and protect against a recurrence. Briggs & Stratton reorganized its operations and made several management changes, including programs that made employees more accountable for their work. These changes proved highly successful, and Briggs & Stratton emerged from a difficult time stronger and more efficient than ever. "That performance was a wake-up call," said Fred Stratton. "There was no time for patience. We had to do things differently."[1]

Several causes for the loss were identified, among the most significant being the nationwide drought of 1988, which slashed engine sales for lawn mowers between 20 to 25 percent. "The simple truth is that this business is very dependent on rainfall," Stratton noted.[2]

"A very high percentage of the engines we build end up on grass-cutting equipment. When it doesn't rain, grass doesn't grow. When grass doesn't grow, it doesn't need to be cut. When grass doesn't need to be cut, people don't replace or repair their lawn mowers. And that happened in the summer of 1988."[3]

Also frustrating were major increases in the cost of raw materials, which triggered increases in engine prices. This price increase triggered further losses of market share, due to increased competition from Japanese companies and domestic companies such as Tecumseh and Kohler. Consequently, major customers like Murray and Toro turned to the competition for engines.

"The Japanese had a tremendous cost advantage," said Stephen Rugg, vice president for sales and marketing, as he recalled the period between 1982 and 1985.

"They could come in this country and bring these products that were, from a quality standpoint, far superior to the stuff we were marketing but at the same price. We started focusing on them, and reaffirmed that our core business is the lawn and garden value business. It's kind of like, if you

---

Above: Though most Casting Division products are used by Briggs & Stratton, the division also casts items such as this crankshaft, which it sells to automobile manufacturers.

In the wake of the 1989 financial downturn, Briggs & Stratton worked harder than ever to improve customer relations. The company filled a trailer with engines for lawn and garden applications and visited dealers and original equipment manufacturers around the country.

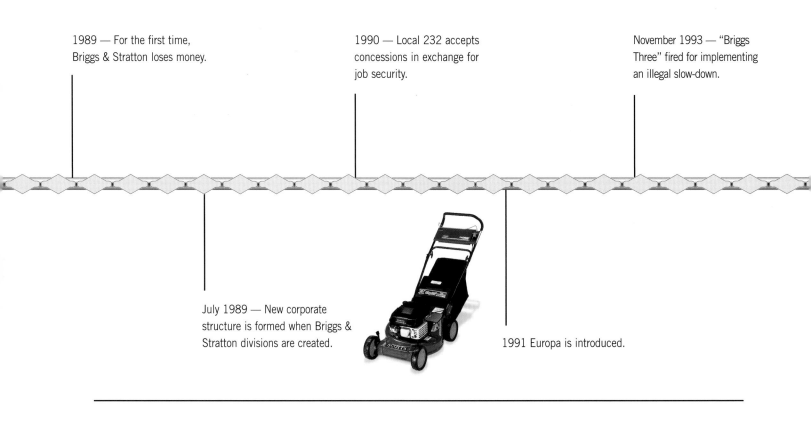

1989 — For the first time, Briggs & Stratton loses money.

1990 — Local 232 accepts concessions in exchange for job security.

November 1993 — "Briggs Three" fired for implementing an illegal slow-down.

July 1989 — New corporate structure is formed when Briggs & Stratton divisions are created.

1991 Europa is introduced.

can stop them at the premium front, they can't penetrate your core business. So we focused on that and took our eye off of Tecumseh, who was doing things to lower its cost and was dealing directly with the merchandisers, and were treating customers in different ways. We treated them all the same. We were not doing business the way business was being conducted by every other company and every other industry in the land."[4]

In the case of Toro, Briggs & Stratton simply didn't have a product line to meet the needs of the customer. "They asked us for this engine and we kept defending and defending what we had," said Rugg.[5] Telephone calls from customers were not answered, and the needs of the equipment manufacturer were ignored. "We lost touch with the marketplace," Rugg admitted. "We lost touch with how people dealt in the marketplace. The biggest challenge was that our market share had slipped by about 15 points."[6]

"I think what happened to us was that we were so good at the old way of doing things that we weren't alert and responsive to new techniques," said Stratton "It took a shock to get us out of our complacency."[7]

For example, recalled Rugg, John Deere had approached Briggs & Stratton about developing a new riding lawn mower engine. "We said that what we have is as good as it's going to get. We didn't listen. I was one of those people."[8]

Briggs & Stratton moved swiftly to remedy the situation. President George Senn and Vice President of Sales Douglas Anderson were asked to resign. Briggs & Stratton executives recognized the need to mend fences. Stratton personally called on customers, doing everything he could to meet their needs. Stratton and other executives went on some 75 overnight trips to mend fences. When Stratton asked Toro's executive vice president in charge of consumer products business, Ralph Murray, why the manufacturer had cut back on Briggs & Stratton engines, he was told, "They don't fit our product, Fred."[9]

"There's much more focus on meeting the needs of our customers," said Kassandra Preston, the corporate compliance officer. "We all provide a service or product to somebody, so we focus on who the ultimate customer is, who the internal customer is. We are aware that just because we

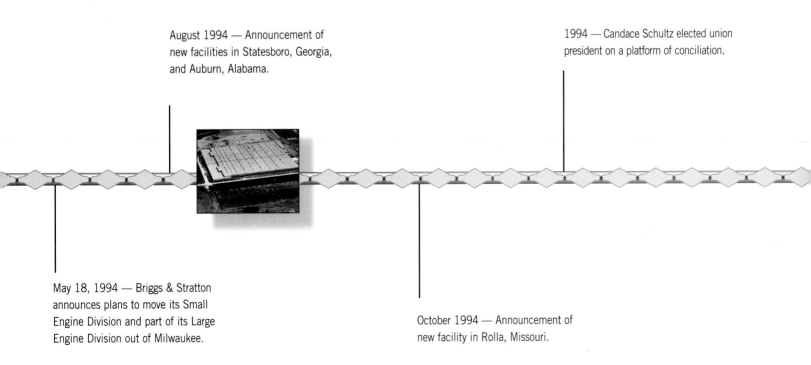

August 1994 — Announcement of new facilities in Statesboro, Georgia, and Auburn, Alabama.

1994 — Candace Schultz elected union president on a platform of conciliation.

May 18, 1994 — Briggs & Stratton announces plans to move its Small Engine Division and part of its Large Engine Division out of Milwaukee.

October 1994 — Announcement of new facility in Rolla, Missouri.

One of the many applications for the Vanguard in the industrial market. This engine is used to power a mud jack, which is used to help restore sunken concrete slabs by pumping concrete underneath the affected area. This unit is manufactured by Voeller Inc., of North Dakota.

"We recognize that we have a basic obligation to provide an adequate return to our capital-providing corporate constituencies. We recognize a further obligation to create value for our shareholders over and above the cost of capital. How is that achieved? Real value creation requires an integrative process of managing the four non-capital providing corporate constituencies (employees, customers, suppliers and community) toward the end of creating value. ... In order to create value for our shareholders, everyone at Briggs & Stratton must be dedicated to creating value in all our relationships with our employees, customers, suppliers and community. These 'value creators' must be the focus of all our efforts."[12]

A Major Corporate Overhaul

In early 1989, Briggs & Stratton laid off 1,000 hourly workers and 150 salaried employees. In July, the company instituted a major corporate overhaul, dividing operations into autonomous business divisions. Each division would focus on a particular product, and would be accountable for everything from initial design to delivery. The role of the corporate office was to oversee divisional operations.

President John Shiely reflected that the company needed to keep pace with the changing competitive environment.

"We had to take apart some of the things that guys like Fred Stratton Sr. and Vincent Shiely and Charlie Coughlin put together. What it takes to be a cost leader today is very different from what it took to be a cost leader in the fifties and sixties. ... The biggest strategic issue for the company in the fifties and sixties was maintaining enough capacity to serve the markets that were growing because of all the home building that occurred after World War II.

"When you get to a billion dollars, it's nice to think you can still manage it by walking around, which was the way Charlie Coughlin could do it. But there comes a point where you have to break it up into manageable pieces, focus your strategy, put in the right people, the right processes, which Fred did, and then let people go and do it."[13]

thought we served them well yesterday doesn't mean we're going to serve them well tomorrow. Their needs may change."[10]

Stratton believed the company invested too much money in large-scale automation. "We learned the lesson that General Motors and lots of other people learned. That just throwing automation at something was not a good answer," he said. "But what is a good answer is taking a good close look at your processes, cleaning them up, getting them really ship-shape and then applying modest, practical automation."[11]

The company implemented the Economic Value Added Program, which linked performance measurement to the goals of shareholders, as said President John Shiely who was general counsel at the time.

In a 1994 speech, Shiely declared the restructuring effort a success.

"The benefits realized from the restructuring have been substantial. Better product line focus, improved financial accountability, more thorough integration of cross-functional initiatives, better assessment of labor/capital tradeoffs, and internal development of experienced operational general managers."[14]

Two divisions had already been established — the Distribution Sales and Service Division and Briggs & Stratton Technologies. The Distribution Sales and Service Division, based in the Menomonee Falls Plant, was responsible for aftermarket sales, distribution and marketing. Also housed within the facility is the Service Repair Center, the Training Center, Customer Service Center and the Graphics Services and Printing Center.

Erik Aspelin, vice president of the Distribution Sales and Service Division, said the goal of that division is to improve service levels at the dealerships. "They are all independent businesses which carry anywhere from five to 20 different product lines. But we show them that their survival is dependent on doing the things that the consumer wants."[15] He noted that the company has 30 training facilities that further this goal.

Customers have questions about using and maintaining lawn mowers, and the dealers are trained to answer these questions and offer assistance.

"The number one problem, which many times isn't really a problem, is that the consumer says it won't start. The consumer buys the bulk of the product through mass retailers They buy something in a box, take it home, don't put oil in or put

too much oil in it. They don't hook up the control right if it's not hooked up already. A lot of simple things and they end up saying it doesn't start."[16]

For more serious problems, Aspelin said, Briggs & Stratton will replace one of more than 8,000 service parts available.

"The company has done a very good job over the years of being able to use universal parts and kits to reduce the number of service parts in the system. At any one point in time, we might have 25,000 to 30,000 parts in production. If you think about the fact that we promise parts will be available for many years after a product is phased out, you would think we would have a lot more than eight thousand parts in service. But we have been able to do a combination of universal parts and kits to keep the number of actual line item inventory down to 8,000. ... Any part that still has a reasonable chance of being used, we will continue to source and stock. But we have parts available for products that are 25 years or older."[17]

The other pre-existing division was Briggs & Stratton Technologies, headquartered at the Glendale Plant, which was responsible for automotive locks. It was named the Technologies Division in 1987 to emphasize that its capabilities were broader than the manufacture of mechanical locks. The division was responsible for the design, manufacture, sales and service of automotive locks, keys, door handles, compartment latches and other components for most North American automobile and truck manufacturers. This division was also responsible for the operations of Tecnologia Briggs & Stratton, its automotive lock assembly plant located in Juarez, Mexico, and a sales office in Detroit, established in the mid-twenties when Briggs & Stratton first developed automotive locks.

Above: Briggs & Stratton Technologies designed and manufactured automotive locks until it was spun off into its own company, STRATTEC Security Corporation, in 1995. The company remains the largest manufacturer of automotive locks in the United States.

A bench inspector examines keys manufactured for the General Motors Corporation.

Jim Wier, executive vice president for operations, ran the lock business for three years. He said moving the assembly to Juarez made sense because the division had always operated independently. "When I was over there running that business you really forget about engines," he said.[18]

Known as the largest suppler of automotive locks and keys in the world, Briggs & Stratton Technologies would also work with it's customers to develop electronic "anti-theft" locking systems, as well as locking systems for use in non-automotive applications.

The new divisions included five manufacturing and three sales divisions. Following the 1995 spin-off of the Technologies Division, the manufacturing divisions now include the Large Engine Division, the Small Engine Division, the Vangurard Division, the Castings Division and the Die Cast Division. Sales divisions are the Lawn and Garden Division, the Industrial Division, the Service Division and the International Division. Anything that doesn't fit into these divisions is referred to as corporate.

Charles Brown, vice president for engineering and quality assurance, explained that each division has its own engineering manager, its own quality manager and its own organization. "What we do at the corporate area is just a small function," he said. "We go out and monitor some of the activities at the division level. We think everybody will do the right stuff, but we just make sure there is consistency and the systems and procedures are in place to make sure they get stuff out. But the day-to-day quality activity is really run by the divisions."[19]

Corporate Offices, Research and Development, the Engine Application Center and the production warehouse all fall under the heading of corporate. Brown described corporate's role as "looking a little further down the road," planning for the future of the company.

"One of the things we try to do in the corporate area is make sure we have proper communication so if somebody has a bright idea in one division, it is shared. That's one of the drawbacks of having a division organization. You have a tendency to do only what you need to do with your organization. It's still necessary to walk down the hall and share it with somebody."[20]

For this reason, he said, Briggs & Stratton has kept the development engineering staffs of the Small Engine division and Large Engine divisions in Milwaukee.

The Large Engine Division

The Large Engine Division occupies nearly one half of the Burleigh Plant in Milwaukee, Wisconsin. It also operates two plants, one in Auburn, Alabama and the other in Statesboro, Georgia.

The division manufactures parts for, and assembles, nine basic horizontal and vertical shaft engines, ranging from 5 to 18 horsepower. The line includes 2,500 different types and trims of aluminum single- and twin-cylinder models for the lawn and garden, commercial, industrial, and agricultural markets. It also produced an older line of cast-iron engines until May 1992, when all cast-iron production was transferred to Puyi-Briggs & Stratton, a joint venture company in Chongqing, China.

Greg Socks, vice president and general manager of the Large Engine Division, began working at Briggs & Stratton in 1978, following in the footsteps of his father, Vern Socks, who was an executive vice president. Gregory Socks reflected on how the company has changed in recent years. "Since my time we have become much less family oriented," he said. "That culture is pretty much gone. It's not as comfortable working here as it was, it's not as fun. But at the same time, it is more rewarding because we are making great progress."[21]

Socks said the division had 2,160 hourly employees and 140 salaried people.[22] He said the division is responsible for 35 percent of Briggs & Stratton volume and half the sales. The division's biggest customer is Modern Tool and Die, which manufactures lawn and garden equipment, along with tractors, riders and tillers.

One of the major challenges of the division is meeting stringent emission laws. But an even larger challenge, said Socks, was "getting our arms around new product development and that cycle with consistent success. We hadn't developed any new product since the mid-eighties and then we did a couple that were unsuccessful. We really didn't know how to introduce products, how to design products. I think today we are very good at that process."[23]

Small Engine Division

Also partially housed in the Burleigh Plant is the Small Engine Division, which manufactures engines of 6 horsepower or less. These operations, occupying a smaller space at the south end of the facility, produce several small industrial/commercial engines, as well as the Sprint and Classic engines used in lower-end lawn mowers. Dick

Fotsch, vice president and general manager of the Small Engine Division, started at Briggs & Stratton in 1975, as a co-op student at Marquette University. In 1977, he worked in product engineering, helping launch the company's first twin engine. He worked as a manufacturing engineer until 1984, when he became plant manager of the Murray, Kentucky, facility.

The Small Engine Division includes the two newest manufacturing facilities in Murray, Kentucky, and Poplar Bluff, Missouri. Both the Sprint and Classic engines are manufactured at Murray, while the popular Quantum line is manufactured at Poplar Bluff. "The Quantum is a phenomenal success," said Stratton "I got a letter from a customer the other day who just bought one and said, 'That's the best lawn mower engine there is.' And he's right."[24]

"Probably our secret weapon over the last five years is that the quality of our end product is substantially better," said Fotsch, "The Quantum engine is a terrific engine."[25]

In 1991, production began on a new overhead valve engine called the Europa, built specifically for the needs of high-end lawn mower manufacturers. Fotsch said the division

Technologia Briggs & Stratton was the only manufacturing plant outside the United States wholly owned by Briggs & Stratton. Eastablished in Juarez, Mexico, in 1988 for automotive lock assembly, it is now part of STRATTEC Security Corporation.

produces about 6 million engines a year in four and a half plants.[26]

"We've invested quite a bit in automating our processes, but of the gains we have made, I would guess 50 percent would be technological in nature. Better processes, quicker processes. And about 50 percent of them would be management-approach-type situations because we have a very flexible work force in our plants outside of Milwaukee. ... We just found better ways to make use of the skills of the folks that we have, and the nice fall-out of doing that is people end up with better jobs. They're more fulfilling jobs. They're jobs where they more fully understand the processes that they're there to maintain and control. So it's really worked out quite well. And we've had some just flat-out productivity gains."[27]

In 1994, the company began a joint venture called SUSA, or Starting USA. Located in Poplar Bluff, the 50-50 joint venture manufactures rewind starters. Briggs & Stratton has operational responsibilities, and Starting Industrial of Japan is responsible for the components and design, Fotsch said.

"We had a situation that was not working out with a former supplier and we needed to move quickly. We could have decided to do it all ourselves and design a rewind. but the bottom line was it was easier, quicker and cheaper for us to do it through a joint venture with these folks. It took a lot of risk out of it. When you make several million of something the first year, you just need one little thing to be wrong and it's a major problem."[28]

The Vanguard Division

Paul Neylon, vice president and general manager of the Vanguard Division, explained

A few of the engines in the popular Industrial/Commercial line, introduced in 1979.

that the division began as manufacturer of components for standard single-cylinder engines. In 1988, the manufacture of overhead-valve single-cylinder engines for the industrial market began. The last single-cylinder overhead-valve Vanguard industrial engine was manufactured in the division in 1994. Now, Neylon said, "We build mostly components, mufflers, and all the ignition systems for Briggs & Stratton engines at the Menomonee Falls plant."[29] The division is also responsible for single-cylinder industrial overhead-valve engines manufactured by Mitsubishi, and V-twin overhead-valve engines manufactured by the DBS joint venture in Japan.

Neylon, a Marquette graduate, started at Briggs & Stratton in 1973, after having served four years in the Navy. He started in the Internal Audit area and moved up to become manufacturing operations manager and then vice president.

Above: An aerial view of the Menomonee Falls Plant. Located on 62 acres, this 850,000-square-foot-plant was constructed in 1980 at a cost of $35 million.

Left: Briggs & Stratton produces more small engines than any other company in the world. The company continually finds new ways to improve production efficiency.

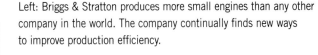

The Die Cast Division

The Die Cast Division, housed completely within the Burleigh Plant, is responsible for such aspects of production as aluminum die casting, die cast trim, finishing and tooling. The division, with more than 600 hourly employees and 65 salaried employees, produced nearly 75 million

pounds of castings in the 1994 fiscal year, supplying aluminum components to the Small and Large Engine divisions. General Manager Allen Nitz, who has a master's degree in physics, was hired by Briggs & Stratton in 1972.

Nitz said some die casting is being moved to southern plants. The Murray, Kentucky, and Poplar Bluff, Missouri plants now provide die casting, he said. The move south is a departure from the original goals of the division when it was established in 1989, he said. Die Casting had been a department before then, he said.

"Top management recognized that die casting was a core technology to our whole business and gave it the visibility of a division. I think that was a good decision. We were then able to focus our resources on that part of the business. Our charter was to become a world-class die caster. We put together a plan called Die Cast '96, which was a five-year plan, meaning in 1996 we were going to get to reach our goals. The decision was made in early 1994 to add more Southern plants. Die cast-

ing is included in these plants, which alleviated most of our Die Cast '96 plan. The Southern die cast operations are more focused and have better facilities. Milwaukee operations will continue to support engine production. Many of the technical improvements made since 1989 will be transferred to the new Southern plants, so progress made during Die Cast '96 will benefit these new facilities."[30]

The Vanguard Division

The Vanguard Division, located in the Corporate Office building, sells the hardest-working engines manufactured by Briggs & Stratton. "These are probably the most gruesome and most demanding applications, including power generating applications used on a standby basis during storm conditions," explained Curt Larson, vice president and general manager of the Industrial Division. "We also power a lot of applications that would be used for farm and industry. For example, crop sprayers and pressure-washing equipment. These are all demanding applications. We also provide engines that power air compressors that are used by contractors, as well as highway tire repair trucks."[31] Larson joined Briggs &

A Vanguard engine powers a riding lawn mower manufactured by Snapper Power Equipment of McDonough, Georgia. Lawn and garden applications remain the largest market for Briggs & Stratton engines.

Stratton in 1986 as manager of after-market sales for the lock division. He was already familiar with the company, having worked as sales manager of *Garden Supply Retailer,* a magazine in which Briggs & Stratton advertised.

Larson said the Industrial Division sells to the commercial market for construction and other heavy-duty work, as well as the consumer industrial side, for pressure cleaners, pumps, generators and other items sold in hardware stores and home centers. The division sells about 100,000 engines to the go-kart industry, he said. "We have logged some very excellent growth in the last three years," he said. "We have grown the business by 50 percent between 1992 and 1995, and we hope to continue that trend."[32]

The Castings Division

The Castings Division, housed in the West Allis and Grey Iron foundries, is responsible for the design and manufacture of such engine components as crankshafts, cam shafts, flywheels and counterweights. The division also manufactures components for use in automotive, agricultural

A rather common application for Briggs & Stratton Industrial/Commericial engines was as the power source for water pumps. This picture, however, illustrates a rather uncommon use for these pumps, as power washers for armored calvalry units fighting in the Gulf War of 1991.

and industrial manufacture. Edward Bednar, vice president and general manager of the Castings Division, started at Briggs & Stratton as a summer intern in 1981, working in the foundries. He was hired to work full-time in 1983.

"I started out working for both foundries during the summer between my sophomore and junior years at Milwaukee School of Engineering. I got started on the very ground floor with both of these facilities. I worked side by side with the machine operators, doing the actual iron testing and qualification, pouring iron, making molds and shaking them out. It was a real hands-on experience."[33]

'The foundries run about 21 hours a day." Bednar said. "The automotive companies are becoming less vertically integrated, which has really opened the doors for us. We have partnered with some good tier-one suppliers to the automotive industry. We cast and they machine, and together we are a pretty good team."[34]

Bednar explained the difference between ductile iron and grey iron.

"The oldest form of cast iron is grey iron. The closest analogy to what a grey iron structure looks like is to imagine a box of corn flakes. Toss the corn flakes in the air, and capture the image in a photograph. Now replace the corn flakes with graphite and replace the air with iron. This structure results in some interesting properties. Grey iron is good at absorbing sound. This is because the flakes of graphite impede the flow of sound waves through the casting. This results in the characteristic 'thud' when striking grey iron. Grey iron is not very ductile because the random graphite flakes act as stress risers. This results in cracks forming before any stretching or elongation can occur. Grey iron is easy to machine because the graphite flakes act as a solid lubricant during the cutting operation. Finally, grey iron is easier to cast because the graphite formation during casting offsets the normal shrinkage that occurs in the solidification of pure iron.

"Nodular iron, also known as ductile iron, is similar to grey iron in the three principal elements are iron, silicon and carbon. The difference is how the graphite forms. By adding a small

One of the most popular applications of the Vanguard engine is in powering generators, such as the one above, manufactured by T&J Manufacturing of Oshkosh, Wisconsin.

amount of magnesium, the graphite becomes a sphere rather than a flake. The most noticeable difference is that ductile iron is not as good at absorbing sound. This results in the characteristic 'ring' heard when striking a ductile iron casting. Ductile iron has significantly higher strength than grey iron."[35]

Improving Quality and Variety

With the new corporate structure in place, and problems associated with customer service under control, Briggs & Stratton was ready to examine the quality and variety of its products. The research and development budget was increased. The company designed the QT4 specifically for the Toro Company, which manufactures Lawn-Boy lawn and garden equipment. The QT4 was a $5\frac{1}{2}$-horsepower overhead-valve engine used exclusively with walk-behind lawn mowers built by Toro. When Toro began using these engines, it dropped a substantial line of foreign-made engines. "The Briggs & Stratton I knew five years ago never would have done that," said

For riding lawn mowers and tractors, Briggs & Stratton produced both a standard and an Industrial/Commercial line of engines, with power ranging from $6\frac{1}{2}$- to 18-horsepower.

Ralph Murray, who was executive vice president in charge of Toro's consumer business.[36]

After almost 10 years of development and testing sponsored by the Gas Research Institute, Briggs & Stratton introduced an engine in 1992 that used natural gas as a fuel source. The engine was used by the York International Corporation, a major manufacturer of heating and air equipment, to power a new building ventilation system, heat pump, and a combination heater/air conditioner system it had developed for residential applications. Because the engine was mounted in a unit that would rest below a window, it needed to run extremely quietly. The 5-horsepower liquid-cooled overhead valve engine was called the Marathon because it was designed to last 15 years. The Marathon, manufactured at the Vanguard Plant in Menomonee Falls, is still considered an experi-

mental product, and the company is uncertain whether a market will develop for it.

Lingering Union Problems

Though the ranks of the Milwaukee-based union had been thinned by the opening of non-union plants in the South, the radical elements of the local union leadership did not abandon their confrontational tactics, and the relationship between management and union remained strained. In late 1989, Local 232 picketed the Briggs & Stratton annual meeting and demanded that Stratton resign. Union President Dick Crofter claimed, "We had profitable operations here until Fred Stratton took over in 1978. ... We feel it's his management that's costing our jobs. Every time we give concessions, they build a new plant."[37]

Union leaders constantly challenged management on cost-cutting and automation efforts, as well as the new cellular production and focus factory concepts. Partly because of labor's refusal to negotiate, heavy layoffs continued to diminish the workforce at the Burleigh Plant.

On November 28, 1990, with negotiations at a standstill, a local newspaper reported that by the end of the year Briggs & Stratton would decide whether to relocate approximately 1,200 Small Engine Division jobs to a third plant in the South. When this information became public, the union members denounced their leadership for inaction, and the leaders responded by opening communication with management. "We were going to move out what was left of the Small Engine Division," recalled Jim Wier, executive vice president of operations.

"At that time, some of the union folks said, 'Give us a crack at staying here.' So we did. We bargained. It was actually very emotional, at least for me, because if it went through it gave us a chance to have labor peace for about four years. It would give us the chance to make the changes

The Burleigh Plant, situated on 82 acres in Wauwatosa, Wisconsin, was the original manufacturing site of the Kool-Bore aluminum block engine. Today, it houses the Large Engine Division, part of the Small Engine Division, the Die Cast Division and the corporate offices. Considered state of the art when it opened in 1955, the plant underwent a $20 million renovation in 1992.

a labor standpoint to ensure the long-term viability of Milwaukee," Wier said.[39]

In an effort to save jobs in Milwaukee, Briggs & Stratton in 1992 began a $20 million renovation at the Burleigh Plant, modernizing machinery that was more than 20 years old.[40] To increase efficiency, the manufacturing concept was changed to a focus factories concept, which shifted the orientation from process to product, so that workers would share responsibility for the final product instead of being responsible for a specific procedure. The goals were lower cost, better quality, reduced inventory and reduced floor space. Despite this good-faith effort on the part of management, its relationship with the union continued to deteriorate.

In 1993, management called for early negotiations, using a bargaining device called "mutual gains," or "win-win." With this method, problems between the two parties are solved through cooperative efforts, focusing on issues rather

we needed to make in Milwaukee to make us financially viable there."[38]

But with the existing contract about to expire, Local 232 squandered valuable time staging rallies and drumming up sympathy with the local media. At the last minute, however, the union accepted contract concessions in exchange for job security. The contract included provisions for the joint establishment of employee involvement, including profit-sharing and pay-for-knowledge programs. Instead of dedicating time to these programs, Local 232 leaders focused on a four-year backlog of grievances. Partly because the union refused to recognize the changing marketplace, Briggs & Stratton in 1992 cut 500 jobs from the Small Engine Division. "For all kinds of reasons, we didn't make the kinds of changes that we had to make in Milwaukee from

The Die Cast Division, in the Burleigh Plant, provides aluminum die casting, die cast trim, finishing and tooling for other Briggs & Stratton departments. Dennis Steeger is one of 600 hourly employees producing nearly 80 million pounds of casting a year in this division.

The Grey Iron Foundry, purchased in 1969 from the Zenith Foundry Company, supplied flywheels and other components to other Briggs & Stratton divisions.

than personalities, and avoiding the standard method of listing positions and demands. Emphasis was placed on solving broad issues, not on petty bickering and accusations. But Local 232 refused to cooperate, arguing that one member of counsel for Briggs & Stratton was a known union-buster.

In the summer of 1993, leaders of Allied Industrial Workers, which in September 1993 would merge with the United Paperworkers International Union and in January 1994 became Local 7232, again resorted to confrontational tactics in the form of a work slowdown. In violation of the collective bargaining agreement, the radical elements of the local union were able to seriously impede the manufacturing process by encouraging members to work slower and boycott overtime work. The slowdown was an attempt to bypass the grievance and arbitration mechanisms of the contract and prevent the implementation of cell pro-

duction and focused factory facilities by placing economic pressure directly on the company. The drop-off in production was immediate, resulting in layoffs and reduced hours for internal and external suppliers to the assembly operations.

The local union leadership later labelled the slowdown "work-to-rule," explaining that the tactic called for the members to "do nothing extra, no cooperation with the company."[41] But this change in name did not disguise the fact that participants were asked to work at a slower pace and attempt to cause bottlenecks in the assembly process. Management appealed to both the local leadership and the international union president to cease the illegal slowdown, finally filing a lawsuit in federal district court seeking an injunction against work-to-rule and damages for the resulting loss in production. Even after the injunction was granted, and the union unsuccessfully appealed to the court of appeals and the United States Supreme Court, the union refused to even discuss the implementation of cell production and focus factory facilities. This refusal continued even after an arbitrator ruled that the company was within its contractual right to implement cell production and focused factories.

Finally, in November 1993, Briggs & Stratton converted the suspension of three people directly involved in implementing and carrying out the illegal work slowdown to discharges. Candy Seib, Laura Drake and Patty Berhardt (the author of a note to her co-workers telling them not to work too hard) immediately became known as the "Briggs Three." Two of the three, who had never attended a union meeting before their discharges, became celebrated union martyrs. With this ammunition in hand, Local 7232 filed charges with the National Labor Relations Board (NLRB) protesting, among other things, the implementation of the focus factories at Burleigh and the termination of the Briggs Three. Despite the charges, management continued to invite the union leadership to participate in discussions regarding facilities relocation issues involving the Small Engine Division as well as part of the Large Engine Division. The union leadership continued to ignore these invitations.

In March 1994, Briggs & Stratton won the arbitration case that had triggered the work-to-rule slowdown that had been enjoined by the federal court. The union continued to file charges with the NLRB, over matters including the effects of the focused factories, the dismissal of the Briggs Three and even the company's right to communicate with employees. After investigation, the NLRB dismissed most charges, but did order an administrative hearing on some of these claims. By then it had become a moot point, particularly after arbitrators had upheld the dismissal of two of the Briggs Three.

On May 18, 1994, Briggs & Stratton formally announced that it would move its entire Small Engine Division and part of its Large Engine Division out of Milwaukee by 1997, and with it would go 2,000 jobs, roughly 37 percent of the Milwaukee workforce. Again, union leadership had rejected any dialogue with the company.

"We'll lose two major product lines out of five," said Gregory Socks, vice president and general manager of the Large Engine Division.[42] Socks noted that the loss would be particularly painful because, "Everybody at the Large Engine Division has always worked here in the Large Engine Division. We haven't had plants outside of Milwaukee before. We've only been a division since 1989, but still we had a plan and we'd been marching along on that plan. So this is a departure from that plan and it affects everybody in the division in one way or another."[43]

Citing the need to stay competitive by reducing transportation and labor costs, and noting that the union refused to cooperate with management, Briggs & Stratton outlined a plan that included three new plants, a $41 million expan-

Here are nine different lawn mowers powered by engines in the Quantum line, one of the most popular engine lines manufactured by Briggs & Stratton.

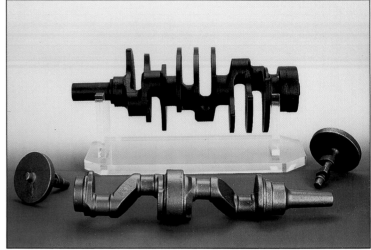

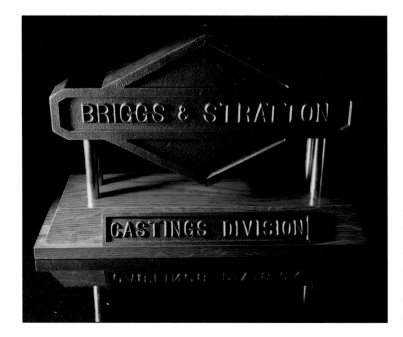

sion and renovation of the Poplar Bluff and Murray plants, increased automation, and the addition of more than 200 jobs to those facilities.

Devastated by the decision and fearful of being criticized for failing to participate in any discussions that could have minimized job loss, labor leaders quickly denounced the company's decision as an example of management greed. The union sought assistance from social activists and local politicians, including Milwaukee Mayor John Norquist and Wisconsin Governor Tommy Thompson. George Thompson, vice president for communications at Briggs & Stratton, noted that

the politicians tend to side with the unions, partly because they want to keep jobs in the city and partly because they recognize that unions comprise a substantial number of voters. Briggs & Stratton's decision to locate facilities out of the state harmed Wisconsin's chances of recruiting new businesses, Thompson reflected.

"The ramifications obviously had a ripple effect on any medium or large company considering Wisconsin. They're going to consider the labor climate. If Briggs & Stratton, one of the largest employers in the state, can't get treated decently in Wisconsin and you are a business person, how do you think that would affect your decision to locate here?"[44]

He also criticized the local newspapers for their coverage of the conflict.

"The newspaper was brutal until we came to an agreement with The Milwaukee Sentinel. *I told them, 'I strongly recommend a policy of discontinuing any type of communication with the*

The Castings Division was created when the company changed its corporate structure in 1989. Operating out of two foundries in West Allis, the division supplies castings for Briggs & Stratton, as well as several outside automobile manufacturers. Above, left: Parts used in drive train assemblies for automobiles. Above: Crankshafts and camshafts for small engines.

paper, with both papers, until we could get what we thought was some balanced and accurate reporting.' The Journal, the afternoon paper, had no interest in doing that whatsoever. As a matter of fact, we had Writers Guild union workers writing about labor activities. There was no possible way to get a fair shake on that one. I appealed to the morning paper, I said, 'Look, we are willing to work with you. We have a difficult situation. We will talk about it, you'll get access. I'll get you access to our top people, but we have to feel like we're getting some balanced and accurate reporting and not a whole lot of inflammatory rhetoric.' ... The Sentinel, the morning paper, appealed more to business people and had much more of a conservative philosophy. I had many conversations with the business editor and we finally struck a deal. I didn't ask them to sugar-coat anything. All I wanted was balanced, objective reporting. I said, 'If we get that, you get the scoops. All we are asking is just a fair hearing in the court of public opinion.' And ultimately we got that. We got a writer replaced, who was the vice president of the Writers Guild, who just wrote some really ugly pieces in his spare time in a union newspaper about companies like Briggs & Stratton. And then he would take that hat off and come to work and write about Briggs & Stratton for the paper."[45]

Finally, Local 7232 sat down with management and proposed a Productivity Partnership Plan, which called for labor and management to work together increasing productivity and profits by improving efficiency. The plan, although a step in the right direction, failed to address any underlying root economic decisions and ultimately was too little, too late.

In August 1994, Briggs & Stratton announced the locations of its new facilities. The first will be located at Statesboro, Georgia, a town of 21,000 people located about 50 miles northwest of Savannah. The 365,000-square-foot-facility will be located on 50 acres and built at a cost of $45 million. The plant is scheduled to open by the end of 1995, with 800 employees responsible for manufacturing engines between 12- and 15-horsepower, for use on lawn and garden tractors.

The second location was announced to be Auburn, Alabama, the small town of 40,000

The Grey Iron Foundry, which allowed Briggs & Stratton to reduce costs through vertical integration, is located in West Allis.

famous for its college and aggressive athletic programs. This 230,000-square-foot facility, scheduled to be in operation by the end of 1995, will be built at a cost of $20 million on a 68-acre lot in the city's new industrial park. The new plant will employ 500 when it begins manufacturing 5-, 7- and 9-horsepower engines for compressors, generators, tillers, and go-karts.

The third location, not announced until October 1994, was Rolla, Missouri, another small town of 15,000 about 100 miles southwest of St. Louis. This plant, also expected to open before 1996, involves a $26 million renovation of an existing 250,000-square-foot facility. This facility will employ 600 people, and, like Poplar Bluff, manufacture the Quantum engine series, along with several other small horsepower engines.

All three sites lured Briggs & Stratton with start-up incentives including tax rebates, training funds, land donations and improvements to area infrastructure. Lower labor costs provided a substantial savings. Additional savings were attributed to proximity of key customers, resulting in reduced transportation expenditures and just-in-time delivery that kept inventory out of storage.

All the plants offered a base salary of about $8 per hour, plus benefits. The plants used focused factory-type manufacturing cells, and provided their own die-casting, machining and painting operations, along with assembly.

Stratton explained some advantages of the new locations.

"We set out to find three new locations, and we settled on Auburn, Statesboro and Rolla. They all have in common the fact that they are towns in which there is a relatively substantial college or university. We like that for three reasons. It's a source of talent that we need in the business. It's a source of students for our seasonal work force, and the quality of the community is better if you have an intellectual standard of the university faculty and the things they like to have in a community."[46]

During this period, Briggs & Stratton also announced that it was purchasing a foundry in Ravenna, Michigan, east of Muskegon, to increase casting capacity to meet the increased production needs of the new plants and outside customers. Acquisition and renovation of the ductile iron foundry would cost approximately $20 million, and add 150 jobs to that area. "It will give us an additional probably 65 million pounds of casting capacity a year. The process is going to be a little bit different, in that it will be the complexity of the job that will determine where it's cast," explained Edward Bednar, vice president and general manager of the Castings Division.[47] "We've got some jobs that are a lot more critical in chemistry certi-

fication and testing requirements and so forth. Those will stay here [in Milwaukee] because this is the division headquarters. This is where we have our metallurgical staff, our divisional quality support, all our design engineers, and so forth."[48]

A multi-million dollar federal lawsuit seeking damages from Local 7232 continued to wind its way through the federal court system. After the Supreme Court refused to hear the case, it was returned to the federal court in Milwaukee for trial. The Briggs Three were denied unemployment compensation benefits by the state of Wisconsin and two remained unemployed as a result of arbitration decisions.

With nearly half of Local 7232 members slated to lose their jobs within the next three years, it seemed likely that the union would at least open a dialogue with the company. But in October 1994, Local 7232 reverted to form and unanimously recommended that the union membership vote down a management proposal for a contract involving the fate of 600 jobs at the Glendale plant. Although the contract offered a generous severance package and extended benefits for those losing their jobs, wage increases for those remaining, and early retirement incentives, Local 7232 leadership recommended rejection of the contract because it did not guarantee that jobs would stay in Milwaukee forever. The union rejected the proposal, but no alternative was presented by the union. The local community and rank-and-file union members pressured the union for a second vote, resulting in overwhelming approval of the contract. All but 240 jobs, already slated to move to the Juarez Plant, were kept in Milwaukee.

At the close of 1994, the union elected Candace Schultz president of Local 7232, making her the first woman to hold that office. Running on a platform of cooperation and communication with management, she may represent the last chance for Briggs & Stratton workers in Milwaukee plants.

When Briggs & Stratton lost Toro business to foreign competition in the mid-eighties, the company realized it needed to work harder tailoring its engines to customer needs. In 1991, Briggs & Stratton introduced the $5\frac{1}{2}$-horsepower QT4 specifically for Toro's walk-behind mowers.

Thompson described Schultz as a welcome departure from previous union leaders.

"The cornerstone of her platform was different from the previous administration, which was confrontational, 'Let's whip them into a frenzy and do anything we can think of, including an illegal slowdown.'... And along comes a person who says, 'We have to stop this. We have to communicate with the company. We have to sit down and get some things hashed out.' That doesn't mean cave in, but at least try to arrive at some things that are mutually agreeable. Well, she didn't win by a landslide, but she won. So evidently, the majority of the people were thinking that same thing."[49]

Gregory Socks, vice president and general manager of the Large Engine Division, said the move south has harmed morale in Milwaukee.

"I don't think morale is very good. It depends on individual little pockets and areas. Some are terrible. Some are still very good. A lot depends on the character of the people, the quality of the manager, how well they are communicating. There are a million variables there, but generally I'd say morale has changed. I think morale wasn't very good prior to the recent announcements anyway."[50]

The Quantum engine, used in walk-behind lawn-mowers, was one of the most lucrative markets for Briggs & Stratton engines.

A Remarkable Comeback

Briggs & Stratton took further steps to streamline operations and find methods to further cut production costs. The company realized it could save money by purchasing materials from outside sources. This procedure, known as outsourcing, was first put into practice when the plastics department at the Glendale Plant was eliminated in the early nineties. This initiative saved the company $4 million, but eliminated 40 jobs.[51] Other outsourced products included electric motors in Mississippi, carburetors in Michigan, pistons in Venezuela, and even the Vanguard twin-cylinder engine to Japan.

When the company was reincorporated in 1924, it became a corporation under the laws of the state of Delaware. In 1992, Briggs & Stratton took advantage of legislation that streamlined corporate operations, and reincorporated under the laws of the state of Wisconsin. The new laws reduced paperwork, allowed more flexibility with dividends, reduced liabilities for company officers and retained rights for stockholders.

By 1992, Briggs & Stratton had made a remarkable comeback. In a relatively short time, the combination of initiatives had taken the company from sales of $876 million in 1989, more than $1 billion in 1992, and returned profitability and competitiveness to all operations. The reorganization and management changes had worked, and the company emerged from the experience with renewed vigor. "We began the 1980s as the world's leading producer of small engines," said Stratton. "We began the 1990s as the world's leading producer. These two simple statements belie the intervening difficulties."[52]

A Briggs & Stratton engine enhances the sleek lines of this go-kart.

CHAPTER FOURTEEN

VISION FOR TOMORROW

"When I sit next to somebody on an airplane, far more often than not, somebody will tell you their Briggs story. Briggs is a neat company to work for as far as heritage goes."

— Dick Fotsch, vice president and general manager, Small Engine Division

AS BRIGGS & STRATTON celebrates its 85th year in 1995, it can reflect on a legacy of triumph over adversity. Briggs & Stratton has survived initial failure, economic collapse, two world wars and international competition, emerging as the profitable and stable leader of the small engine industry. It owns eight manufacturing and testing facilities in the United States, and shares joint-venture partnerships with three facilities in Asia. Briggs & Stratton also has offices and warehouses in Australia, Canada, Sweden, France, Germany, Great Britain, the Netherlands, Singapore, Switzerland, the United Arab Emirates and New Zealand.

The company offers its customers nearly 100 different models of engine, ranging from 2 to 20 horsepower, which can be serviced at more than 32,000 authorized service facilities in 102 countries. To keep up with the worldwide demand for parts, Briggs & Stratton manufactures nearly 24,000 active and sub-assembly parts, with 35,000 parts maintained in active inventory. To produce these parts and engines, Briggs & Stratton uses a remarkable 175 tons of aluminum, 125 tons of steel, 35 tons of zinc and 270 tons of ductile and grey cast iron every day of operations. Briggs & Stratton has

become a highly regarded brand name by producing high-quality, durable, reasonably priced products. The company has continued to grow in stature by focusing on technological improvements, without relying on flashy slogans and advertising. A trained awareness of rapidly changing market needs, and an enviable continuity in leadership are among factors contributing to the present success of Briggs & Stratton.

New Leadership

On August 16, 1994, John S. Shiely was elected president and chief operating officer of Briggs & Stratton. Shiely is the son of Vincent Shiely, who was president from 1971 to 1977 and chairman of the board from 1976 until his death in 1977. Like his father, Shiely is an extrovert, and even plays in a rock and roll band called Live Band. He performs five or six times a year, raising money for charities or entertaining at Briggs & Stratton holiday gatherings.[1]

Shiely joined the company in 1986 as general counsel, and was promoted to vice president

Above: A 5-horsepower engine used in industrial and commercial applications.

and general counsel in 1990. In 1991, he was named executive vice president of administration. Before joining Briggs & Stratton, Shiely worked at Arthur Andersen & Company, Hughes Hubbard & Reed Law Firm, and Allen Bradley/Rockwell International. He graduated from Notre Dame in 1974 and earned a law degree from Marquette University in 1977. He explained that his father had convinced him to attend law school.

"I didn't want to be a lawyer, and in fact I had applied to business schools. But around Christmas of my senior year, I was sitting around talking to my dad, and he said, 'You're not married. You don't have much in the way of responsibilities. If you have the time and the inclination, you ought to go to law school, because lawyers are going to have more and more to say about how corporations are going to be run.'"[2]

John S. Shiely, president and chief operating officer of Briggs & Stratton since August 1994. He joined the company in 1986, after working as a tax and corporate lawyer.

August 16, 1994 — John S. Shiely is elected president and chief operating officer.

February 1995 – Line of power tool accessories is introduced.

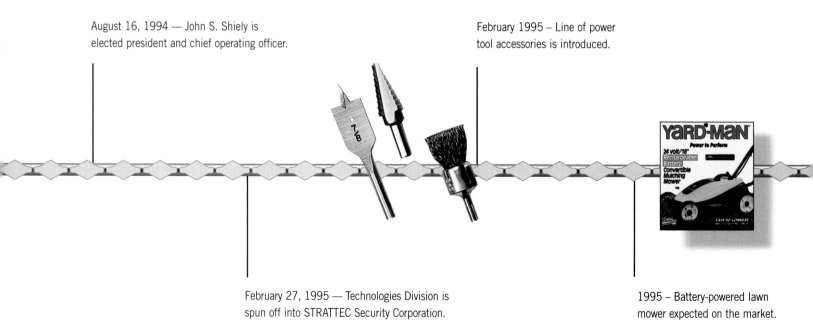

February 27, 1995 — Technologies Division is spun off into STRATTEC Security Corporation.

1995 – Battery-powered lawn mower expected on the market.

Following law school, Shiely earned a Master of Management degree from the Kellogg Graduate School of Management at Northwestern University. Fred Stratton commented that it was unusual for two sons of company presidents to follow so closely in the footsteps of their fathers.

"It's interesting he ended up here. First he was a tax lawyer and then he became a corporate lawyer. ... I learned that he might be available. We talked him into coming here and it's been a terrific addition. I think he might not have been so interested if it hadn't been for the fact that his father worked here."[3]

Shiely said he had not intended to join Briggs & Stratton, "because you certainly don't want to live your life in someone else's shadow."[4]

"I had an interest because it was one of the largest companies in Milwaukee. I came here in

Fred Stratton Jr. has been chief executive officer of Briggs & Stratton since 1977, when he was elected president at the age of 38. He has been chairman of the company since 1987.

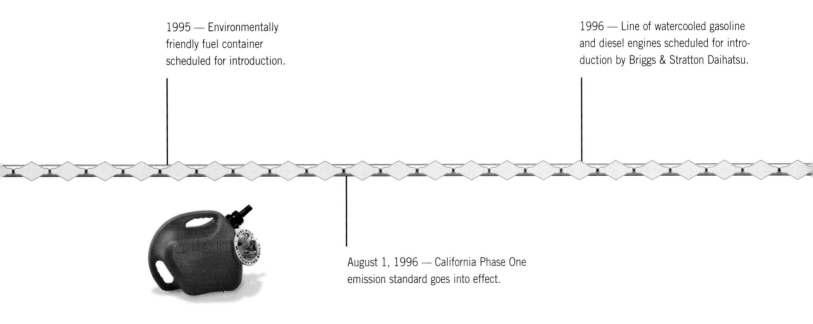

1995 — Environmentally friendly fuel container scheduled for introduction.

1996 — Line of watercooled gasoline and diesel engines scheduled for introduction by Briggs & Stratton Daihatsu.

August 1, 1996 — California Phase One emission standard goes into effect.

1986, nine years after my father died. I felt comfortable that I wouldn't have to deal with that. I was flying on a somewhat different vector than he was, being a lawyer, being a deal guy, a corporate development guy. Plus, public corporations have a pretty short memory. It's performance that matters. You have to deliver value each year. My old man used to tell me, 'A couple of bad years and they don't have much use for you.' ... So I don't think there was any thought in my mind of manifest destiny. As a matter of fact, this is one of the places I thought I was least likely to end up at."[5]

STRATTEC

One of the company's most significant changes has been the February 27, 1995 spin-off of the Technologies Division into a separate company called the STRATTEC Security Corporation. Harold Stratton II, vice president and general manager of the division, became president and chief executive officer of Strattec. He explained that Briggs & Stratton shareholders receive one share of the new corporation for every five in Briggs & Stratton.[6] STRATTEC stock is traded on the NASDAQ exchange under the symbol STRT.

"One of the reasons for the spin-off is that some dramatic things have changed in the auto industry relative to our product. We have some neat new opportunities plus some challenges, because there will be a transition from a straight mechanical product to electronic enhancements. Some day we may go to total electronic products. We want to be around to drive that change and react to it."[7]

Before becoming STRATTEC, Briggs & Stratton Technologies developed a new anti-theft electronic locking system that disconnects the ignition from a car's electrical system if the steering column is broken or it is disturbed another way.

Although the Technologies Division had represented only 7 percent of overall Briggs & Stratton revenues, the division led the world in automotive lock production and sales, providing quality assemblies to General Motors, Chrysler, Ford and every major truck manufacturer in North America. Since automotive lock manufacturing has little in common with small engine manufacture, the division has

Harold Stratton II, president and chief executive officer of STRATTEC, a company that was formed when Briggs & Stratton's Technologies Division was spun off.

always been relatively autonomous. Dick Fotsch, vice president and general manager of the Small Engine Division, said the spin-off gives Strattec an identity of its own.

"Spinning it off and making it its own separate entity would give it the opportunity to be recognized in the market place for its value. Not just mixed in with the main part of Briggs & Stratton. I think there's merit to that."[8]

As a new company, STRATTEC will be able to access its own capital, fund its own ventures, and maintain a tighter control over its fate. Stratton said he is not leaving behind the heritage of Briggs & Stratton. "The heritage end of the business is still there, even if they don't have the same name," he said. "The important thing is there is a connection there. We're talking about a customer base that is not large. It is pretty concentrated on our end of the business. They have stuck with us for years and years because for 80 years we have done pretty much the right things for them as well as for ourselves. We aren't going to lose that as a result of a name change."[9]

Improved Customer Service

A computer network subsidiary, POWER-COM 2000, allows Briggs & Stratton to communicate with dealers, distributors and equipment manufacturers. "This subsidiary now has three different product lines with a lot of different modules in each one," said Erik Aspelin, vice president in charge of the Distribution Sales & Service Division. "One is the computer business management system, one is the electronic communications, so we could have a standard way of communicating with any of our suppliers, and the third is electronic cataloging, putting all illustrated parts in the repair manuals, service books, sales catalogs, all on disk."[10] Within a few years, the majority of these agencies will be utilizing POWERCOM 2000.

"The concept has been very well accepted with 27 original equipment manufacuters," said Aspelin. "It's starting to really gain momentum. What this system does is allows a large number of small, non-computerized dealers, to develop a dealer business management system."[11] By the summer of 1995, 1,800 dealers had signed on.

New Emissions Standards

New emission standards established by the Environmental Protection Agency and the California Air Resources Board are playing an

important role in the future of Briggs & Stratton. An EPA Phase One rule, patterned after the CARB Phase One rule, will be effective for the 1997 model year. Negotiations on the EPA Phase Two continue.

California Phase One, which went into effect August 1, 1995, calls for a 70 percent emission reduction, which Briggs & Stratton has already achieved in many of its engine families. Charles Brown, vice president of engineering and quality assurance, said Briggs & Stratton has been working continuously to improve emissions.

"Probably since 1988 or 1989, when California initially started thinking about passing an emissions regulation, it has occupied an increasing amount of time for the engineers, technicians, designers and everybody associated with it. We've learned an awful lot over the last two or three years, and we continue to learn. There's a good mix of the responsibilities between the division engineering folks and the corporate engineering folks. The divisions are looking at what they are going to do over the next year or two, and the corporate folks are looking more at the 1999, 2000 time frame."[12]

Brown noted some ways that Briggs & Stratton is improving its emissions performance.

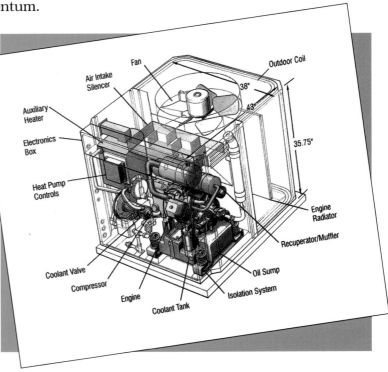

The 5-horsepower Marathon engine is powered with natural gas. Designed in cooperation with the Gas Research Institute, it is used to power the Triathlon Heat Pump developed by York International Corporation.

"In general, we split the problem into two parts. There is a fuel system problem that has to be dealt with, and what we call the engine power head. The piston, cylinder head, those types of things. The things that we have done from a power head standpoint result in a better product that is emission compliant. A lot of people in our industry don't want to talk about that too much because it is forcing the way we make our engine, design our product and manufacture our product to comply with the regulations. When you put it all together, it's going to result in a better product than if we didn't have the emission regulations."[13]

The real challenge will be the California Phase Two, Brown admitted. "There's a California Phase Two standard that we don't think anybody in our industry is going to be able to meet," he said. "The standards as they are right now are not technically feasible. They are way too low."[14]

Aspelin said the emissions standards create challenges for every department in the Briggs & Stratton organization.

"It's going to put more pressure on the whole system. There is no way we are going to be able to put the new test equipment in the field at the dealer level like you would with automobiles. So what we

will depend on is one extensive test of what comes off the manufacturers' line."[15]

Briggs & Stratton is experimenting with engines that run on methanol, and has already produced the Marathon engine, which runs on natural gas. But Brown said the use of alternative fuels is limited by availability.

"We have not done any work on anything beyond what will likely show up at the gas pumps because people who buy our products usually use whatever they find at the gas station."[16]

Another solution to the problem of emissions is a battery-powered lawn mower, expected to be marketed by MTD's Yard Man division and by Snapper in 1996. Briggs & Stratton plans to target this product toward urban homeowners with small yards. Stratton discussed the evolution of the battery-powered unit.

"There was a little bit of an internal debate. Some of us thought, 'We make power equipment, and the power can be electric as well as gasoline. Let's see what we can do.' One side of the argument was that we might be making our own product obsolete. And the other side of the argument was, 'If we don't do it, somebody else will.' So I decided it better be us. Besides, we were interested in being electrical suppliers. ... I think the best concept that the guys came up with, is that we want to make this thing light, but we want to give it long enough cutting time so people are happy with it. We designed it so that it has about half the battery power necessary, and build it so the battery is easily replaceable, and then sell it with a couple of batteries. ... That way the consumer can have a light product that's easy to push around, and when you get to your half-hour running time, if there's still more lawn to cut, you just take out your battery and drop in another one and go. If you want to cut for 24 hours, you can get more batteries and have them all charging up. It takes about 18

Overhead valve engines such as the one on the left are growing in popularity because of their superior fuel efficiency and power.

Briggs & Stratton's 1988 line of engines for rotary lawn mowers.

hours to fully charge a battery. You can mow forever with enough batteries."[17]

Marketing Director William Reitman said the battery-powered lawn mower is not, however, as powerful as a gas-powered engine. To make the product more efficient, the weight of the deck was reduced from 76 pounds to 46 pounds.[18] He noted that 55 percent of consumers cut their lawns in less than an hour.

"Then you have to factor out people who use self-propelled mowers, and it becomes a smaller and smaller segment that this would appeal to. We view it as a niche opportunity. We don't know how large the niche will get. We think it's somewhere between 5 and 15 percent of the market as the technology gets better. It's an opportunity, but it's also a risk, because a battery electric mower takes market share away from a gas-powered mower."[19]

"That has enormous potential ramifications," said board member Peter Georgescu, chairman of the prestigious New York-based Young & Rubicam advertising firm. "Briggs & Stratton is not going to be in the battery business, that's for sure. ... The issue is, what role will they play in that industry?[20]

New Products on the Horizon

The Briggs & Stratton Daihatsu joint venture will market a line of watercooled gasoline and diesel engines designed and manufactured by Daihatsu. This will be the first diesel engine for Briggs & Stratton since the Farymann venture of 1984. The full line, ranging from 18-horsepower to 31-horsepower, is expected to be on the market by January 1996. Paul O. Farny, who worked for Farymann Diesel, is now president and general manager of Briggs & Stratton Daihatsu.

"We know that the diesel process has become very sophisticated. Daihatsu has small cars with diesels and they have maintained technology on the forefront of that development, so we are very optimistic that we are going to offer diesel engines which are very state of the art and very competitive in the market."[21]

In February 1995, Briggs & Stratton introduced a line of power tool accessories, including drill bits, hole saws, wire end brushes, Reitman said.

"Our niche here is our dealer network. The lawn and garden dealer has continued to lose a share of equipment sales over the years, so they are looking for new revenue opportunities. Accessories are very much an impulse purchase item. If you're a heavy do-it-yourselfer, you always want to make sure you have enough drill bits and saw blades and those types of things available. So here is an opportunity for a dealer to gain some incremental volume."[22]

Georgescu also likes the new line. "I think it is the right thing for them to explore. I've been very supportive of that."[23]

A Better Fuel Container

The company plans to introduce a unique new design of fuel container that will protect the environment and save fuel. Scheduled for introduction in late 1995, this revolutionary container won't leak, spill or vent vaporized fuel that is being poured into a tank, said Stratton.

"The fuel cans that are out there are imperfect in a number of ways. One of the problems is that they create a lot of evaporative emissions in the process of taking the fuel from the gas pump to the can, in the process of filling the fuel tanks of equipment, and just in storage, because most cans are vented. And that is a volatile organic compound that contributes to smog. Plus, people have a tendency to spill when filling any kind of equipment. For example, any time you spill fueling a boat, you see this

The overhead-valve Europa, used in premium walk-behind mowers, meets and exceeds the highest government standards of noise and emission reduction.

Briggs & Stratton has developed an environmentally friendly fuel container that won't leak, spill or vent vaporized gasoline.

film on top of the water. And I always feel guilty about it. So we told our R&D people to design a fuel can that won't spill and is as environmentally friendly as you can make a fuel can. They came up with a nozzle and a can-nozzle combination that really solves a lot of the problems.

"You still have to take it to the gas station and take the nozzle off and fill the can. But once you get it in the can it is sealed. Operation of the can is quite simple. First, you turn the nozzle, which releases any pressure in the can. If there's pressure, you hear a 'psst.' Then comes what for first-time users is the great leap of faith. You lift it up and hold the nozzle [down]. Psychologically, it's hard to do the first time. The nozzle has a kind of a spring mounting. You lower the nozzle into your filler neck, and the weight of the can starts the flow of fuel, and you can get a fairly decent seal at the lip of the nozzle on the filler opening. And it fills, glub, glub, glub, not as fast as you might like it, but at a reasonable pace. When the fuel level reaches the tip of the nozzle, the flow is cut off. The glubbing

The premium market for walk-behind mowers continues to grow, supplied by engines such as the Europa.

stops and you know it won't pour any more. When you lift the can, the spring-loading closes and seals the can again. I've been using prototypes for the past year at home for fueling the lawn and garden equipment, and I'm in love with it. Now, it's going to cost more than your every-day gas can, but I've been using the prototypes for the last year and I haven't spilled a drop."[24]

Reitman said sales efforts will focus on distinguishing the container from more conventional models. It will be sold in lawn and garden departments, not automotive sections of retail outlets.

"We're trying to get ourselves into some high-profile catalogs and high-profile retail outlets. We're going to have to rely on some creative point-of-sale ideas to differentiate it. Today, a can just sits there. Our goal will be to have a sell piece attached to the can. The design of the can itself is appealing. One of the reasons we took a design approach is that we wanted it to look different on the shelf so it would catch the consumer's eye.

"As with the battery-pow-ered electric

engine, it has strong environmental attributes, but that's not what the consumers are going to buy. They buy the battery engine because it's incredibly easy to start and it's quiet to operate. They'll buy the fuel can because it doesn't spill, doesn't make a mess. You avoid that gas smell on the ride back from the gas station."25

Improving Production

Briggs & Stratton will be producing more overhead valve engines, which are more efficient and therefore produce less emissions. But overhead valve engines are more difficult to produce. These engines simply can't be manufactured as easily as L-head counterparts.

The company also plans to continue producing higher-horsepower engines. Stratton said the trend toward higher horsepower is good for Briggs & Stratton.

"Higher horsepower means more sales dollars. It works because people are switching to riding equipment. That's one trend. Within the walk-behind category there is a trend toward higher horsepower. In recent years, that has been largely environmentally driven. Particularly because of the fact that municipal landfills have stopped, or are soon going to stop, accepting yard waste and grass clippings. So, people have to deal with that themselves.

Rather than put it in bags, mulching mowers require a little more horsepower because you are not just cutting it once. You are cutting it and re-cutting it and actually doing more work. With the riding equipment, people just like to get the job done faster. Plus, I think people like the idea of higher horsepower. It's a lot more fun. So gradually, you have not only a trend from walk-behind to riders, but within the walk-behind category and within the rider category you have trends to higher horsepower. You put all those factors together and this will keep the revenue line growing pretty nicely."26

Assisting Briggs & Stratton in these design and production goals is computer design software called PRO E, which, in tandem with a CAD/CAM system, will build a plastic model of components with a quality suitable for limited testing and analysis.

Changing Marketplace

Briggs & Stratton pays close attention to the evolving marketplace for its products. The role of mass merchandisers in the sales and marketing of lawn and garden equipment will continue to present both challenges and opportunities for Briggs & Stratton. The company plans to introduce more mid-level and premium engines to this segment. Stephen Rugg, vice president of sales and marketing, said discount retailers such as Kmart and Wal-Mart are distorting the marketplace.

"The biggest challenge that we have today is the consolidation of the business and the overall power of the merchandisers. They are in the lawn and garden business to do a number of things. They sell low-price lawn and garden stuff to give their store a low-price image. Then people come in and they'll sell other things at higher prices. If they create a lawn and garden department so they can sell fertilizer and live goods, they'll make a lot more money on fertilizer and live goods than on lawn and garden equipment. ... Another thing is that the major brands have been withheld from most mass merchandisers. Toro and Snapper and John Deere are sold almost exclusively at dealerships."27

Reitman said maintaining product loyalty is a continuing challenge for the company. "In order to do that, we need to continue to have good, solid relationships with customers and retailers, and we need to continue developing products that address consumer needs."28

Georgescu believes "the future of the organization will depend on their ability to market. And that means establishing and managing the relationship, not necessarily with their immediate customer, but their ultimate customer, which is the user of the product."29 He noted that the Briggs & Stratton name "is one of the strongest assets the corporation has, even though it is not on the balance sheet."30

New Challenges

Briggs & Stratton is constantly looking for new markets for its products. Hugo Keltz, vice president of the International Division since

1991, said the company has identified markets that show potential for future growth.

"We have identified markets like, obviously, Russia. And then we talk about the region of Eastern Europe as well. We have identified markets like Indonesia. And we have identified Brazil as another market where we seek tremendous growth potential. India is another market with tremendous growth potential sooner or later. China obviously is another market. Just about a year ago, we established our own regional office in Shanghai."[31]

Keltz said the biggest challenge in the international market is to gain market share in industrial businesses and in developing nations. "The developing world is dominated today by Honda. So that certainly is a big challenge for us. We are going to be successful with our Vanguard engines against Honda and some other Japanese companies."[32]

President John Shiely noted that the company is constantly striving for improvement, and he described some of the challenges facing individual divisions.

"The primary challenge of the Small Engine Division has been identified by its management as being substantial additional cost reductions, continuous product improvement and addressing the 'mass marketization' of their product. For the Large Engine Division, the challenges are to accomplish focused factory deployment to improve quality and substantially reduce indirect labor and inventories, effective assessment of labor/capital tradeoffs, and new product development. The major challenges

for the Vanguard Division are appropriate product positioning and achievement of competitive costs in a low-volume environment."[33]

Briggs & Stratton has come a long way in 85 years. Starting in a one-room office in the old Pfeiffer Machine Shop, Briggs & Stratton has grown into the largest manufacturer of small four-cycle engines in the world. Peter Georgescu said the company has fought hard to stay on top.

"The reason that Briggs & Stratton has succeeded, in my opinion, is because of the power of the brand, and because they took aggressive action to streamline themselves, to take the fat out, to become competitive. So there was not enough room for a Japanese company to come in and attack, on the basis of either cost or reputation. That is something that should not go unnoted in the history of this company, and I give Fred Stratton enormous credit for recognizing the challenge and doing whatever was necessary to meet it."[34]

A new line of power tool accesories offered by Briggs & Stratton boosts revenues by increasing impulse buying at retail outlets.

NOTES TO SOURCES

Chapter One

1. *Genealogy of Briggs Family.* Codington County Historical Society, Watertown, South Dakota: July 5, 1988), p. 3.
2. *Shakopee Courier,* September 12, 1888, and *Watertown Courier News,* [no date], cited in Genealogy of Briggs Family, p. 3.
3. *The Milwaukee Journal,* October 7, 1962.
4. *Ibid.*
5. Colet Coughlin, interviewed by the author, June 15, 1995. Transcript, p. 1.
6. *Ibid.,* p. 3.
7. Wright's Directory of Milwaukee, Wisconsin for 1908, p. 866.
8. *Ibid.*
9. Letter from Frederick P. Stratton Jr. to the author, August 28, 1995.
10. *Ibid.*
11. *The Milwaukee Journal,* October 7, 1962, p. 1.
12. Letter of Patent granted to Stephen F. Briggs, of Milwaukee, Wisconsin, from the United States Patent Office. Assignor to the firm of Briggs & Stratton of Milwaukee, a Co-partnership, Patent No. 950,126, Serial No.475,957, February 22, 1910, p. 1.
13. *Auditors' Report on Investigation of Accounts and Organization,* prepared for Briggs & Stratton by Arthur Andersen & Co., June 30, 1919, p. 1.
14. *Return of Annual Net Income for the Briggs & Stratton Company,* 1911, p. 1.
15. *Monthly Sales Summaries,* Briggs & Stratton Company, March and June through December 1912.
16. *Monthly Sales Summaries,* Briggs & Stratton Company, 1913.
17. *Monthly Sales Summaries,* Briggs & Stratton Company, 1914.
18. Lease with Briggs & Stratton Company, Feister-Owen Press (Incorporated), November 1, 1912.
19. *The St. Petersburg (Fl.) Times,* Personality section, August 17, 1958, p. 23.
20. Agreement between the Briggs & Stratton Company (through the General Sales Company, Detroit, Michigan) with the Barr Manufacturing Company, Detroit, Michigan, March 6, 1912.
21. Agreement between the Briggs & Stratton Company, (through the General Sales Company, Detroit, Michigan) and the Morton and Morton Company, March 18, 1912.
22. *Monthly Sales Summaries,* 1912, for nine months including March and May through December, Briggs & Stratton Company.
23. *Monthly Sales Summaries,* 1913, Briggs & Stratton Company.
24. *Monthly Sales Summaries,* 1912-1916, Briggs & Stratton Company.
25. Contract between the Briggs & Stratton Company and Arthur Storz Auto Supply Company of Omaha, Nebraska, May 15, 1912, p. 1.

Chapter Two

1. *Monthly Sales Summaries,* 1912-1916, Briggs & Stratton Company.

2. *Ibid.*

3. Contract between the Briggs & Stratton Company and the Willys-Overland Company, Toledo, Ohio, October 28, 1912, and *Contract,* between the Briggs & Stratton Company and the Dodge Brothers, Hamtramck, Michigan, September 1, 1915.

4. *Monthly Sales Summaries,* 1915, and January through March, May through June and August through November, 1916, Briggs & Stratton Company.

5. *Monthly Sales Summaries,* 1913, 1914 and 1915, and January through March, May through June and August through November, 1916, Briggs & Stratton Company.

6. Copy of advertisement in *Automotive Electrical Engineer,* November 1922, p. 5.

7. Automotive electrical supply catalog, published by the Briggs & Stratton Company, October 1916, p. 6

8. *Monthly Sales Summaries,* May 1915 through December 1916, Briggs & Stratton Company.

9. *Profit and Loss Account,* 1915, Briggs & Stratton Company.

10. *Profit and Loss Account,* 1916, Briggs & Stratton Company.

11. *Monthly Sales Summaries,* 1912-1916, Briggs & Stratton Company. See also, *Return of Annual Net Income* for the Briggs & Stratton Company, year ending December 31, 1911, United States Internal Revenue Service.

12. *Auditors' Report on Investigation of Accounts and Organization for the Briggs & Stratton Company,* prepared by Arthur Andersen & Company, June 30, 1919.

13. *Bulletin No. 600,* January 1929, published by Briggs & Stratton, p. 4.

14. Memo from O. Weymier to L. Regner, October 20, 1952, p. 2. See also, *Briggs & Stratton Corporation Building Summary as of December 31, 1949,* March 15, 1950.

15. Memo O. Weymier, p. 3.

16. *History, Policies, Manufacturing Facilities, Products and Distribution,* published by the Briggs & Stratton Company, 1923. p. 3.

17. *Ibid.,* p. 5.

18. *Report,* covering Balance Sheet Income Statement and Supporting Schedules as of December 31, 1920, Briggs & Stratton Company, p. 2.

19. *Ibid.* See also *Final Balance Sheet Income Statement and Supporting Schedules for Month/Year Ended December 31,* for 1921 through 1930, "Schedule A, Net Sales."

20. Minutes of organization proceedings, Briggs Loading Company, May 7, 1918, "Article I, Section 2," p. 2.

21. Contract with the United States of America, Ordnance Department, U. S. Army, Order No. WAR-ORD. P8015-1913Tw. First Supplemental Contract, September 19, 1918, "Amendments #1 and #2, Article II," Briggs Loading Company, p. 2.

22. *Ibid,* "Article IV," p. 3.

23. Award from the Secretary of War of the United States of America, to the Briggs Loading Company, under "An Act to Provide Relief in Cases of Contracts Connected with the Prosecution of the War, and for other Purposes," December 16, 1919, pp. 1-2.

24. *Special Report,* prepared by Herbert J. Brooks & Company, September 15, 1922. (Chicago), pp. 6-7.

Chapter Three

1. "The Auto Wheel Saves Pedaling," *Auto Wheels Limited,* published by International Auto Wheel Company, Ltd., Russell Road, Kensington, London, 1910.

2. Jim Altman, "The Motor Wheel." *Antique Automobile,* March-April, 1971, pp. 19-20.

3. *Ibid,* 19-20. See also A.O. Smith Company, "Motor Wheeling", pamphlet published in 1917.

4. Contract between A.O. Smith Company and Stephen F. Briggs, May 19, 1919. (Milwaukee), p. 1.

5. Altman, "Motor Wheel", p. 20.

6. *The Briggs & Stratton Motor Wheel,* published by

the Briggs & Stratton Company-Motor Wheel Division, 1920. p. 5.

7. *Creating a Bigger Bicycle Market,* pamphlet, published by the Briggs & Stratton Company-Motor Wheel Division. pp. 2-3.

8. *Ibid,,* p. 12.

9. These magazines included *The Saturday Evening Post, Boy's Life, The Youth's Companion, American Boy,* and *Popular Mechanics.* The advertisements began in March 1920.

10. *Motor Wheel Age,* magazine published by Briggs & Stratton, May-June 1920. Inside back cover.

11   *Motor Wheel Age,* February 1920, inside front cover.

12. *Motor Wheel Age,* April 1920, p. 12, and May-June 1920, p. 13.

13 *Motor Wheel Age,* February, 1920, p. 9.

14. *Briggs & Stratton Motor Wheel,* pamphlet by the Briggs & Stratton Company-Motor Wheel Division. p. 6.

15. *It's Plumb Wonderful How You Like It,* pamphlet by Briggs & Stratton.

16. *Motor Wheel Age,* April 1920, p. 15.

17. *Ibid,,* p. 13.

18. *Harbor Light,* Harbor Springs, Michigan. December 28-January 3, 1978.

19. Edwin Ketchum, "Fifty Miles an Hour on a Motor-Skate." *Popular Science Monthly,* December, 1925, p. 32. Although the Motor Wheel is not mentioned by name, an accompanying photograph shows a motor/wheel combination nearly identical to the Briggs & Stratton Model D Motor Wheel.

20. *Creating a Bigger Bicycle Market,* p. 4.

21. Robert Gorman, "The World's first Sports Car." *Popular Science,* June, 1960. p. 126.

22. John Matras, "1920 Auto Red Bug: Small, Light, Cheap and Built by Briggs & Stratton." *Autoweek,* January 2, 1989.

23. *Motor Wheel Age,* May-June 1920. p. 19.

24. *Land and Buildings as of 1919, 1920, 1923, East Plant, "Charts 3-5",* document produced by the Briggs & Stratton Corporation.

Chapter Four

1. Contract between the Briggs & Stratton Company and Frank Held, December 27, 1920, pp. 1-3.

2. *Ibid.,* p. 1.

3. Agreement between the Briggs & Stratton Company and the Gilson Manufacturing Company, December 31, 1924. p. 1.

4. *Approximate Build Dates,* a listing compiled by Andrew Cochrane, with information on Engine Model Series and corresponding dates of manufacture, 1991. p. 1.

5. Bulletin from Briggs & Stratton regarding the General Utility Engine Type P, 1920, p. 2.

6. *Final Balance Sheet,* Income Statement and Supporting Schedules for Briggs & Stratton Company, 1921, "Schedule A."

7. *Engine Sales Data,* showing unit sales, dollar sales and horsepower. 1924 to date. Produced by the Briggs & Stratton Corporation, August 12, 1974.

8. Letter from John I. Beggs, chairman of the Board of Directors, to the stockholders of Briggs & Stratton, February 14, 1923, p. 1.

9. *Briggs & Stratton Company Trust Agreement,* October 1, 1921, p. 1.

10. *History, Policies, Manufacturing Facilities, Products and Distribution,* catalog published by the Briggs & Stratton Company, 1923, p. 14.

11. *Ibid.,* pp. 14-15.

12. Basco Automotive Equipment, Catalog No. 1,000, January, 1933.

13. "What 21 Years Have Accomplished" *The Master Locksmith,* June, 1930, p. 15.

14. *Balance Sheet Income Statement with Supporting Schedules,* year ending December 31, for years 1925-1930. "Schedule A."

15. Harold M. Stratton II, interviewed by the author, Milwaukee, Wisconsin, February 17, 1995. Transcript, p. 27.

16. *Bulletin No. 600,* Briggs & Stratton Corporation, January 1929, p. 3.

17. *Balance and Income Statements,* "Schedule A," 1926-1930, Briggs and Stratton Corporation.

18. *Brief History of the Briggs & Stratton Corporation,* written for the New York Stock Exchange, May 20, 1929, p. 2.

19. Contract between the Briggs & Stratton Corporation and Nash Motors, June 12, 1930.

20. *Balance Sheet Income Statement with Supporting Schedules,* for Briggs & Stratton, 1925-1930, "Schedule A."

21. *The Brooklyn Eagle,* Brooklyn, New York, September 23, 1929.

22. *Wall Street Journal,* April 28, 1930.

23. *History, Policies,* pp. 23-24.

Chapter Five

1. *Mellowes Electric Frigerator,* promotional pamphlet, p. 2.

2. *Ibid.,* p. 3.

3. *Ibid.,* p. 2.

4. *Ibid.,* p. 4.

5. *Ibid.,* p. 2.

6. *Balance Sheet Income Statement and Supporting Schedules,* for 1921 and 1922, "Schedule A."

7. *Milwaukee Journal,* November 29, 1931.

8. *Balance Sheet Income Statement,* 1927, "Schedule B."

9. *Building Summary* as of December 31, 1960, East Plant, "Charts 6 through 9."

Chapter Six

1. *Producing the "Evinrude" - "Elto" - "Lockwood",* Outboard Motors Corporation, p. 2.

2. *Statement of Facts Re: Acquisition of Outboard Motors Corporation,* p. 1.

3. *Ibid.,* p. 1.

4. *Auditor's Report,* for the three months ending March 30, 1929, Elto Outboard Motor Company, p. 2.

5. *Auditor's Report,* for the three months ending March 30, 1929, Lockwood Motor Company, p. 2.

6. *Ibid.,* pp. 2-3.

7. For a detailed history of the Outboard Motors Corporation see *Evinrude-Johnson and the Legend of OMC,* Jeffrey L. Rodengen, Write Stuff Syndicate, Inc: Ft. Lauderdale, 1993.

8. *Milwaukee Journal,* October 7, 1962.

9. *Wagemaker Company-Boat Division, Wolverine Boats,* sales brochure, 1938.

10. *Do You Need ... A Motor?* sales pamphlet published by Marine Sales and Service Limited, (Vancouver, British Columbia, Canada).

11. For more information on Briggs & Stratton marine engines and transmissions, see the company's pamphlet, "Briggs & Stratton 4-Cycle Air-Cooled Inboards for All Small Boats..."

12. *The Last Word in Sports: Sea Scoot,* sales pamphlet published by the Moto-Scoot Manufacturing Company, (Chicago, Illinois).

13. *Ibid.,* pp. 2-3.

14. Letter from Fred Stratton Jr. to the author, August 31, 1995.

Chapter Seven

1. *Powered By Briggs & Stratton,* sales promotion booklet, Briggs & Stratton, 1937, p. 6.

2. *Fullpower* became something of a generic trade name for all Briggs & Stratton engines manufactured during the twenties and thirties.

3. Report to Charles C. Coughlin, president, Briggs & Stratton Corporation. "Comparative Total Net Sales to Washing Machine Manufacturers, 1927-1946."

4. *Ibid.*

5. *Summary of Gasoline Motor Shipments per Month,* from 1924 to 1932 inclusive according to type, published by Briggs & Stratton.

6. The first Briggs & Stratton engine to come equipped with the "L"-head was the *Model Q,* introduced in February 1929, about one year prior to the introduction of the *Model L.* For a list of engine introduction dates and descriptions see *Record of Production in the Engine Division of Briggs & Stratton Corporation,* published May 12, 1943 by Briggs & Stratton.

7. *Briggs & Stratton Flywheel,* published March 1930 by Briggs & Stratton, p. 3.

8. *Yearly Analysis of Motor Division Production and Service Sales,* published in 1935 by Briggs & Stratton, p. 1.

9. *Summary of Power Charger Production and Service*

Sales by Model, for January 1, 1936 to June 30, 1936, published by Briggs & Stratton.

10. *Summary of Income Statement,* 1939, published by Briggs & Stratton.

11. *Power Charger,* promotional booklet published in 1936 by Briggs & Stratton.

12. *Powered by 4-Cycle Briggs & Stratton Gasoline Motor,* promotional booklet for the farm washer, published by Briggs & Stratton, pp. 2-3.

13. *Ibid.*

Chapter Eight

1. Dr. Alan Axelrod and Charles Philips, *What Every American Should Know About American History,* (Holbrook, Massachusetts: Bob Adams, Inc., 1992), pp. 274-275.

2. *Comparative Total Net Sales -- Washing Machine Manufacturers,* 1927-1942, published by Briggs & Stratton.

3. *Analysis of Cost of Sales, Gross Profit and Percentage of Gross Profit to Net Sales by Division,* for 1926 through 1929.

4. *Ibid.,* 1930 and 1940.

5. *Ibid.*1929-1933.

6. *Sales Summary,* 1940, "Summary of Motors," published by Briggs & Stratton.

7. Report to Charles L. Coughlin, "Comparative Total Net Sales, Lawn Mower Manufacturers, 1927-1946."

8. *Commando: The Aristocrat of Light Motorcycles,* sales brochure for Merx Products, Inc.

9. *Ibid.*

10. *Summary of Sales,* 1939, summary of engines, "Production and Service Net Sales by Use."

11. *Yearly Analysis of Motor Division Production and Service Sales* 1935 and 1936, published by Briggs & Stratton.

12. *Briggs & Stratton Flywheel,* published by Briggs & Stratton, p. 1.

13. *Land and Buildings as of 1941: East Plant,* "Chart #13," documents published by Briggs & Stratton.

14. Charles Graf, interviewed by the author, June 1, 1995. Transcript, p. 10.

15. Graf interview, p. 11.

16. Jack Ebershoff, interviewed by Robert Carter, Milwaukee, Wisconsin, June 2, 1995. Transcript, p. 24.

17. Leo Lechtenberg, interviewed by Robert Carter, June 2, 1995, Elm Grove, Wisconsin. Transcript, p. 1.

18. Lechtenberg interview, p. 2.

19. *Sales Summary,* 1939, "Summary of Motors," documents published by Briggs & Stratton.

20. *Analysis of Oil Cleaners Production and Service Sales for 1936,* Briggs & Stratton.

21. *The Problem Solver,* sales booklet by Air-Saver Valve Company, Birmingham, Michigan.

22. *ITW Fastex, A Solution That Works For Briggs & Stratton,* advertisement.

23. *Sales Summary,* 1939-1945, "Summary of Specialties/Graham Transmissions."

24. *Sales Summary,* 1939-1950, "Summary of Automotive."

25. *Flywheel,* December 1930, published by Briggs & Stratton, p. 2.

26. *Ibid.*

Chapter Nine

1. Edward Mueller, interviewed by the author, February 16, 1995, Milwaukee, Wisconsin. Transcript, p. 2.

2. Jack Ebershoff, interviewed by Robert Carter, June 2, 1995, Milwaukee, Wisconsin. Transcript, p. 9.

3. *Sales and Profits during the War Effort,* 1942 through 1945, Briggs & Stratton Corporation. See also, *War Sales by Product Lines,* 1942 through 1945, and *Ordnance Fuse Shipments,* 1940 through 1943.

4. *Airplane Magneto Shipments,* 1943 through 1945, Briggs & Stratton.

5. *War Sales by Product Lines,* 1942 through 1945, Briggs & Stratton.

6. *Sales and Profits during the War Effort,* 1942 through 1945.

7. Leo Lechtenberg, interviewed by Robert Carter, June 2, 1995, Elm Grove, Wisconsin. Transcript, p. 12.

8. *Ibid.*

9. *History of Airplane Ignition Switches Manufactured by*

the Briggs & Stratton Corporation, published by Briggs & Stratton, p. 3.

10. *Recap of Airplane Switch Shipments for the Years 1942-1944,* published by Briggs & Stratton.
11. Letter from Edward V. Oehler, vice president of Briggs & Stratton, to John A. Deverey, deputy chief, War Production Board, Automotive Division, January 5, 1944, p. 4.
12. Letter from O.L. Sickert, Briggs & Stratton Corporation, to the War Production Board, February 2, 1944.
13. *Summary of Equipment Purchased and Used in the Manufacture of Various Items on War Contracts,* published by Briggs & Stratton.
14. *Engine Information/War Business/Payroll Information,* report prepared for Charles Coughlin.
15. *Nets Sales & Net Profit Split Between War & Non-War Years,* 1942 through 1945, prepared by Briggs & Stratton.
16. "200 Companies with Biggest Arms Orders." *Financial World,* February 5, 1941, p. 13.

Chapter Ten

1. Harold Stratton II, interviewed by the author, February 17, 1995, Milwaukee, Wisconsin. Transcript, p. 29.
2. *Comparative Total Net Sales, Lawn Mower Manufacturers,* and

Summary of Sales for 1946, "Summary of Engines," published by Briggs & Stratton.
3. John Shiely, interviewed by the author, June 14, 1995, Milwaukee. Transcript, p. 4.
4. Michael E. Porter, *Competitive Strategy,* (Free Press: 1980), p. 36.
5. Colet Coughlin, interviewed by the author, June 15, 1995. Transcript, p. 5.
6. Coughlin interview, p. 10.
7. *South Dakota State University Centennial,* February 1981.
8. Coughlin interview, p. 20.
9. Ed Mueller, interviewed by the author, June 13, 1995, Milwaukee, Wisconsin. Transcript, pp. 6-7.
10. Leo Lechtenberg, interviewed by Robert Carter, June 2, 1995, Elm Grove, Wisconsin. Transcript, p. 5.
11. Jack Ebershoff, interviewed by Robert Carter, June 2, 1995, Milwaukee, Wisconsin. Transcript, p. 18.
12. *Shipment Recap Record, Gas Motor Department,* published by Briggs & Stratton, 1953.
13. Ebershoff interview, p. 15.
14. *Sales Summary,* 1955 through 1960, "Summary of Engines."
15. *Condensed Profit & Loss Statements,* audit reports prepared by Arthur Andersen & Co.
16. *Analysis of Sales By Product Line,* "Total Government," published by Briggs & Stratton.

17. *Engine Sales Data,* 1924 to date, published August 12, 1974 by Briggs & Stratton.
18. *Briggs & Stratton Newsletter,* August-September 1959, p. 6.
19. *Floor Space and Acquisition Dates of Various Plants,* published September 30, 1965, and *Land and Buildings as of December 31, 1950, East Plant,* "Charts 17-24."
20. *The Milwaukee Sentinel,* March 19, 1954.
21. *The Milwaukee Sentinel,* April 4, 1956.
22. *Wilmington, Delaware Newspaper,* March 26, 1951 and March 30, 1951.
23. The *Milwaukee Journal,* January 2, 1957.
24. Lechtenberg interview, p. 24.
25. The *Milwaukee Sentinel,* February 16, 1960.
26. Ebershoff interview, p. 19.
27. *Ibid.,* p. 20.
28. *Ibid.,* p. 29.
29. *The Milwaukee Sentinel,*and *The Milwaukee Journal,* April 7, 1946.
30. *The Milwaukee Journal,* May 13, 1946.
31. Agreement between the Briggs & Stratton Corporation and the United Automobile Workers of America, Local 232, May 16, 1938, p. 6.
32. Supplemental Agreement between the Briggs & Stratton Corporation and the United Automobile Workers of America, Local 232, September 11, 1946.
33. *The Milwaukee Journal,* October 18, 1946 and June 10, 1946.
34. *Ibid.*

35. *The Milwaukee Sentinel,* April 14, 1950.
36. Charles Graf, interviewed by the author, June 1, 1995. Transcript, p. 8.
37. *The Milwaukee Journal,* March 17, 1950.
38. *The Milwaukee Journal,* March 22, 1950.
39. Coughlin interview, p. 12.
40. *Ibid.,* p. 13.
41. *The Milwaukee Journal,* February 11-13, 1950. Stories of threats, violence and vandalism are reported in both *The Milwaukee Journal,* and *The Milwaukee Sentinel,* between January and March 1950.
42. *The Milwaukee Journal,* February 15, 1950, March 8, 1950, and April 11, 1950.
43. *The Milwaukee Journal,* April 21, 1950.
44. Agreement between the Briggs & Stratton Corporation and the United Automobile Workers of America, Local 232, August 1, 1950.
45. *AFL Auto Worker,* newsletter published August 1950.
46. The *Milwaukee Journal,* July 12, 1950.
47. Lechtenberg interview, p. 30.
48. Annual Reports, 1955 and 1959, Briggs & Stratton.
49. Lechtenberg interview, p. 49.
50. *Factory Service Training Center,* booklet published by Briggs & Stratton.
51. *Service the World Over,* sales brochure published by Briggs & Stratton.

Chapter Eleven

1. *Speech,* by Vincent R. Shiely at the Baird Investment Seminar, 1973. Transcript, p. 2.
2. *Letter.* from Frederick P. Stratton Jr. to the author, August 31, 1995.
3. *Ibid.*
4. Leo Lechtenberg, interviewed by Robert Carter, June 2, 1995, Elm Grove, Wisconsin. Transcript, p. 43.
5. John Shiely, interviewed by the author, June 14, 1995, Milwaukee, Wisconsin. Transcript, p. 8.
6. Colet Coughlin, interviewed by the author, June 15, 1995. Transcript, p. 8.
7. Shiely interview, p. 6.
8. *Ibid.,* p. 7.
9. *Briggs & Stratton Newsletter,* September-October 1956, pp. 1 and 4.
10. Quiet News from Briggs and Stratton, sales brochure published by Briggs & Stratton.
11. *Memo,* from Fred Stratton to L.W. Dewey and I. Kamulkin, March 28, 1979.
12. *Quiet News.*
13. *The Milwaukee Sentinel,* August 30, 1972.
14. Vincent Shiely, Baird speech, p. 14.
15. "The Little Engine That Coins Money." *Forbes,* October 1, 1977, p. 85.
16. *The Wall Street Journal,* March 16, 1960.
17. *The Milwaukee Journal,* September 5, 1969.
18. *Annual Report,* 1967, Briggs & Stratton.
19. *Engine Sales,* 1924 to date, published in 1974 by Briggs & Stratton.
20. *The Wauwatosa News-Times,* August 17, 1967.
21. *The Milwaukee Journal,* August 21, 1968, *The Milwaukee Sentinel,* September 19, 1968, and The *Menomonee Falls News,* September 25, 1968.
22. *Engine Sales,* 1924 to date, published in 1974 by Briggs & Stratton.
23. *Annual Report,* 1973, Briggs & Stratton.
24. *Sales Summary,* 1973, Briggs & Stratton.
25. Vincent Shiely, Baird speech, p. 5.
26. The *Milwaukee Journal,* June 27, 1973.
27. *The Brookings (S.D.) Register,* March 19, 1952.
28. *South Dakota State University Centennial,* February 1981.
29. Frederick P. Stratton Jr., interviewed by the author, February 17, 1995, Milwaukee, Wisconsin. Transcript, p. 3.
30. *Ibid.,* p. 4.
31. *Ibid.,* p. 7.
32. Lechtenberg interview, p. 70.
33. *Ibid.,* p. 71.
34. Jack Ebershoff, interviewed by Robert Carter, June 2, 1995, Milwaukee, Wisconsin. Transcript, p. 25.
35. *Wall Street Journal,* October 10, 1978.
36. Stratton interview, p. 24.
37. Stratton interview, p. 2.

Chapter Twelve

1. *Speech,* by Fred Stratton at the Baird Award Ceremony, printed in the *Annual Report,* 1994, Briggs & Stratton.
2. Mike O'Neal, "Briggs & Stratton to Sell West

German Diesel Plant." *The Business Journal,* July 23, 1984, p. 3.

3. Hugo Keltz, interviewed by the author, June 2, 1995, Milwaukee, Wisconsin. Transcript, p. 9.

4. Frederick P. Stratton Jr., interviewed by the author, June 13, 1995, Milwaukee, Wisconsin. Transcript, p. 9.

5. *The Menomonee Falls News,* May 24, 1979.

6. James Wier, interviewed by the author, February 17, 1995, Milwaukee, Wisconsin. Transcript, p. 3.

7. *Letter,* from Frederick P. Stratton Jr. to the author, August 31, 1995.

8. *Speech,* by Vincent R. Shiely at the Baird Investment Seminar, 1973. Transcript, p. 25.

9. *The Milwaukee Sentinel,* August 1, 1974.

10. Paul Neylon, interviewed by the author, June 13, 1995, Milwaukee, Wisconsin. Transcript, p. 6.

11. *Ibid.,* p. 7.

12. Brian Barlow, "Briggs & Stratton Plans Move of Lawn Mower Engine Business." *The Business Journal,* December 31, 1984.

13. *Milwaukee Journal,* September 6, 1983.

14. *Letter,* from Frederick P. Stratton Jr. to the author, August 31, 1995.

15. *The Milwaukee Journal,* October 25, 1983.

16. *The Milwaukee Journal,* November 9, 1983.

17. *The Milwaukee Journal,* October 31, 1983.

18. Fred Stratton interview, p. 1.

19. Dick Fotsch, interviewed by the author, June 12, 1995, Milwaukee, Wisconsin. Transcript, p. 5.

20. *Ibid.,* p. 6.

21. *Ibid.,* p. 6.

22. Neylon interview, p. 8.

23. *Ibid.*

24. Stephen Rugg, interviewed by the author, February 16, 1995, Milwaukee, Wisconsin. Transcript, p. 13.

25. George Thompson, interviewed by the author, June 7, 1995. Transcript, p. 15.

26. Michael Hamilton, interviewed by the author, June 1, 1995. Transcript, p. 28.

27. Fred Stratton interview, June 13, 1995, pp. 4-5.

28. *The Milwaukee Journal,* July 17, 1973.

29. Kassandra Preston, interviewed by the author, February 16, 1995, Milwaukee, Wisconsin. Transcript, p. 3.

30. *Briggs & Stratton Newsletter,* July 1990, p. 11.

31. Wier interview, p. 5.

32. Fred Stratton interview, June 13, 1995, pp. 17-18.

33. *Ibid.,* pp. 6-7.

34. Paul Farny, interviewed by the author, June 13, 1995, Milwaukee, Wisconsin. Transcript, p. 4.

35. Neylon interview, p. 14.

36. Farny interview, p. 7.

37. *Ibid.,* p. 6.

38. Fred Statton, letter to the author, August 31, 1995.

39. Hamilton interview, p. 19.

40. *Ibid.,* p. 21.

41. Fred Stratton interview, June 13, 1995, p. 1.

42. *Ibid.,* p. 4.

43. John Connole, "Briggs & Stratton is Rolling After Greasing Its Squeaky Wheels", *The Business Journal,* May 26, 1986.

44. John Shiely, interviewed by the author, June 14, 1995, Milwaukee, Wisconsin. Transcript, p. 22.

45. "Briggs & Stratton is Rolling."

46. Charles O. Brown, interviewed by the author, February 16, 1995, Milwaukee, Wisconsin. Transcript, p. 18.

47. *The Milwaukee Journal,* March 23, 1982.

48. Fred Stratton interview, p. 16.

49. *The Milwaukee Journal,* May 29, 1977.

50. Fred Stratton interview, p. 15.

Chapter Thirteen

1. Fred Stratton, interviewed by the author, June 13, 1995, Milwaukee, Wisconsin. Transcript, p. 30.

2. *Ibid.,* p. 21.

3. *Speech,* by Fred Stratton at the Baird Award Ceremony, printed in the *Annual Report,* 1994, Briggs & Stratton.

4. Stephen Rugg, interviewed by the author, February 16, 1995, Milwaukee, Wisconsin. Transcript, p. 5

5. *Ibid.,* p. 8.

6. *Ibid.,* p. 3.

7. Fred Stratton interview, p. 34.

8. Rugg interview, p. 7.

9. *The Milwaukee Journal,* August 26, 1990.

10. Kassandra Preston, interviewed by the author, February 16, 1995, Milwaukee, Wisconsin. Transcript, p. 10.
11. Fred Stratton interview, p. 16.
12. *Speech*, by John Shiely, "Managing for Value Creation at Briggs & Stratton," 1994. Transcript, pp. 7-8.
13. Shiely interview, pp. 22-25.
14. Shiely speech, "Value Creation," p. 13.
15. Erik Aspelin, interviewed by the author, February 17, 1995, Milwaukee, Wisconsin. Transcript, p. 4.
16. *Ibid.*, p. 6.
17. *Ibid.*, p. 13.
18. James Wier, interviewed by the author, February 17, 1995, Milwaukee, Wisconsin. Transcript, p. 9.
19. Charles O. Brown, interviewed by the author, February 16, 1995, Milwaukee, Wisconsin. Transcript, p. 2.
20. *Ibid.*, pp. 19-20.
21. Gregory Socks, interviewed by the author, February 16, 1995, Milwaukee, Wisconsin. Transcript, pp. 8-9.
22. *Ibid.*, p. 2.
23. *Ibid.*
24. Fred Stratton interview, June 13, 1995, p. 26.
25. Dick Fotsch, interviewed by the author, June 12, 1995, Milwaukee, Wisconsin. Transcript, p. 11.
26. Socks interview, p. 5.
27. Fotsch interview, p. 12.
28. *Ibid.*, p. 10.

29. Paul Neylon, interviewed by the author, June 13, 1995, Milwaukee, Wisconsin. Transcript, p. 15.
30. Allen Nitz, interviewed by the author, June 14, 1995, Milwaukee, Wisconsin. Transcript, p. 10.
31. Curt Larson, interviewed by the author, February 17, 1995, Milwaukee, Wisconsin. Transcript, 2.
32. *Ibid.*, p. 9.
33. Edward Bednar, interviewed by the author, February 16, 1995, Milwaukee, Wisconsin. Transcript, p. 1.
34. *Ibid.*, p. 4.
35. *Ibid.*, p. 5.
36. *The Milwaukee Journal*, August 26, 1990.
37. *The Milwaukee Sentinel*, October 19, 1989.
38. Wier interview, p. 10.
39. *Ibid.*, p. 11.
40. Rich Kirchen, "$20 million Renovation Set at Briggs Plant." *Business Journal*, May 16-23, 1992, p. 1.
41. *The Milwaukee Sentinel*, September 17, 1993.
42. Socks interview, p. 11.
43. *Ibid.*, p. 12.
44. George Thompson, interviewed by the author, June 1, 1995. Transcript, p. 21.
45. *Ibid.*, pp. 8-9.
46. Fred Stratton interview, p. 2.
47. Bednar interview, p. 4.
48. *Ibid.*
49. Thompson interview, pp. 12-14.
50. Socks interview, p. 10.
51. *The Milwaukee Sentinel*, May 10, 1991.
52. *Speech*, by Fred Stratton at Baird Award Ceremony, 1994.

Chapter Fourteen

1. John Shiely, interviewed by the author, June 14, 1995, Milwaukee, Wisconsin. Transcript, p. 11.
2. Shiely interview, p. 12.
3. Fred Stratton Jr. interviewed by the author, February 17, 1995, Milwaukee, Wisconsin. Transcript, p. 21.
4. Shiely interview, p. 17.
5. *Ibid.*
6. Harold Stratton II, interviewed by the author, February 17, 1995, Milwaukee, Wisconsin. Transcript, p. 26.
7. *Ibid.*, p. 30.
8. Dick Fotsch, interviewed by the author, June 12, 1995, Milwaukee, Wisconsin. Transcript, p. 16.
9. Harold Stratton interview, p. 34.
10. Erik Aspelin, interviewed by the author, February 17, 1995, Milwaukee, Wisconsin. Transcript, p. 15.
11. *Ibid.*, p. 14.
12. Charles O. Brown, interviewed by the author, February 16, 1995, Milwaukee, Wisconsin. Transcript, p. 4.
13. *Ibid.*, pp. 5-6.
14. *Ibid.*, pp. 9-10.
15. Aspelin interview, p. 20.
16. Brown interview, p. 11.
17. Fred Stratton Jr., interviewed June 13, 1995, pp. 12-13.
18. William Reitman, interviewed by the author, June 13, 1995, Milwaukee, Wisconsin. Transcript, p. 8.

19. *Ibid.,* p. 9.
20. Peter Georgescu, interviewed by the author, July 6, 1995. Transcript, pp. 8-9.
21. Paul Farny, interviewed by the author, June 13, 1995, Milwaukee, Wisconsin. Transcript, p. 16.
22. Reitman interview, pp. 15-16.
23. Georgescu interview, p. 10.
24. Fred Stratton, interviewed June 13, 1995, pp. 14-16.
25. Reitman interview, p. 11.
26. Fred Stratton, interviewed February 17, 1995, p. 26.
27. Stephen Rugg, interviewed by the author, February 16, 1995, Milwaukee, Wisconsin. Transcript, p. 10.
28. Reitman interview, p. 7.
29. Georgescu interview, p. 2.
30. *Ibid.,* p. 10.
31. Hugo Keltz, interviewed by the author, June 2, 1995, Milwaukee, Wisconsin. Transcript, p. 19.
32. *Ibid.,* p. 24.
33. *Speech,* by John Shiely, "Managing for Value Creation at Briggs & Stratton," 1994. Transcript, 13-14.
34. Georgescu interview, p. 12.